PICTORIAL HISTORY OF NORTH AMERICAN RAILROADS

CONSULTANTS AND CONTRIBUTING WRITERS
WALTER P. GRAY III AND JOHN P. HANKEY

CONTRIBUTING WRITERS
PAUL HAMMOND
JIM WRINN
KARL ZIMMERMANN

PUBLICATIONS INTERNATIONAL, LTD.

Walter P. Gray III is Director of the California State Railroad Museum in Sacramento. A historical railroad lecturer, consultant, and writer, he is co-author of *Rails Across America* and a contributing writer for many railroad publications, including *Locomotive & Railway Preservation, Trainline,* and *On Track* magazines.

John P. Hankey is a historian, veteran railroader, and former curator of the B&O Railroad Museum in Baltimore. He writes regularly for *Railway Preservation Magazine* and other historic preservation publications and has authored numerous works on railroad history. Presently, he divides his time between teaching, research, and museum consulting projects. He also serves as a lecturer and study leader for the Smithsonian Institution Associates program.

Paul Hammond is editor of *Locomotive & Railway Preservation* magazine. He is the former general manager of the Orange Empire Railway Museum and author of *Railway Odyssey.*

Jim Wrinn writes about railroads for the *Charlotte Observer* newspaper. He is a frequent contributor to popular railroad magazines, including *Trains* and *Locomotive & Railway Preservation.* He also works as a volunteer with the North Carolina Transportation Museum.

Karl Zimmermann is the author of 11 railroad books, including *Santa Fe Streamliners: The Chiefs and Their Tribesmen; CZ: The Story of the California Zephyr;* and *Paradise Regained: A South African Steam Diary.* He is a contributing writer for *Trains, Passenger Train Journal, Locomotive & Railway Preservation, International Railway Traveler, Railfan and Railroad,* and *Travel & Leisure* magazines.

Copyright © 1996 Publications International, Ltd. All rights reserved. This book may not be reproduced or quoted in whole or in part by any means whatsoever without written permission from:

Louis Weber, C.E.O.
Publications International, Ltd.
7373 North Cicero Avenue
Lincolnwood, Illinois 60646

Permission is never granted for commercial purposes.

Manufactured in USA.

8 7 6 5 4 3 2 1

ISBN: 0-7853-1776-7

Library of Congress Catalog Card Number: 96-69043

Editorial Assistant: Kevin Bunker

C O N T E N T S

CONTENTS

Both as an economic force and as a cultural icon, the railroad is unique in the extent and depth of its influence upon the development of this continent. In fact, it is nearly impossible to explore the history of the United States, Canada, and Mexico since 1850 without crossing a few railroad tracks.

The great overlapping national themes of westward expansion, industrialization, and the rise of big business, as well as the inevitable conflicts that arose among agrarian, labor, industrial, and governmental interests, all come together in the story of the railroad. The industry provides a kind of shorthand to the national experience.

The railroads have also given us much of the inventory of heroes and villains that populate the mythology of the Industrial Age. No workingman was stronger than John Henry; no engineer was braver than Casey Jones; and no businessmen were more unscrupulous or voracious than the railroads' own "robber barons." For North Americans, they have become the stuff of legend.

DURING THE 1930S, M-K-T KATY LINES FEATURED A PIONEER THEME IN ITS ADS, MENUS, AND OTHER PROMOTIONAL ITEMS.

Still, it is fair to ask why there is yet another book about a subject so well documented. The story is a good one—and, we believe, an essential one—but past tellings have often failed to capture more than the heaviest outlines of this vital history, and there is much more that can and should be said.

This also happens to be a good time to observe and comment on railroading. The industry is undergoing important changes as the twentieth century draws to a close, making this an opportune moment to revise some of the earlier interpretations and otherwise bring the story up-to-date. Fortunately, we have the opportunity to hear from some of

A CLASSIC SOUTHERN PACIFIC "DAYLIGHT" 4-8-4 PASSES A VINTAGE STEAM LOCOMOTIVE FROM AN EARLIER ERA.

the most capable and thoughtful scholars working in railroad history, who have collaborated to produce the present volume.

Pictorial History of North American Railroads brings together five knowledgeable authors to tell the story of railroads in North America. Railroad historian John Hankey, former curator of the B&O Railroad Museum in Baltimore, is credited with giving the book its shape and focus. Paul Hammond, editor of *Locomotive & Railway Preservation* magazine, together with well–known railroad author Karl Zimmerman and *Charlotte Observer* transportation reporter Jim Wrinn, have brought their distinctive experiences and perspectives to the writing as well, making this a durable addition to railroad history. As for myself, I can only say that I am honored to be in the company of these distinguished writers.

STATION AGENT KEYS, SUCH AS THESE FROM AROUND 1930, WERE A SYMBOL OF TRUST EARNED BY YEARS OF LOYAL SERVICE.

Thanks are also due to Kevin Bunker at the California State Railroad Museum for writing most of the captions; Ralph Justen of the National Railroad Museum in Green Bay, Wisconsin, as well as Rob and Nancy Hofer, for their assistance in acquiring memorabilia; and to Kurt Bell, Gary Schlerf, John Gruber, Richard Steinheimer, and Shirley Burman for photographic research.

None of us pretends that this is the ultimate railroad history, for such a thing cannot exist. We can only hope you will find it an interesting and worthwhile contribution to the literature and are stimulated to learn more about this fascinating subject.

Walter P. Gray III
Director, California State Railroad Museum
Sacramento

THE NEW YORK CENTRAL USED STREAMLINED "HUDSON" LOCOMOTIVES LIKE THIS ONE TO PULL ITS FABLED TWENTIETH CENTURY LIMITED.

PETER COOPER'S "TOM THUMB" 1829-30 BALTIMORE & OHIO R.R.

Chapter 1

HOORAY FOR THE RAILROAD!

To nineteenth-century Americans, the United States seemed unimaginably vast. Yet they lacked the one thing they needed most to fulfill their destiny: reliable, all-weather transportation. Common roads, canals, and steamboats merely whetted the country's appetite for mobility. One technology in particular—the "rail road"—offered dependable, year-round transport anywhere a narrow path for two rails could be carved. It was the tool Americans had been waiting for, and they used it vigorously to settle the continent.

*I*magine, for a moment, how Americans of the early nineteenth century must have felt gazing westward toward two million square miles of fledgling country. Promoters estimated there to be *a thousand million acres* available for settlement and exploitation, and practically every acre held the promise of freedom, prosperity, and the chance for a new life built on hard work and initiative.

Wealth, in the form of good farmland and grass for stock grazing, or metals like lead and gold, was there for the taking. Better yet, the United States tolerated no aristocrats, and there were no centuries-old traditions limiting what a man and his family could do in pursuit of life, liberty, and happiness. Yet with few exceptions, there was no effective way to reach that promised land, or to ship back the fruits of human toil.

George Washington recognized the need for some kind of transportation network. "Smooth the road and make easy the way," he

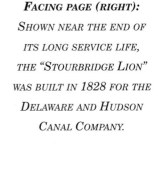

FACING PAGE (RIGHT): SHOWN NEAR THE END OF ITS LONG SERVICE LIFE, THE "STOURBRIDGE LION" WAS BUILT IN 1828 FOR THE DELAWARE AND HUDSON CANAL COMPANY.

THROUGHOUT THE LATE NINETEENTH CENTURY, RAILROADS BOTH KNOWINGLY AND UNWITTINGLY CREATED A MYTHOLOGY OF EARLY RAILROADING. THERE WERE NO "FIRST RAILROAD CARS" LIKE THIS IN THE UNITED STATES, BUT THE IMAGE PROVIDED A NICE CONTRAST WITH LUXURY TRAINS BEING ADVERTISED TO THE PUBLIC AFTER THE CIVIL WAR.

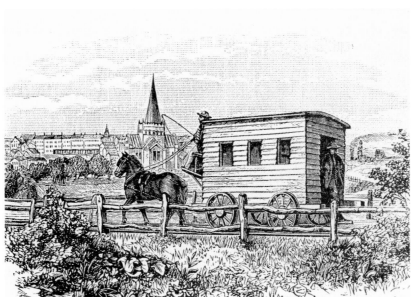

EARLY TRAVEL BY COACH WAS ARDUOUS UNDER THE BEST OF CIRCUMSTANCES. PASSENGERS WERE WEDGED INTO CRAMPED, HARD SEATS, WITH LITTLE PROTECTION FROM HEAT, DUST, COLD, OR RAIN.

wrote, "and see how amazingly our exports will be increased and how amply we shall be compensated for the expense of effecting it."

Railroads intensified a transportation revolution, the results of which were astonishing. At no other time in history has a people settled so large an area and wrested from it so much wealth in so short a time. Both the conquests of Alexander the Great and the rise of the Roman Empire pale in comparison with the expansion of the United States and Canada across the North American continent. Admittedly, that incredible growth came at great cost. Native Americans were displaced from their ancient lands, nature was continuously assaulted during the rush to build an industrialized society, and the United States suffered one Civil War and many smaller skirmishes in the struggle to define itself. Yet the undeniable result was a continent that, despite its ongoing turmoil, has enjoyed a degree of power, affluence, and accomplishment unprecedented in human history.

THE ERA IN REVIEW

1800:
Quarry tramways are introduced in the United States.

1815:
John Stevens receives a state charter for a tramroad in New Jersey.

1818:
Stevens is granted a charter to build a railroad in Pennsylvania.

1826:
The Granite Railway near Boston opens as the first U.S. railroad to carry passengers and freight.

1827:
The Baltimore & Ohio Railroad is chartered to build a railroad between the Atlantic seaboard and the Ohio River in western Virginia, a distance of more than 350 miles.

1830:
The B&O inaugurates the first regularly scheduled passenger trains in the United States—coaches hauled by horses for a distance of 13 miles.

By year's end, the South Carolina Railroad begins offering regularly scheduled, steam-powered passenger service; a railroad boom commences nationwide.

None of that would have been possible without effective, cheap, fast transportation. The railroad provided just that, making it possible to have truly national markets, cultures, languages, and governments. In the United States, those bonds of steel helped fulfill the national motto *E Pluribus Unum*, or "From Many, One."

Until the "Age of Steam," neither land nor water transport had changed much for two thousand years. Americans still relied on sheer muscle, using animals to pull wagons laden with as much as eight tons of freight. A traveler on horseback might manage 40 miles per hour in short spurts, but seldom exceeded that distance in a day's travel.

For most people, transportation on land meant walking. On a good road in good weather, a hearty person could cover 20 miles in a single day; in bad weather, or over rough terrain, half of that was normal. By the early nineteenth century, coach travel was available over

IN 1828—BEFORE AMERICA HAD ITS FIRST RAILROAD—ENGLISH POTTERY MAKER ENOCH WOOD & SONS WAS OFFERING A VERSION OF ITS FAMOUS "FLOW BLUE" DINNERWARE WITH A RAILROAD THEME.

THE ERA IN REVIEW

1835:
The B&O Railroad's Washington Branch opens, providing the first rail line to the nation's capital.

1837:
Henry R. Campbell completes the first 4-4-0 locomotive; later named the "American" type, it became the most popular nineteenth-century locomotive.

1844:
Samuel F. B. Morse makes the first successful tests of his "magnetic telegraph," inaugurating the age of instantaneous electronic communication over long distances.

1852:
Railroads open routes from New York to Chicago and across the Allegheny Mountains to make connections with

midwestern railroads and the Ohio and Mississippi Rivers.

1854:
Congress hires surveyors to locate possible rail routes to California.

1857:
Financial panic temporarily halts most railway construction. Regional disputes lead to talk of civil war.

main routes along the eastern seaboard and inland to burgeoning cities like Pittsburgh and Cincinnati. The roads of the period were muddy in spring, dusty and rutted in summer, and often impassable in winter.

The canal boom of the 1820s sought to lace populated areas together with "ditches" three to six feet deep and anywhere from 20 to 40 feet wide, along which sturdy freighters and packet boats could be towed by animals. Canal transport was cheap and effective, although canals were expensive to build, especially if they required costly stone locks or complex engineering. Traffic was slow, averaging three miles per hour, and canals often froze in winter. More critically, the Appalachian Mountains posed an insurmountable barrier to east-west links. The lack of water in large sections of the country precluded the use of canals, so that despite the immediate success

FEW OF THE EARLIEST AND MOST SIGNIFICANT EXAMPLES OF LOCOMOTIVES AND CARS WERE PRESERVED. MANY YEARS LATER, RAILROADS AND THEIR SUPPLIERS CREATED A VARIETY OF SOUVENIR AND PROMOTIONAL PIECES PAYING HOMAGE TO EARLY AMERICAN RAILROADING. PAPERWEIGHTS LIKE THIS WERE ESPECIALLY POPULAR.

ONE OF THE EARLIEST, AND MOST BASIC, MEANS OF TRANSPORTATION IN NORTH AMERICA WAS THE FLATBOAT. LITTLE MORE THAN A RAFT, IT COULD CARRY A SUBSTANTIAL CARGO—BUT ONLY DOWNSTREAM.

of the Erie Canal (opened from the Hudson River to Lake Erie in 1825), shippers and travelers recognized the limitations of canals as they sought an effective means to reach the rapidly advancing western frontier.

Americans had more success with steam navigation. Both Atlantic coastal and Ohio-Mississippi, or "western," steamboats introduced the nation to fast, cheap, comfortable transportation. The first steam-powered trans-Atlantic crossing and the introduction of steamboat service between Pittsburgh and New Orleans both took place in 1819. By the mid-1820s, well-appointed boats were plying most of the Mississippi River system, the Great Lakes, the Chesapeake Bay, Hudson River, and anywhere else there was enough water to float a hull and

FROM THE VERY BEGINNING OF RAILROADING THERE WAS "INTERMODAL" TRAFFIC. THIS PHOTOGRAPH SHOWS COAL BEING DUMPED FROM RAILROAD CARS INTO A WAITING CANAL BOAT. FOR TRANSPORTING MINERALS, WATER WAS STILL THE LEAST EXPENSIVE OPTION.

enough traffic to attract an entrepreneur.

Yet like canals and roads, river traffic was seasonal and subject to the vagaries of weather. Water routes often were roundabout, and there simply were not enough rivers in the right places to serve the entire country. For the prevailing tide of traffic between the East and West, water transportation was important, but at best inconvenient and often inadequate. What Americans really wanted was a steamboat that could run on dry land, anywhere they needed it to go. And that is what they proceeded to build, using ideas stretching back to antiquity.

No one actually "invented" the railroad, nor can any one place claim its birth. Ancient Corinthians cut grooves in stone pavement to guide wagon wheels, as did the Romans. In late-medieval Central Europe, miners crafted tramways (later, "tramroads") with crude wooden wheels rolling on equally crude wooden rails. By the 1500s, tramways were in use in Germany and Great Britain, and by the time of American independence there were hundreds of miles of fairly sophisticated tramroads and railroads operating throughout the mining districts of England and Wales, using gravity and animal power. A man by the name of Richard Trevithick built the first successful steam locomotive in 1804, operating it on the Penydarren tramroad in Wales.

By 1825 and the opening of the Stockton & Darlington Rail-

THIS BYPASSED SECTION OF THE CAMDEN & AMBOY RAILROAD IN NEW JERSEY SURVIVED AS AN EXAMPLE OF EARLY 1830S RAILROAD TRACK. LIKE ENGLISH IRON RAILS OF THE PERIOD, THEY WERE SUPPORTED UPON BLOCKS OF STONE, WHICH MADE A STURDY—BUT EXPENSIVE—RAILROAD. MOST COMPANIES SOON ADOPTED THE WOODEN CROSSTIE AS STANDARD.

THE WORK OF BUILDING THE FIRST RAILROADS WAS ACCOMPLISHED WITH HUMAN MUSCLE AND DOGGED ENDURANCE. THIS CONSTRUCTION TRAIN FROM THE 1850S ILLUSTRATES THE LABORIOUS PROCESS OF MOVING EARTH BY HAND AND THE RELATIVELY CRUDE STATE OF ANTEBELLUM RAILROADING.

way in northern England, there was little doubt that the combination of iron rails, steam locomotion, and trains of cars would develop rapidly as a form of freight and passenger transportation. Nicholas Wood's *Practical Treatise on Railroads,* published in 1825, was widely read and available to interested Americans. The success of Robert Stephenson's locomotive "Rocket" at the 1828 Rainhill Trials held by the Liverpool and Manchester Railway proved the potential of steam power. Present at that contest—which pitted the most novel and advanced locomotives of the day against each other—were representatives of America's earliest railroads. Ross Winans of the Baltimore & Ohio Railroad and Horatio Allen of the South Carolina Railroad watched attentively as the "Rocket" raced by with heavy trains at what to them were dizzying speeds. They returned to the United States with the conviction that railroads were exactly what the new nation needed.

There were at least a few quarry tramroads in the United States by 1800, and well-known examples were in use outside Philadelphia and Wilmington by 1810. As early as 1812, Revolutionary War veteran and indefatigable promoter Colonel John Stevens published a pamphlet entitled *The Superior Advantages of Railways and Steam Carriages over Canal Navigation.* By 1815, he had secured a charter from the State of New Jersey to build a tramroad—in effect, an early, com-

BEFORE THE RAILROADS, THOUSANDS OF PEOPLE MADE THE TREK TO THE FRONTIER OVER A CIRCUITOUS ROUTE BY COMMON ROAD AND RIVER. SEVERAL FAMILIES MIGHT BUILD AN "ARK" LIKE THIS, LOAD UP THEIR GOODS AND ANIMALS, AND SET OUT FOR "THE WEST"—WHICH USUALLY MEANT ILLINOIS, MISSOURI, OF SOME OTHER PRAIRIE STATE.

mon-carriage railroad—from Trenton, on the Delaware River, to New Brunswick, at the head of tidal navigation on Raritan Bay opposite New York City. In 1825, Stevens made a demonstration "steam waggon" to operate on a circular wood track in Hoboken. He and other visionaries, such as Oliver Evans, planted the seeds that eventually found fertile soil in the United States.

From the handful of railroad charters granted by state legislatures in the late 1820s, the number of railroads proposed or under construction increased rapidly through the 1830s. At first, large cities wanted railroads to connect with other cities or improve their status as trading centers. Then smaller cities and towns clamored for a railroad link that would join them to emerging trunk routes, and before long, population centers of all sizes at least dreamed of having some kind of railroad connection.

Track mileage in 1830 totalled around 100, with several thousand miles of track planned or under construction. That compared with roughly 1,300 miles of canals in use and several thousand miles of established river routes. Just 10 years later, the number of railroad and canal miles were almost identical—a little over 3,300 for each—but few people were promoting canals in 1840.

FOR AT LEAST A DECADE, SOME AMERICAN RAILROAD MANAGERS REGARDED BRITISH LOCOMOTIVES AS MECHANICALLY SUPERIOR TO NATIVE EXAMPLES. THIS IS THE "ROCKET," BUILT IN ENGLAND FOR THE PHILADELPHIA & READING RAILWAY IN 1838.

JOHN C. STEVENS (1785–1857) WAS THE MAN WHO FIRST SAW THE RAILROAD AS A TOOL OF ECONOMIC PROGRESS IN NORTH AMERICA. MORE THAN ANYONE, HE DESERVES THE TITLE "FATHER OF THE AMERICAN RAILROAD."

THESE REPLICA FREIGHT CARS FROM 1830 ILLUSTRATE THE RELATIVE SCALE OF EARLY RAILROADING. EACH FOUR-WHEEL CAR COULD CARRY UPWARDS OF 10 TONS OF CARGO. FLOUR WAS AN ESPECIALLY IMPORTANT COMMODITY ON THE B&O; IT WAS SHIPPED IN BARRELS AS SHOWN HERE. HORSES ALSO HAULED CARS SUCH AS THESE.

Instead, despite the financial panic of 1837 and a general lull in business, tens of thousands of miles of railroad were under construction in all settled parts of the country. The railroad had arrived on the American scene.

The first two decades of railroading were a period of experimentation and rapid technological evolution. By the 1820s, the United States could claim a small but competent group of surveyors, engineers, and builders with experience constructing roads, canals, and bridges. The field of civil engineering did not yet exist, but the U.S. Military Academy was training military officers as engineers based on the well-established French engineering curriculum.

To assist in locating and developing our first railroads, the federal

EVER SINCE THE B&O FINISHED ITS MAINLINE BETWEEN CHESAPEAKE BAY AND THE OHIO RIVER IN 1852, THIS SPOT NEAR WHEELING, WEST VIRGINIA, HAS BEEN KNOWN AS "ROSEBY'S ROCK," NAMED AFTER A CONSTRUCTION BOSS.

government often permitted these military engineers to assist railroad companies. Other needed skills came from wagon makers, millwrights, stonemasons, and machinists familiar with the crude marine steam engines of the day. In fact, almost anyone with a craft, or experience with machinery or construction, found opportunity in railroading.

There were fundamental questions to be answered. Should the flanges be on the inside of the wheels, or the outside? Should rails be of wood, iron, or of more permanent stone? Were steam locomotives practical for U.S. railroads? Should railroads minimize curvature at the expense of grades, or vice versa? Some of the best engineering minds of the day soon began devising answers. Jonathan Knight, a skilled mathematician and engineer, made calculations as to the rolling characteristics of railway vehicles and proposed a wheel with a slight taper to the tread—the shape still in general use. The versatile

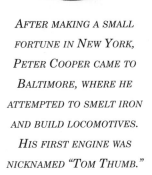

AFTER MAKING A SMALL FORTUNE IN NEW YORK, PETER COOPER CAME TO BALTIMORE, WHERE HE ATTEMPTED TO SMELT IRON AND BUILD LOCOMOTIVES. HIS FIRST ENGINE WAS NICKNAMED "TOM THUMB."

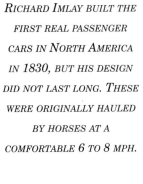

RICHARD IMLAY BUILT THE FIRST REAL PASSENGER CARS IN NORTH AMERICA IN 1830, BUT HIS DESIGN DID NOT LAST LONG. THESE WERE ORIGINALLY HAULED BY HORSES AT A COMFORTABLE 6 TO 8 MPH.

"John Bull" Steams Again

In 1980, John H. White, Jr., and his colleagues at the Smithsonian Institution pondered how to mark the 150th anniversary of the locomotive "John Bull." Dare they carefully steam up and actually operate the oldest locomotive in America? After all, it did spend 35 years in rough railroad service, and the best way to learn how machinery actually worked is to operate it. There were risks, but much to be learned in the process.

The firm of Robert Stephenson in England constructed the locomotive for the Camden and Amboy Railroad and delivered it in August of 1831. By 1866, the "John Bull" was out of service—but the railroad recognized its historic importance and preserved it intact. After the Pennsylvania Railroad absorbed the C&A in 1871, it exhibited the "John Bull" at various expositions and in 1885 presented the locomotive to the Smithsonian Institution.

Almost a hundred years later, Smithsonian staff and volunteers completely disassembled and inspected the ancient engine. After many tests and lots of tender care, the "John Bull" steamed again, hauling its companion passenger car over branch lines near Washington, D.C. Over a period of several weeks in the fall of 1981, the locomotive taught its keepers more about early steam power than any textbook possibly could. It looked, smelled, sounded, and behaved exactly like the thousands of steam locomotives that followed it—to the delight of curators and rail fans alike.

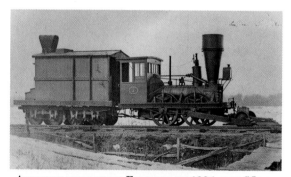

ARRIVING HERE FROM ENGLAND IN 1831, THE "JOHN BULL" WAS MODIFIED SUBSTANTIALLY TO MAKE IT BETTER SUITED TO AMERICAN CONDITIONS.

Robert Stevens of New Jersey (John Stevens's son) conceived of the "T" rail design that is still the standard for American railroads. Inventions such as the swiveling four-wheel truck, designs for switches and turntables, and all sorts of basic engineering challenges kept these pioneers busy for years. Many railroads paid dearly for their initial mistakes, with the entire country watching. But even mistakes provided valuable lessons.

Railroad promoters and officials had their hands full, too. First they had to convince skeptical legislators and investors of the practicability of railroads; then they had to manage the explosive growth after the idea caught on.

Most of the early lines were modest in their aspirations. The 1826 Mohawk & Hudson Rail Road built a 17-mile line between Schenec-

PLACING THE SYMBOLIC FIRST STONE OF THE BALTIMORE & OHIO RAILROAD WAS A MONUMENTAL AFFAIR FOR THE CITY OF BALTIMORE. THE MAN WITH THE SHOVEL IS CHARLES CARROLL, BY 1828 THE ONLY SURVIVING SIGNER OF THE DECLARATION OF INDEPENDENCE. BALTIMORE AND MARYLAND STAKED THEIR ECONOMIC FUTURE ON THE RAILROAD.

tady on the Mohawk River and Albany on the Hudson River as a shortcut for traffic on the Erie Canal. Finished in 1830, the railroad served as a portage route between the two rivers and saved 40 miles of slow canal travel. Another early railroad, John Stevens's 1830 Camden & Amboy Railroad and Transportation Company, was built to carry passengers and freight across the neck of New Jersey separating the Delaware River from New York Harbor.

AMERICANS WERE JUSTLY FAMOUS FOR THEIR INGENUITY, AND RAILROADERS WERE NOTORIOUSLY PRACTICAL MEN. BUT SOME ANTEBELLUM LOCOMOTIVES—LIKE THIS 6-2-0 BUILT BY THE CAMDEN & AMBOY—WERE SPECTACULAR ODDITIES AS WELL AS MISERABLE FAILURES.

More ambitious was the South Carolina Canal and Railroad Company, which intended to connect interior points to coastal cities as a way to enhance port commerce. When it opened in 1833 to the city of Hamburg, South Carolina, it had the distinction of being the longest continuous railroad in the world (136 miles) and the first to use a steam locomotive in regular passenger service.

The Baltimore & Ohio Railroad gets credit for commencing the first truly modern railroad, even though John Stevens had predated the B&O with what was for its time an audacious plan to build a railroad across Pennsylvania. The B&O originated in the minds of leading Baltimore merchants in 1826, and it was chartered in early 1827. Three years later, the B&O opened America's first common-carriage railroad (13 miles to Ellicott's Mills) as the first leg of a proposed 380-mile, double-tracked line over the Allegheny Mountains intended to tap into the burgeoning

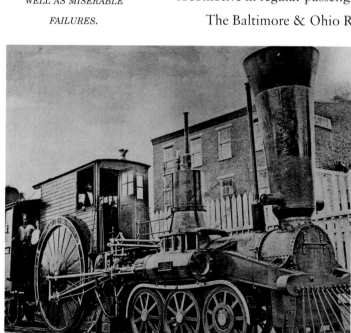

SHOWN HERE LATE IN THE NINETEENTH CENTURY, ELLICOTT CITY WAS THE B&O'S FIRST TERMINUS. THE STONE BUILDING ON THE LEFT DATES FROM 1831, MAKING IT AMERICA'S FIRST RAILROAD STATION. TODAY, IT HAS BEEN MAGNIFICENTLY RESTORED AND IS OPEN AS A MUSEUM.

western traffic moving on the Ohio-Mississippi River system. This was different in scale, intent, and risk from the short railroads that were its contemporaries. So different, in fact, that the B&O was a tremendous gamble.

Only at the beginning did British technology play a substantial role in American railroading. The first locomotive in the U.S. was an import from the machine works of John Rastrick of Stourbridge, England, which delivered the "Stourbridge Lion" to the Delaware and Hudson Canal Company. After a nearly disastrous trial on the company's 18-mile tramroad in eastern Pennsylvania in August of 1829, the "Lion" and its sister engine were set aside. Later British locomotives, such as the "Planet" type locomotives built by Robert Stephenson, were far more successful. In 1831, the Camden & Amboy imported the "John Bull," now preserved at the Smithsonian Institution.

THESE OHIO RIVER STEAMBOATS, PHOTOGRAPHED IN CINCINNATI SHORTLY AFTER THE CIVIL WAR, ARE TYPICAL OF THE HUNDREDS OF CRAFT THAT PLIED THE WESTERN RIVERS IN COMPETITION WITH THE EMERGING RAILROAD NETWORK. THEY CARRIED PASSENGERS WITH MORE COMFORT, BUT LESS RELIABILITY, THAN TRAINS.

ALTHOUGH INITIAL COSTS WERE HIGH, STONE BRIDGES WERE A BETTER INVESTMENT THAN TIMBER ONES BECAUSE THEY REQUIRED MUCH LESS MAINTENANCE AND WERE IMPERVIOUS TO FIRE.

Iron rails, too, initially came from Great Britain because domestic forges could not deliver inexpensive, high-quality wrought iron in the immense quantities needed. British mechanics were likewise a significant import. The ranks of railroad mechanical departments were filled with men who had learned their crafts in British mills and factories and then emigrated to North America to find a better life.

In those days, almost anyone could find work on the railroad. The hardest, lowest-paying jobs were in railroad construction. Shovels, wheel barrows, mules, and black powder were the primary tools with which hundreds of thousands of men moved millions of tons of earth. With axe and adz they transformed countless trees into ties, bridge timbers, and lumber for cars. Often, immigrants from Ireland, Germany, and other northern European countries drifted from one railroad job to another, supporting their families as best they could. In the South, both slaves and free men worked to build and maintain railroads. Surprisingly, women also found work on the railroad in these early years. Most often they worked as charwomen in railroad buildings, car cleaners, cooks at railroad eating houses, and doing other traditionally "women's" work that paralleled their duties in the home.

A few lucky men had skilled railroad jobs as

STILL SPRY AFTER 50 YEARS OF SERVICE ON THE B&O, THIS 1836 "GRASSHOPPER" IS TYPICAL OF THE FIRST SUCCESSFUL AMERICAN-BUILT STEAM LOCOMOTIVES. WITH VERTICAL BOILERS AND INDIRECT GEARING, THEY WERE SLOW BUT SURPRISINGLY POWERFUL.

THIS DECORATIVE FLASK FROM THE LATE 1820S IS TYPICAL OF THE SOUVENIRS AND COMMEMORATIVE OBJECTS PRODUCED TO MARK THE OPENING OF THE "RAILWAY AGE" IN NORTH AMERICA.

machinists, painters, carpenters, boilermakers, and similar craft-oriented occupations. Almost all companies started apprentice programs, and railroad jobs were often handed down from father to son or uncle to nephew. Train and engine service carried with it high status and considerable risk. Locomotive engineers in particular were heroes to the general public and small boys alike, and the conductor was a man of great authority who had charge of the train as a captain does his ship. To attain those coveted positions, men had to work their way up from the bottom, starting as brakemen or engine wipers and serving an indefinite apprenticeship.

Brakemen performed especially hazardous work. They had to ride the tops of freight cars in all weather for as long as it took to traverse the standard 100-mile division. Sometimes railroaders were required to go right back out on another run, working 20 or 30 hours straight. The toll of death and injury was great, as it was in many mining and industrial occupations.

BY THE LATE 1840S, LOCOMOTIVES HAD ATTAINED THEIR FAMILIAR FORM. THIS 1848 FREIGHT ENGINE COULD HAVE HAULED AS MANY AS 30 CARS ON LEVEL TRACK. IT BURNED COAL AND REPRESENTED THE STATE OF THE ART IN ITS DAY.

The Death of a Railroad Fireman

Railroaders faced many hazards in the course of an ordinary run, as this account, taken from D.C. Prescott's *Early Day Railroading From Chicago* (1910), attests:

"In those days the only way to oil the cylinders of a locomotive was for the fireman to walk out on the running board of the engine with a can of melted tallow in his hand [and] ... use both hands to open the cup on top of the steam chest and pour in the tallow; and this, too, when the engine is going down grade possibly thirty to forty miles an hour, for the tallow could not be poured when the engine was working steam.... Roger[s] engines had no running boards, but were provided with low down side bars extending along just outside the driving wheels. These bars were only three and one-half inches wide ... and the fireman had to walk out on those bars with one hand hold of a round bar above him and the tallow can in the other, with the side rods playing like lightning within six inches of his feet. They were rightly called man killers; and Rodney Hathaway, roused from slumber by Horace [the engineer] to go out and oil the cylinders as they went down Clinton grade, started on a trip he had often made before, but that night he fell in between that rail and the drivers, and Horace hearing his bones cracking whistled down brakes; and they picked up poor Rodney in fragments."

THIS NINETEENTH-CENTURY CARTOON DEPICTS THE POPULAR VIEW OF CALLOUS RAILROAD AND STEAMBOAT INTERESTS DANCING OVER THE CORPSE OF THE TRAVELING PUBLIC.

Railroaders accepted those risks for a number of reasons. Above all, railroading was one of the first industrial occupations to offer the possibility of lifetime employment. If a man followed the rules, served faithfully, and was careful for his own safety, he might have a well-paying job for life. That was an almost revolutionary development for the common working man, who at this point in history was accustomed to working on a daily basis and experiencing feast or famine—literally—for the effort.

Railroaders also took great pride in their craft and their role in building up the country. Too often overlooked in the scholarly studies of railroad work is the fact that railroading could be downright enjoyable. Compared with repetitive factory work or following a mule and plow for a lifetime, railroad work offered genuine challenge, the chance for meaningful advancement, and a constantly changing work environment.

FACING PAGE (RIGHT): THE RAILROAD BROUGHT THE INDUSTRIAL REVOLUTION TO EVEN THE MOST REMOTE CORNERS OF THE CONTINENT. IN MANY RURAL AREAS, THE LOCOMOTIVE WAS THE MOST POWERFUL AND COMPLEX MACHINE ANYONE HAD EVER SEEN. IT WAS A SOURCE OF AWE AND RESPECT, AND SOMETIMES, FEAR.

ALTHOUGH MOST LIKELY FROM AFTER THE WAR, THIS VIEW CAPTURES THE UNFINISHED QUALITY OF MANY ANTEBELLUM RAILROADS. THE LOCOMOTIVE CREW IN THE FOREGROUND IS ALMOST CERTAINLY AMERICAN-BORN; THE MEN ON THE FLAT CARS ARE ALMOST CERTAINLY IMMIGRANTS MAKING A DOLLAR OR TWO FOR A TWELVE-HOUR DAY.

As railroads grew larger throughout the antebellum period, the basis of railroad employment shifted from traditional crafts and paternalistic relations to a more hard-nosed and impersonal style of industrial relations. In response, railroaders began banding together for their own protection. Early railroaders' mutual benefit societies—insurance plans—emerged in the 1850s as the men found it difficult or impossible to secure regular insurance. Those voluntary societies formed the nucleus of the major railroad craft unions that would emerge after the Civil War. The companies regarded any kind of activism as treason, and they responded swiftly with dismissal, fines, imprisonment, or blacklisting, depending on how powerful that particular company happened to be.

Even before the wrenching changes of the Civil War, American railroads attained an almost sovereign status, and they were so pow-

MANY EARLY RAILROADS HAD LOCOMOTIVES NAMED "PIONEER," SYMBOLIC OF THEIR ROLE IN OPENING THE CONTINENT. THE CUMBERLAND VALLEY RAILROAD IN PENNSYLVANIA USED THIS TINY 2-4-2 ON ITS LINE OUT OF HARRISBURG. IT IS NOW PRESERVED AT THE SMITHSONIAN INSTITUTION IN WASHINGTON.

erful a force in American life that writers as diverse as Henry David Thoreau and the editors of *The American Railroad Journal* regarded the railroad as the defining American technology, if not the apogee of American accomplishment.

By the 1840s, the ultimate form of the nineteenth-century American railroad was beginning to emerge. Many lines had started out as government-assisted works or as joint ventures between local governments and private investors. It soon became apparent that there was so much money to be made in railroading that the private sector could go it alone.

This was the period in which the railroad industry emerged as "America's first big business," devising new management techniques and creating capital markets and mechanisms of finance. Railroading gave hundreds of thousands of Americans steady employment. By providing cheap transportation, it helped shape the rapidly growing domestic economy. The railroad speculator, too, became a familiar figure as railroads pioneered many of the cutthroat business practices that would flower in the latter half of the nineteenth century under the likes of W. H. Vanderbilt, Jay Gould, and many others.

Railroad technology advanced rapidly. A clever mechanic or inventor could become wealthy, as railroads constantly sought ways to boost efficiency and profits. There were countless hare-brained proposals, but

THE BRITISH TENDED TO BUILD RAILWAYS AS A COMPLETE UNIT. AMERICAN PRACTICE MORE OFTEN INVOLVED BUILDING A LIGHTLY CONSTRUCTED LINE TO OPEN THE RAILROAD FOR BUSINESS, THEN RETURNING AS MONEY AND TRAFFIC WARRANTED TO IMPROVE AND FINISH THE WORK. HERE, TEAMS WORK TO "FILL" A TRESTLE WITH ROCK.

BEFORE THE CIVIL WAR, THERE WAS NO SUCH THING AS "STANDARD TIME." ALTHOUGH RAILROADS ISSUED TIMETABLES AND RAN TRAINS BY THE CLOCK, THERE WAS A GREAT DEAL OF UNCERTAINTY IN THE SYSTEM. THIS E. HOWARD TIMEPIECE IS AN EXAMPLE OF AN EARLY STATION OR OFFICE CLOCK.

many ideas had real merit: the classic "American" locomotive (the 4-4-0 of Civil War fame); new kinds of inexpensive iron bridges; innovative car designs; and techniques for building and equipping railroads cheaply and quickly.

Even basic equipment, such as cabs for locomotive crews, bells, headlights, whistles, and a rudimentary series of operating rules had to be created, for railroading truly was a new undertaking. Americans soon turned away from British practice and devised methods and materials far better suited to the near-wilderness conditions facing so many railroads here.

Some inventions were well ahead of their time. In 1851, Dr. Charles Grafton Page tested an experimental electric locomotive on the B&O's tracks out of Washington, D.C. Ross Winans patented a crude kind of roller bearing in 1828, and the pages of the trade press were filled with fantastic mechanical schemes.

RAILROADS WERE THE CONTINENT'S LARGEST CONSUMERS OF IRON AND ALSO PRODIGIOUS USERS OF WOOD, PAINT, WIRE, MACHINE TOOLS, AND ALL KINDS OF SPECIALTY PRODUCTS. CONSTRUCTION TRAINS LIKE THIS CONSTANTLY SHUTTLED MATERIAL TO FAR-FLUNG LOCATIONS.

On the other hand, railroads acutely felt the lack of other, more basic, inventions. Throughout the antebellum period, freight and passenger trains had only crude hand brakes, manned by stout trainmen and brakemen, to stop them. Couplings between early railroad cars consisted of solid drawbars or pieces of chain with so much slack in them that the cars continually crashed into each other as the train accelerated and decelerated. Until the development of the injector, locomotives relied on mechanical pumps to replenish boiler water, which meant that a locomotive standing still for any length of time had to be run back and forth at intervals to keep from exhausting its water supply.

Operating practices generally conformed to the limitations of the equipment and track. As the "American standard" track of "T" rails laid on wooden crossties became widespread, train speeds crept up

LOCOMOTIVE BUILDER WILLIAM MASON OF MASSACHUSETTS TURNED OUT SOME OF THE MOST BEAUTIFUL MACHINES EVER CONSTRUCTED. THIS CLASSIC "AMERICAN" TYPE 4-4-0 FOR THE BOSTON & WORCESTER RAILROAD POSES FOR ITS BUILDER'S PORTRAIT OUTSIDE THE MASON'S SHOP.

throughout the period. Passengers were astounded at first to exceed 15 miles per hour; alarmists expressed fear that the human body could not withstand such velocities, and some men took out pencil and paper and wrote coherent sentences as they whizzed along to prove that the brain could function at speeds near 20 miles per hour.

Freight trains initially operated at between 5 and 10 miles per hour, about the same as wagons but with much greater efficiency and ease. By the time of the Civil War, well-maintained railroads were running passenger trains in excess of 40 miles per hour, and freight trains often above 20 miles per hour.

Railroads borrowed techniques for management and employee discipline from the military, devising elaborate sets of rules to govern the running of trains. Steamboats had followed somewhat flexible timetables for years, but the precision with which railroads had to be operated for safety reasons gave America the concept of "railroad time," meaning the rest of the country had to adhere to the railroad's

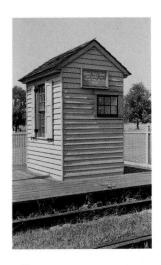

THE EARLIEST RAILROAD BUILDINGS WERE OFTEN STARKLY SIMPLE, LIKE THIS TINY 1832 TICKET OFFICE FOR THE NEW CASTLE & FRENCHTOWN RAIL ROAD IN DELAWARE.

AMERICANS LOVED TO EXPRESS INDIVIDUALITY AND THEIR SENSE OF AESTHETICS THROUGH THEIR MACHINES. MANY PRE-CIVIL WAR LOCOMOTIVES WERE EITHER HEAVILY DECORATED OR INCORPORATED NOVEL FEATURES THAT GAVE THEM GREAT INDIVIDUALITY, LIKE THIS VAGUELY GOTHIC-REVIVAL 4-2-0.

The Magnetic Telegraph: News by "Lightning"

Samuel Finley Breese Morse was an artist and visionary who was fascinated with electricity and its possibilities for long-distance communication.

Morse conceived the idea of using electrical pulses to send messages long distances over wires, and he patented the idea in 1837. After years of tinkering and political lobbying, Congress appropriated $30,000 for a demonstration project.

The Baltimore & Ohio Railroad gave Morse permission to bury a prototype telegraph wire alongside its tracks between Washington, D.C., and Baltimore, Maryland. Morse and associates Alfred Vail and Ezra Cornell (who later founded the university bearing his name) spent most of 1843—and at least $15,000—figuring out that underground wires shorted out, and that the best chance of success was to string the copper line above ground, from pole to pole. After starting over in the spring of 1844, they quickly completed a continuous wire from the basement of the building housing the Supreme Court to the Baltimore & Ohio's Mt. Clare and Pratt Street depots in Baltimore, approximately 44 miles to the north.

NORTH AMERICANS AND THEIR RAILROADS CAME TO RELY ON THE RAPID LONG-DISTANCE COMMUNICATION THAT TELEGRAPHY AFFORDED.

On May 24, 1844, Miss Anne Ellsworth (daughter of the Commissioner of Patents) had the honor of composing the first ceremonial telegraphic message.

Morse slowly tapped out, and Vail eagerly received, the Biblical admonition that would inaugurate the age of instantaneous long-distance communication and, along with the railroad, change the world: "What Hath God Wrought."

schedule—a fact resented by many. Before long, railroads had the power to make or break towns and direct the course of industry.

As the 1850s dawned, travelers demanded better equipment, closer coordination between railroads, and higher levels of comfort. The crowded, tiny coaches of railroading's first two decades gave way to more spacious and comfortable cars with padded seats, stoves for winter travel, and even primitive sleeping cars for long overnight runs. The public used the comparatively comfortable steamboats, with their sleeping cabins, dining rooms, salons, and pleasing decorations as standards against which to measure the comfort of train travel.

The growth of the railroad network made life different—and better—for almost everyone. When flour had to be hauled over the National Road from Wheeling, on the Ohio River in western Virginia, to Baltimore for export to Europe, the farmer was lucky to receive $1 a barrel. Wagon freight charges amounted to $4. After the B&O Railroad opened its main line to Wheeling in 1853, the price at the docks remained about the same, $5 or so. But the railroad charged only $1 to haul that barrel of flour the 380 miles over the mountains in one-tenth the time. The farmer pocketed $4, which in turn allowed him to purchase manufactured goods brought in from the East by railroad and to improve his farm for still higher yields.

These brief vignettes do not do justice to the change wrought by the railroad in the 30 years before the Civil War. In half a lifetime, this one technology helped push the extent of settlement a thousand miles westward. It made possible one national market, no matter how vast the continent. That market would arise only after the intense sectional rivalries had been settled by war, but even in the 1850s, western grain and cattle found ready buyers in the big cities of the East, while the railroad permitted the concentration of the steel industry in just a few eastern locations.

Railroads brought fresh food, fuel, and raw materials to the burgeoning cities, materially improving the quality of life for countless Americans. With the means for adequate transportation at hand, politicians seriously proposed an all-rail link across the country to California. Railroad development started simultaneously in dozens of isolated areas, all awaiting the completion of a national system.

Perhaps most important, those first decades of railroading in America changed people's perceptions about time, space, and their relationships with each other and their country. All across the land, people spoke of the way trains had accelerated and intensified life in America. Yet for most people, the railroad was good; it improved their lives and enhanced the opportunities that nature presented.

In the coming years, the nation would even see its railroads change the course of war, proving yet again how powerful the combination of iron, steam, and human determination could be.

THIS EARLY SCENE ON THE CAMDEN & AMBOY RAILROAD SHOWS A DRAWBRIDGE, AN "AMERICAN" TYPE 4-4-0, AND A PASSENGER CAR TYPICAL OF THE 1840S. EXCEPT FOR THE LOCOMOTIVE AND PARTS OF THE CAR AND BRIDGE, EVERYTHING IS MADE OF WOOD.

Chapter 2

WESTWARD THE COURSE OF EMPIRE...

Three forces reshaped the United States between 1860 and the end of the century. First was the Civil War; second was the continuing tide of westward expansion; third was the American Industrial Revolution. Common to all was the railroad. It not only enabled the preservation of the Union, but also permitted the kind of rapid industrialization that made the United States a world power.

The Civil War was the defining event for nineteenth-century America, and railroads played an important role in the conflict. As the North industrialized rapidly between 1820 and 1860, railroads helped create—and prospered from—the rise of factory production and diversified large-scale agriculture.

In the South, railroads played a marginal role in the cotton and tobacco economy. With little industry to support them, the railroads that did crisscross the inland South were lightly built, often poorly maintained, and generally inferior to those in the North. In the end, the North's industrial superiority—epitomized by its superb railroad system—enabled it to pummel the Confederacy into submission.

Both Abraham Lincoln and Jefferson Davis recognized the need for an effective railroad system in the war effort, and military men on

THE AMERICAN CIVIL WAR WAS AS UGLY, BRUTAL, AND DESTRUCTIVE AS ANY EVER FOUGHT. IN APRIL OF 1865, VICTORIOUS UNION TROOPS POSE BESIDE A RUINED RICHMOND & PETERSBURG RAILROAD LOCOMOTIVE AND SHOP IN THE FORMER CONFEDERATE CAPITAL.

ON THE ORANGE & ALEXANDRIA RAILROAD—A KEY LINE PROVIDING THE UNION WITH ACCESS TO THE CONFEDERATE STRONGHOLD OF VIRGINIA'S SHENANDOAH VALLEY— U.S. MILITARY RAILROAD FORCES POSE BEFORE A RECENTLY COMPLETED TEMPORARY BRIDGE. AS THEY BECAME MORE PROFICIENT, SMALL UNITS COULD COMPLETE A BRIDGE LIKE THIS IN A DAY OR LESS.

both sides used railroads skillfully. The South, however, had neither the factories capable of building new locomotives in wartime nor the political will to forge the existing railroad network into a smoothly functioning system.

The North, on the other hand, quickly created the United States Military Railroad to expropriate and operate any railroad it needed. The Union Army appointed Daniel C. McCallum and Herman Haupt as ranking officers, giving them extraordinary powers to provide railroad support for northern troops.

Throughout the war, opposing forces recognized the tactical advantages of either controlling or destroying railroad supply lines. But it was not until Union General William Rosecrans found himself under siege at Chattanooga, Tennessee, in 1863 that leaders discovered the true strategic value of railroads. Over the ob-

BEFORE THE WIDESPREAD USE OF PETROLEUM OILS IN THE LATE NINETEENTH CENTURY, TALLOW—ANIMAL FAT—WAS A USEFUL LUBRICANT FOR STEAM LOCOMOTIVES. FIREMEN AND ENGINEERS USED TALLOW POTS MUCH LIKE THIS TO LUBRICATE THE CYLINDERS OF MOVING LOCOMOTIVES.

THE ERA IN REVIEW

1860–1865:
The Civil War causes unprecedented traffic for northern railroads, destruction of most southern railroads, and new appreciation for railroads' capabilities.

1863:
Twelve enginemen form the Brotherhood of Locomotive Engineers, the first successful railroad labor organization.

1868:
Confederate veteran Eli Janney patents a design for an automatic knuckle coupler, the basis for today's standard couplers.

1869:
The Union Pacific Railroad meets the Central Pacific Railroad at Promontory Summit, Utah, forming a continuous railroad line from coast to coast.

1870:
Gen. William Jackson Palmer organizes the Denver & Rio Grande Railway.

1873:
George Westinghouse perfects the triple valve and the automatic air brake.

1883:
On November 18, "The Day of Two Noons," when railroads (and many

jections of cabinet members and even some generals, Lincoln approved a daring plan to send two entire Army corps on a circuitous rail route to reinforce Rosecrans. Despite the short notice and complexity of the plan, railroad convoys carried 20,000 men, their full equipment, ten batteries with horses, and more than 100 cars of baggage and supplies 1,100 miles in just seven days (11 days from idea to execution).

ON RAILROADS OPERATING THROUGH WAR-TORN COUNTRY, SOLDIERS OFTEN HELPED DEFEND KEY LINES AND JUNCTIONS. WHEN TELEGRAPH CIRCUITS WERE DOWN AND NO LOCOMOTIVE WAS AVAILABLE, A HANDCAR ON THE RAILROAD MIGHT OFFER THE ONLY MEANS OF COMMUNICATION.

Fifteen months later, 17,000 men made the reverse movement in an equally timely fashion on their way to complete the Union victory at Richmond, Virginia. War would never be the same again, for the railroad had proved to be a powerful military weapon as well as an agent of civilization.

As the Civil War intensified, Lincoln and the country wrestled with the question of how to connect the existing railroad network in the Midwest with California. During the spring of 1862, the House and Senate passed the Pacific Railroad Act, authorizing land grants and

cities) adopt Standard Railway Time— the basis for our time zones today.

1885:
The Canadian Pacific Railway completes Canada's first transcontinental line.

1887:
The Interstate Commerce Act becomes effective, marking the first federal regulation of railroads.

A record total of 12,876 miles of track is laid in the United States; the amount would never be surpassed.

1893:
The Railway Safety Appliance Act is signed into law, improving worker safety over the next two decades.

New York Central locomotive 999 sets an unofficial speed record of 112.5

mph—supposedly the first time man exceeded 100 mph.

1894:
A strike at the Pullman Palace Car Company spreads nationwide.

1895:
General Electric installs the first mainline railroad electrification in America on the B&O in Baltimore.

loans varying from $16,000 per mile of flat prairie railroad to $48,000 per mile of difficult mountain track. That made the project a "pay-as-you-go" program, creating wealth out of the very land made accessible by the railroad.

In California, four transplanted Yankee businessmen—Leland Stanford, Charles Crocker, Collis Huntington, and Mark Hopkins—formed the Central Pacific Railroad to begin carving a path for the iron horse through the granite Sierra and the hauntingly beautiful high desert of Nevada. Meanwhile, Congress incorporated the Union Pacific Railroad to build a line from the Missouri River to a connection with the Central Pacific.

AMERICA'S RAILROADS PERMITTED LARGE-SCALE, INTENSIVE AGRICULTURE BEYOND ANYONE'S WILDEST DREAMS. WHEAT-PRODUCING TOWNS LIKE MORO, OREGON, SHOWN HERE IN 1890, BEGAN TO FEED THE WORLD.

IMMEDIATELY AFTER THE CIVIL WAR, THE NATION CLIMBED ABOARD ITS RAILROADS LIKE NEVER BEFORE. THIS EARLY SLEEPING CAR SUGGESTS THE SPARTAN ACCOMMODATIONS TO BE FOUND FOR OVERNIGHT TRAVEL AT THE TIME.

There was nothing technologically novel about the project. Railroad engineering by that time was well understood, and the hardware available "off the shelf." It was the sheer scale of the endeavor that was audacious, as virtually every scrap of iron and tool for both railroads had to be hauled thousands of miles to the remote railheads. On the Central Pacific line, almost everything came by ship—a 17,000-mile journey around Cape Horn. But the race was on, and each railroad became so proficient that it sometimes laid more than five miles of track a day at the rate of 2,500 ties, 350 rails, 10,000 spikes, and 1,400 bolts per mile—every one put in place by hand.

But whose hands? Because of a labor shortage in the West, the Central Pacific hired Chinese immigrants as laborers, finding them to be such skilled, diligent, and efficient railroad

UNLIKE EUROPE, NORTH AMERICA DID NOT SEGREGATE PASSENGERS ON THE BASIS OF CLASS. HOWEVER, IN DIFFERENT PARTS OF THE COUNTRY THERE MIGHT HAVE BEEN SEPARATE WAITING ROOMS FOR MEN, WOMEN, IMMIGRANTS, PULLMAN PASSENGERS, BLACKS, WHITES, NATIVE AMERICANS, SMOKERS, AND NONSMOKERS.

RAILROAD STATIONS WERE OFTEN THE OUTPOSTS OF CIVILIZATION. THE PRESENCE OF THE RAILROAD GAVE HOPE. FOR ISOLATED PEOPLE, THE STATION MEANT CONTACT WITH THE REST OF THE COUNTRY BY TELEGRAPH, AND TRAINS MEANT THE FREEDOM TO COME AND GO—EVEN IF IT WAS A LONG WAIT.

To a working railroader of the 1890s, a sturdy railroad lantern provided illumination, a means to signal, and on the coldest nights, a tiny bit of warmth.

builders that the C P began recruiting workers from southern China. At one point, more than 14,000 men were at work on the CP—mostly Chinese, along with a handful of Irish- and American-born railroaders. They battled incredible winter snows, granite that yielded only grudgingly to black powder, and some of the roughest terrain on the continent.

On the Union Pacific, Irish and other European immigrants joined former Confederates, Union veterans, and anyone else who could work from sunup to sundown for a dollar or two per day. The men ate beef, bread, and pie; liquids were limited to bad whiskey, boiled coffee, and whatever water was at hand. Ferocious summer heat, terrific storms, and sporadic Indian attacks made hard physical work even worse.

More than a hundred years separate these sections of rail, yet laid at the proper width, both could carry the same train. The "John Brown" rail on the right was imported from Great Britain. The standard "T" rail on the left came in many different sizes and remains standard to this day.

Bear River City, Wyoming, at the railhead of the Union Pacific, in 1868. Like many other "Hell on Wheels" towns, it provided railroad workers with both civilization and vice.

West by Emigrant Train

Only a fraction of the millions of European immigrants landing at America's East Coast ports wished to remain there. A substantial portion headed west, where they could hope to farm, own land, and prosper in a way unimaginable in the Old World.

TODAY'S TRAVELERS CAN ONLY IMAGINE THE DISCOMFORT IMMIGRANTS MUST HAVE FELT SPENDING DAYS AT A TIME ABOARD CROWDED "EMIGRANT" CARS SUCH AS THIS. THE ONLY CHEAPER ALTERNATIVE WAS A RUDELY FITTED-OUT BOXCAR.

Many immigrants had saved for years to make the journey, arranging for railroad transportation while still in Europe; others were met by relatives already here. They wanted to reach their destinations as inexpensively as possible, and railroads tried to accommodate them. Immigrants were not demanding; there were a lot of them; and some day, they would likely become more affluent railroad customers.

Most large railroads provided spartan "emigrant" cars, some of which were merely boxcars with benches. Others were old or stripped-down coaches, into which the new Americans were crowded with all their belongings. Usually, they cooked their meals right in the cars and attempted to sleep as best they could. After a harrowing two-week ocean voyage in steerage on an aging steamship, they could breathe fresh air and dwell upon the future.

For much of the nineteenth century, railroads charged as little as one cent per mile for transportation, or about $8 from the docks of Baltimore to Chicago. In America, even a peasant could ride the rails.

As the tracks advanced farther away from civilization, portable towns dubbed "Hell on Wheels" followed the UP railhead, providing women, gambling, cheap liquor, and the roughest amenities. Some, like Cheyenne, Wyoming, became permanent towns, transforming themselves into respectable communities. Others disappeared without a trace.

The ceremony marking the connection of the two railroads at Promontory Summit, Utah, on May 10, 1869, was small and simple. The Union Pacific had built 1,086 miles of main line; the Central Pacific, 690 miles. After prayers, speeches, and placement of the last rails, dignitaries took turns gently tapping gold and silver spikes into a predrilled laurel tie. The estimated 600 men and women gathered at the site cheered as the telegraph flashed the news to an anxiously waiting

LOCOMOTIVE WHISTLES RANGED FROM THIS SMALL SINGLE-NOTE EXAMPLE FROM THE MID-NINETEENTH CENTURY TO ELABORATE FIVE-NOTE AND "CHIME" WHISTLES COMMON AROUND 1900. SKILLFUL ENGINEERS PLAYED THEM LIKE MUSICAL INSTRUMENTS. TODAY, COLLECTORS PRIZE THEM.

SPREAD PHOTO (NEXT PAGE): WHERE TREES WERE PLENTIFUL, SO WERE WOOD TRESTLES LIKE THIS RECENTLY COMPLETED BRIDGE OVER THE GREEN RIVER ON THE WEST SLOPE OF THE CASCADE MOUNTAINS NEAR SEATTLE. RAILROAD CONSTRUCTION GANGS BROUGHT MEN FROM ALL OVER THE WORLD TOGETHER IN SOMETIMES UNLIKELY PLACES.

ON MAY 10, 1869, RAILROAD DIGNITARIES MINGLED WITH A SMALL CROWD OF A FEW HUNDRED WORKERS AND ONLOOKERS TO CREATE ONE OF THE MOST WELL-KNOWN RAILROAD PHOTOGRAPHS IN HISTORY. AT PROMONTORY SUMMIT, UTAH, THE PACIFIC RAILROAD HAS JUST BEEN COMPLETED.

country: Done! Across the United States, Americans cheered what they regarded as the most important project of their lifetimes—and a sure sign of the prosperity to come.

The Central Pacific and Union Pacific were not long without competitors. In 1864, President Lincoln signed a bill authorizing the construction of the Northern Pacific Railroad from the upper Great Lakes to the Pacific Northwest. A generous land grant of nearly 60 million acres provided collateral for construction mortgages and new lands for Easterners and immigrants hungry for a new life. A lavish gold-spike ceremony marked the completion of this second transcontinental railroad on September 8, 1883.

Just ten years later the indomitable James J. Hill completed the parallel Great Northern Railway, built to the highest standards without government subsidy. It also linked Chicago and the Great Lakes with the forests, farms, and ports of Oregon and Washington. Both railroads reached up into Canada, providing an impetus for the construction of a true Canadian transcontinental.

By the time Canada attained partial independence from Great Britain in 1867, it had a little less than 2,500 miles of track, mostly in the East. The American trans-

THESE MEN ARE BUILDING A PIER FOR THE UP'S GREEN RIVER, WYOMING, BRIDGE THE SAME WAY THEY BUILT THE ENTIRE RAILROAD: BY HAND. SKILLED STONECUTTERS SHAPE THE ROCK, WHILE MASONS AND LABORERS WRESTLE IT INTO PLACE WITH THE HELP OF A HAND DERRICK. A WOOD AND IRON BRIDGE WILL CARRY THE TRACKS ACROSS THE RIVER.

THE CREW OF THIS 1880S SOUTHERN PACIFIC "EMIGRANT" TRAIN IS TYPICAL OF TENS OF THOUSANDS OF THEIR BRETHREN: THE CONDUCTOR, IN UNIFORM; THE ENGINEER, LEANING ON THE LOCOMOTIVE; THE TRAINMEN, WEARING HATS WITH BADGES; THE FIREMAN WITH A MASCOT. THIS WAS HARD, DANGEROUS WORK— BUT IT WAS SOME OF THE BEST WORK TO BE HAD.

continental railroads posed a real threat to the young Dominion of Canada, for its western provinces—most notably British Columbia—demanded the completion of a true Canadian cross-continent railroad as a condition of continued participation in the confederation.

After a few false starts, the Canadian Pacific Railway in 1881 began an astounding push west across the Canadian Rockies that would tie the two oceans with yet another rail route in just four years. A poster celebrating the 1885 feat summed up Canada's feelings: "A Red Letter Day...Our Own Line...No Customs, No Delays, No Transfers, Low Rates, Quick Time." As in the United States, the railroad helped make Canada one country.

Throughout the 1880s, another round of railroad fever swept the United States, as Chicago claimed the title of "Railroad Capital of the

FOR MUCH OF ITS LENGTH, THE UP HAD TO HAUL IN EVERY STICK OF WOOD IT NEEDED FROM DISTANT FORESTS. CARPENTERS (NOTE THE SQUARE IN THE MAN'S HAND) USED SAWS, ADZES, CHISELS, AND MALLETS TO WORK TIMBERS INTO SHAPE. DRAGGED BY HORSES TO THEIR NEEDED LOCATION, THEY WERE SET INTO PLACE WITH DERRICKS AND HUMAN MUSCLE.

The Robber Barons

Like the Gilded Age itself, the so-called "robber barons" flourished only briefly, but they left an indelible mark on nineteenth-century America.

Jay Gould was reviled by the press as one of the most amoral figures in business history. However, at least one scholarly biography suggests that the wily financier was merely doing business according to the prevailing ethics of his time. Gould was simply more aggressive and a better strategic thinker than most of his contemporaries.

Daniel Drew, on the other hand, epitomized the worst the Gilded Age had to offer. As a cattle drover he perfected the technique of watering stock—that is, feeding cattle salt before a sale and

THERE IS NO DOUBT THAT ROBBER BARONS MANIPULATED STOCK AND CONDUCTED BUSINESS IN WAYS THAT WOULD BE PATENTLY ILLEGAL TODAY. BUT IN THE NINETEENTH CENTURY, BOTH BUSINESS LAW AND ETHICS WERE FAR LESS DEVELOPED THAN AT PRESENT, AND THEY WERE OPERATING IN A SOCIETY THAT ENCOURAGED AUDACIOUS BEHAVIOR.

allowing them to drink their fill of water just before being weighed. Drew also made a crooked fortune in steamboats, and then conspired with New York's Boss Tweed to defraud railroad investors.

Drew's greatest contest was with Cornelius Vanderbilt over control of the Erie Railroad. Working with partners Jay Gould and Jim Fisk, Drew used subterfuge, bribery, theft, and every trick known to Wall Street to bankrupt Vanderbilt and control the Erie. The scale of his crimes was breathtaking even in that age of corruption.

In the end, Drew lost his fortune; by the time he died, in 1879, he was dependent on the charity of others.

World" and former frontier outposts such as Denver and Kansas City became bustling railroad centers. Before long, the reach of railroads provided a truly nationwide market for industrial and agricultural goods, allowing regional economic specialization. For example, steelmaking concentrated in the area around Pittsburgh, while the Northern Plains states engaged in large-scale grain production.

Southern railroads worked hard to rebuild so they could connect with the burgeoning national system. At the end of May of 1886, every railroad in the South not built to standard gauge made a marathon effort to change tracks, cars, and locomotives to the national standard of 4'8½". Over a few days, thousands of men shifted rails and moved wheels on their axles to make it possible for true car interchange throughout the nation.

Mineral wealth in the West lured iron rails to the most remote and inaccessible corners of the land. Between 1860 and 1890, Nevada's Comstock Lode alone yielded $340 million in gold and silver. Railroads carried machinery and consumer goods in, ore and metal out, and thousands of treasure seekers in both directions.

Gen. William Jackson Palmer built a Colorado railroad empire to the innovative gauge of three feet between the rails. By century's end,

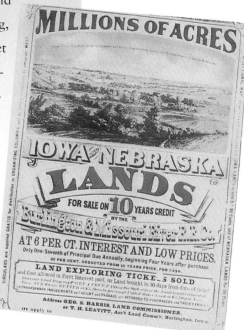

THE B&O'S DIVISION LOCOMOTIVE SHOP COMPLEX AT MARTINSBURG, WEST VIRGINIA, REPRESENTS A TYPICAL MIDSIZED RAILROAD FACILITY OF THE 1870S. THE COVERED ROUNDHOUSE WAS A GARAGE FOR ENGINES; THE RECTANGULAR BUILDINGS HOUSED WORKSHOPS AND MACHINERY.

ADVERTISING POSTERS SUCH AS THIS ONE FROM 1873 CALLED ATTENTION TO THE MILLIONS OF ACRES OF RAILROAD AND GOVERNMENT LAND AVAILABLE AT REASONABLE PRICES. IT IS DIFFICULT TO OVERESTIMATE THE LURE OF CHEAP, FERTILE LAND TO AMERICANS AND IMMIGRANTS SEEKING A BETTER LIFE.

narrow-gauge tracks reached across the Continental Divide at elevations in excess of 10,000 feet to link remote mountain mining towns like Monarch, Ouray, Telluride, and Aspen with cosmopolitan Denver.

Gold also spurred impressive feats of railroad construction in Montana and Idaho. Eventually, less glamorous (but equally valuable) metals such as lead, copper, and nickel, supplemented the boom-and-bust precious metals economy and made yet another generation of miners and railroaders wealthy.

Railroads also opened up the Southwest, where men sought fortunes in cattle, cotton, and wheat. The Atchison, Topeka & Santa Fe Railway completed a through-line from Chicago to the Pacific coast in 1884, the same year Collis P. Huntington and Leland Stanford—two of the "Big Four" who built the Central Pacific—finished the Southern Pacific Railroad from Los Angeles to New Orleans. Finally, the main lines envisioned by the Pacific Railroad Act of 1854 were in place. At about that time, Yankee railroaders turned their attention to Mexico.

Neither the culture nor the economy of Mexico favored the development of railroads, nor was the dry, mountainous country hospitable to the iron horse. The country's first attempt at railroad building began in the mid-1840s;

RAILROAD MACHINISTS LEARNED THEIR CRAFT AS APPRENTICES, AND THEY OFTEN MADE THEIR OWN TOOLS AND THE CASES TO STORE THEM. THIS CHEST REPRESENTED THOUSANDS OF YEARS OF SKILL DISTILLED INTO HARD-WON "FINGER KNOWLEDGE."

LARAMIE, WYOMING, GREW FROM A SMALL TOWN ALONG THE RAILROAD TO A MAJOR WESTERN CITY. EARLY PASSENGERS PAUSED AT RAILROAD HOTELS AND EATING HOUSES SUCH AS THIS ONE FOR MEALS, REST, AND PERHAPS A SIDE TRIP TO HUNT BUFFALO. THE FOOD RANGED FROM SIMPLE BUT SUBSTANTIAL TO UTTERLY WRETCHED, AND TRAVELERS SOMETIMES HAD TO SHARE A BED WITH STRANGERS.

40 years later, less than 400 miles of track were in service. Mexican President Porfirio Díaz set out to change that in 1880, offering concessions to U.S. companies willing to fund and build Mexican railroads. Over the next few decades, rail lines gradually radiated from Mexico City to connect interior points with the U.S. railroad network at Nogales, Arizona, and the Texas towns of Laredo and El Paso.

Many Mexican railroads were in fact controlled by American and British companies, which operated them primarily for north-south commerce. In the traditional agrarian economy of Mexico, railroads did not have the same transforming effect that the railroads of the north did. Only in the twentieth century

BETWEEN THE END OF THE CIVIL WAR AND ABOUT 1900, RAILROADS BUILT PERHAPS 40,000 BUILDINGS OF ALL TYPES THROUGHOUT THE CONTINENT. MANY STATIONS LOOKED ALIKE IN THAT THEY WERE SIMPLE AND SHARED FEATURES LIKE THE AGENT'S BAY WINDOW, THE PLATFORM, AND A FREIGHT ROOM.

would Mexico's railroad network come into its own as a genuine national system.

Americans traveled more than Europeans even before the coming of the railroad. After the Civil War, they created the most mobile society the world had ever known. But it was not without risk or accident. Until the 1850s, serious railroad accidents had been relatively rare, and the few that did occur—such as the 1853 Norwalk disaster, in which a train ran through an open drawbridge, killing 45 persons— usually were the result of a combination of human error and unusual circumstances. That changed as the general pace of life in America accelerated and trains became faster, longer, and more frequent, reducing the margin for error.

The public responded with increasing alarm to railway disasters such as the 1871 Revere, Massachusetts, collision, which killed 29 and seriously injured many more, and the Ashtabula, Ohio, wreck of 1876,

RAILROADS DEVELOPED ELABORATE RULES FOR THE SAFE OPERATION OF TRAINS. LANTERNS AND COLOR SIGNALS PLAYED A LARGE PART IN THOSE RULES. THIS IS A REAR-END MARKER LAMP, USED TO IDENTIFY THE BACK END OF A TRAIN.

FACING PAGE (RIGHT): THE PENNSYLVANIA RAILROAD'S BROAD STREET STATION IN PHILADELPHIA DISPATCHED A TRAIN EVERY FEW MOMENTS DURING BUSY PERIODS. BY THEN, RAILROADING WAS A GIANT TRANSPORTATION MACHINE, AND A TRAIN SUCH AS THIS MIGHT CARRY MAIL, SMALL FREIGHT, AND BOTH COACH AND SLEEPING CAR PASSENGERS.

SARATOGA, NEW YORK, WAS A PLAYGROUND FOR THE WEALTHY IN THE LATE NINETEENTH CENTURY, AS WELL AS HOME OF A FAMOUS RACETRACK AND SPRINGS FREQUENTED BY MIDDLE-CLASS PATRONS WITH MONEY AND PRETENSIONS. THE ORNATE FRENCH-INSPIRED ARCHITECTURE OF THE LARGE STATION WAS INTENDED TO IMPRESS.

which left 80 dead. Even though steamboat accidents killed many more passengers, they were thought to be acts of God. Railroad wrecks were sensational and thought to be examples of human failure or the consequences of corporate greed. It took railroads several decades to improve train-control practices and adopt safety devices sufficient to make railroad travel truly safe.

Eli Janney, a Civil War veteran and store clerk in Alexandria, Virginia, conceived and patented the first "knuckle" coupler in 1868. His design, the basis for the couplers of today, resembled two hands clasped together when joined. Able to close and lock automatically, they could be opened from the side of the car, greatly reducing the number and severity of casualties suffered by brakemen using the treacherous link-and-pin couplers. By the 1890s, there were many different styles of so-called Janney couplers in use, but many of them would not join with each other. A prudent conduc-

WHEN RAILROADS BORROWED THE IDEA OF THE DINING CAR FROM STEAMBOATS, THEY ALSO BORROWED A TRADITION OF HEAVY, DECORATED HOTEL-GRADE CHINA. THIS EXAMPLE FROM THE 1880S FEATURES AN ELABORATE "B&O" AND BORDER PATTERN.

AS THIS BEAUTIFULLY RESTORED VIRGINIA & TRUCKEE RAILROAD COACH SHOWS, EVEN PASSENGERS IN THE REMOTEST PARTS OF THE COUNTRY ENJOYED COLOR AND FINE CRAFTSMANSHIP IN THE 1870S. THE RELATIVELY LOW COST OF LABOR MADE FANCY STENCIL WORK AND PAINTED CLOTH HEADLINERS AFFORDABLE FOR EVEN THE MOST BUSINESSLIKE RAILROAD.

tor might have to carry a dozen different spare "knuckles" on his caboose.

In 1869, George Westinghouse patented his first air brake. By 1873, he had developed the triple valve, the key component in the creation of an "automatic" air brake. Instead of using compressed air directly from the locomotive to provide the force for pressing brake shoes against the wheels, his system placed a reservoir of air under each car and charged them from a continuous brake pipe linked to the locomotive. That way, if the air pump failed or the train parted, air stored on each car could apply the brakes automatically—an especially useful fail-safe feature.

During competitive trials in 1887–1888, the Westinghouse design proved so superior that it was made the universal standard. It was

SOME CARS WERE TASTEFULLY PLAIN, AS WAS THIS COACH BUILT FOR THE NORFOLK & WESTERN RAILWAY. THE "WALKOVER" SEATS COULD BE REVERSED. THE CAR HAD TOILETS, STOVES, SLATTED SHUTTERS TO KEEP OUT CINDERS, GAS LIGHTS, AND PROBABLY STEAM HEAT—ALL THE AMENITIES OF COACH TRAVEL IN THE LATE NINETEENTH CENTURY.

THE PULLMAN PALACE-CAR COMPANY BUILT THE ALEXANDER FOR A. A. MCLEOD, PRESIDENT OF THE PHILADELPHIA & READING RAILWAY. THIS 1890 VIEW SHOWS THE CAR OUTSIDE THE SHOPS AT PULLMAN, ILLINOIS, SITE OF A MAJOR STRIKE FOUR YEARS LATER.

The Birth of Standard Time

Before railroads, America was a largely agrarian nation with widely dispersed settlements. Each place of consequence observed its own "sun" time, determined when the sun passed directly overhead. Thus when it was 9 A.M. in Boston, it was only 8:36 A.M. in Washington, and 12 minutes earlier in Pittsburgh. That was fine for farmers, but railroads needed something less complicated.

Before the Civil War, railroads in New England had agreed to use a common time, and small regions throughout the country gradually saw the merits of such a system. It fell to the railroads, however, to create the Standard Time we all use today.

In 1883, after much discussion, the General and Southern

A REFLECTION OF COMPANY PRIDE, THIS E. HOWARD CLOCK WAS MADE IN BOSTON FOR A RAILROAD IN WISCONSIN.

Railway Time Conventions—representing all of the railroads in the United States—adopted a plan dividing the continent into "zones," within which all railroads would operate to a common standard time. Each zone was an hour different from its neighbors, and the boundaries were fixed based on longitude adjusted for local features.

November 18, 1883, was "The Day of Two Noons," when railroads across the country reset their clocks. Despite howls of protest from citizens who thought time to be God's alone to regulate, standardized time simplified railroad operations and made travel safer. The rest of the country quickly adopted Railway Standard Time, and Congress made it official in 1918.

adopted early for passenger trains, but it took an act of Congress (the Railway Safety Appliance Act of 1893) to force the railroads to speed its application to freight trains. The air brake was perhaps the most important single railroad invention of the period.

George Pullman, who had vastly improved the quality of sleeping and dining cars, popularized the vestibule for passenger cars beginning in 1887. Previously, cars had open platforms, making it dangerous to cross from car to car when the train was in motion. The vestibule enclosed the platform and joined the cars with the familiar flexible-canvas diaphragm, making the train into one continuous unit and encouraging the development of specialized lounge, dining, and other cars.

A German tinsmith by the name of Julius Pintsch devised a lighting system based on compressed petroleum gas. It gave brighter light with less smoke than the old kerosene lamps. Advances in hygiene (water coolers, flush toilets), comfort (window screens, larger and better-ventilated berths), and safety (anti-telescoping devices, stronger wheels) made rail travel more safe and comfortable for all passengers.

Freight trains grew longer and more productive, with larger cars operating at higher speeds. Coal drags might still be run at a leisurely 15 miles per hour by the 1890s, but perishable freight such as fruit and livestock might wheel along at 40—

THE BEST TRAINS CARRIED CARS WITH OBSERVATION OR "SUN" ROOMS. HERE, IN LESS FORMAL SETTINGS, PASSENGERS MIGHT CONVERSE, ENJOY A LIBATION, OR SIMPLY SETTLE BACK TO WATCH THE SCENERY. EVEN THEN, AMERICAN TRAVELERS WERE A VARIED AND OFTEN CONTENTIOUS LOT.

RAILROADS USUALLY ASSIGNED "OFFICER'S" (OR "OFFICE") CARS TO SENIOR EXECUTIVES, WHO LIVED ABOARD THEM DURING INSPECTION TRIPS AND DISTANT MEETINGS. THEY HAD COMFORTABLE LIVING, DINING, AND SLEEPING SPACES, BUT THEY WERE MEANT FOR BUSINESS. THE FIREPLACE HELPED HEAT THE CAR WHEN IT WAS PARKED ON A SIDING AWAY FROM A SUPPLY OF STEAM.

or even 50—miles per hour. Throughout the 1860s and '70s, railroads adopted the caboose, giving brakemen and the conductor some shelter and safety, and in the process creating a symbol of American railroading. The increasing use of iron and steel in freight cars, as well as new types of cars—such as tank cars for the transport of petroleum used to make lamp fuel—dramatically changed the very nature of freight transportation. By the last quarter of the century, it was possible to ship almost anything, almost anywhere, by rail.

Locomotives, too, grew larger and more sophisticated. A new generation of trained mechanics and engineers virtually reinvented the locomotive and made railroading the "high technology" of its day. The highly decorated wood-burning 4-4-0s of the Civil War evolved by 1900 into starkly black, no-nonsense coal-burning behemoths weighing twice as much. By 1900, builders in the United States, Canada, and

KEROSENE LAMPS, POLISHED DARK WOOD, AND BOLDLY PATTERNED UPHOLSTERY CHARACTERIZE THIS SLEEPING CAR FROM THE EARLY 1890S. THE FOLDING UPPER BERTHS ARE VISIBLE ABOVE. WHILE THE CAR WAS OF WOOD, ITS SIZE, WEIGHT, AND LEVEL OF COMFORT WOULD HAVE APPROACHED THAT OF MODERN STEEL CARS.

CROWDED WITH HEAVY METALWORKING MACHINERY AND TEEMING WITH SKILLED EMPLOYEES, THE HUNDREDS OF RAILROAD SHOPS ACROSS NORTH AMERICA REPRESENTED A CONSIDERABLE PORTION OF THE CONTINENT'S INDUSTRIAL CAPACITY. ALMOST ANY SHOP OF THIS SIZE COULD BUILD LOCOMOTIVES FROM SCRATCH.

Mexico had turned out more than 70,000 locomotives of all shapes, sizes, and types.

Elijah McCoy was one of several black inventors and mechanics active in the railroad industry. Advertising for the mechanical lubricator he developed gave us the expression "the real McCoy." Other inventors relentlessly pursued the quest for more power, more speed, and greater efficiency. Railroading was an industry in which small economies added up over the long haul, so the locomotive was subject to constant tinkering.

In the turbulent 1870s and 1880s, people throughout the United States came to regard railroads with a mixture of admiration and hatred. The Credit Mobilier scandal provides but one example. Certain

POSED FOR ITS FORMAL BUILDER'S PORTRAIT OUTSIDE THE WILMINGTON, DELAWARE, SHOP OF JACKSON & SHARP, THIS COACH IS TYPICAL OF CARS BUILT FOR SHORTLINE AND NARROW GAUGE RAILROADS IN THE 1860S AND 1870S. IT WAS MADE MOSTLY OF WOOD AND REQUIRED A HIGH DEGREE OF SKILLED LABOR.

RAILROADS OPENED FLORIDA FOR DEVELOPMENT IN THE LATE NINETEENTH CENTURY. HENRY PLANT WAS ONE OF SEVERAL SOUTHERN RAILROAD TYCOONS WHO USED NORTHERN MONEY TO BUILD SUBSTANTIAL SYSTEMS. THIS WOOD-BURNING 4-4-0 WITH TWO COACHES IS TYPICAL OF THE PERIOD.

officers of the Union Pacific formed a separate construction company to raise capital and ensure that influential backers received a suitable return on their investment—which in one year alone totaled 348 percent. Investigations held after the scandal broke in 1872 revealed that key congressmen had accepted Credit Mobilier stock as a gratuity. Ulysses S. Grant and future President James A. Garfield were among those implicated.

Rate wars and rate discrimination were other examples of the railroads "not playing fair." In a vicious cycle leading some railroads to near-ruin, competing lines would undercut each other's rates to capture traffic. Conversely, railroads often charged whatever the traffic would bear, without regard for what seemed reasonable to the traveler or shipper. Some companies granted rebates or kickbacks to powerful shippers such as John D. Rockefeller and Standard Oil. The

ALTHOUGH IT WAS A WELL-PLANNED, BUT UNOFFICIAL, PUBLICITY STUNT, THERE IS LITTLE DOUBT NEW YORK CENTRAL NO. 999 AND CARS FROM THE EMPIRE STATE EXPRESS REACHED A SPPED OF 112 MILES PER HOUR IN MAY OF 1893. CRACKING THE CENTURY MARK SPURRED A QUEST FOR EVEN GREATER SPEED.

ON EACH FLANK OF ALMOST EVERY STEAM LOCOMOTIVE, A BRASS OR BRONZE PLAQUE SUCH AS THIS PROVIDED THE ENGINE'S PEDIGREE. THIS WAS ITS "BIRTH CERTIFICATE," IMPORTANT BECAUSE A LOCOMOTIVE COULD BE RENUMBERED MANY TIMES. THIS PLAQUE WAS FROM THE 2,475TH LOCOMOTIVE BUILT BY THE BROOKS LOCOMOTIVE WORKS.

unfairness of these practices so enraged the public that Congress created the Interstate Commerce Commission in 1887 to bring some order to the unruly industry. This marked the first time the federal government attempted the direct regulation of American business.

Railroads also varied between fairness and harshness in their dealings with their workers. Some executives believed in paying a living wage and accepted the right of employees to form labor organizations and bargain collectively. Others took the view that labor was a commodity to be purchased at the lowest cost without regard for the individuals involved.

The economic depression of the 1870s brought these practices into sharp relief, when the Pennsylvania Railroad and other roads in 1877 reduced wages by 10 percent while preserving dividend payments. Train and engine crews went on strike in protest, and violence flared as state militias were dispatched to keep the trains running. So great was workers' hostility towards the Pennsylvania Railroad that riot damage to its property totaled more than $2 million.

The social discontent revealed by the Strike of 1877 frightened leaders and citizens alike. Serious strikes in 1888 and

THE LATE NINETEENTH-CENTURY PRESS VILLIFIED JAY GOULD AND WILLIAM H. VANDERBILT FOR THEIR PERCEIVED IMMORALITY AND RAPACIOUS BUSINESS METHODS. IN FACT, THEIR VAST ACCUMULATIONS OF WEALTH AND POWER VIOLATED DEEPLY HELD AMERICAN NOTIONS OF EQUALITY AND "FAIR PLAY."

A SKILLFUL MANIPULATOR, JAY GOULD BECAME A NATIONAL CELEBRITY BECAUSE OF HIS CRAFTY DEALINGS IN RAILROAD SECURITIES—OFTEN AT THE EXPENSE OF SMALLER INVESTORS.

1894 further polarized railroad labor and management, as they revealed the human cost of laissez-faire capitalism and rapid industrialization.

Throughout the period, crafty railroad promoters manipulated Wall Street and found ingenious ways to fleece investors. Rascals such as Daniel Drew, who bled the Erie Railroad of tens of millions of dollars, gave rise to the term "Robber Baron" and personified corporate America to the average worker.

In fairness, it should be noted that most executives were honest and sincerely interested in building their companies. And although railroading created millionaires at a fantastic pace, many railroad fortunes were the basis for great philanthropic works. Stanford University, The Johns Hopkins Hospitals, and art museums throughout the

MUCH OF THE STRIFE CONNECTED WITH THE RAILWAY STRIKE OF 1894 CENTERED IN ILLINOIS. OVER THE OBJECTIONS OF THE STATE'S GOVERNOR, PRESIDENT GROVER CLEVELAND SENT IN FEDERAL TROOPS TO SUPPRESS THE STRIKE. THIS IS COMPANY "C" OF THE 15TH U.S. INFANTRY AT BLUE ISLAND, ILLINOIS.

country are just some of the institutions created from the bequests of nineteenth-century railroad leaders.

As the country emerged from the Civil War, perhaps 150,000 men and women worked for railroads, with thousands more (no one knows how many) engaged in collateral work. By 1900, the number of railroad employees exceeded one million, with tens of thousands making a living in related fields, such as producing railway supplies. These railroaders were men and women of all races, faiths, and political persuasions.

There was discrimination, to be sure. Blacks and Latinos could be firemen but not engineers; skilled trades and union membership were open to a select few; sometimes jobs were assigned on the basis of religion; and the most recent immigrants usually held the dirtiest, most hazardous, and lowest-paying jobs. The railroad was a mirror of American society at large, with all of its imperfections and opportunities, but it was also a tool for nation-building.

Nowhere was that more evident than in the task of carrying immigrants to their new homes. Some railroads actually employed agents in Europe to recruit entire families and villages to settle the vast tracts of farmable land served by the company's tracks. Other lines provided special

During the Railway Strike of 1894, hunger, despair, and anger sometimes drove mobs to acts of violence against railroad property. In response, National Guardsmen sent to protect that property fired upon the mobs, killing and wounding many. The bloodshed so appalled the nation that new ways were sought to settle labor disputes.

Virtually unchanged for more than a century, the bell-pattern spike maul remains one of the most basic and useful tools on the railroad. The long head allows the hammer face to strike the spike over the top of the rail, while its considerable weight helps drive the spike home.

The Electric Railroad

*C*harles Grafton Page made the first trip on a battery-powered locomotive in America in 1851, but only after Thomas Edison, Werner von Siemens, and others had perfected dynamos and motors was modern electric traction made practical for railroads. The basic knowledge was available by 1880, and in 1884 an electric streetcar was being tested in Kansas City.

In 1888, a brilliant young electrical engineer by the name of Frank Sprague completed the first successful electric railway system in Richmond, Virginia. Forty streetcars operated over 12 miles of track, starting a boom in electric railway construction. Almost 15,000 miles were in service by 1900.

The B&O Railroad traditionally claimed the honor of being the first steam railroad to use electric locomotives over a portion of its line. In 1895, the B&O developed a system that allowed it to switch power to an overhead third rail so that pioneer General Electric locomotives ("motors," as they are often known) could begin hauling trains through long tunnels without asphyxiating passengers or crew.

In reality, the first standard-gauge electric locomotive to replace a steam locomotive in regular service was an odd-looking, 21-ton contraption built in 1889 for the Whitinsville Machine Company in Massachusetts. It hauled freight between a railroad main line and a manufacturing plant 1½ miles away.

CINCINNATI WAS ONE OF THE FIRST MAJOR CITIES TO FULLY EMBRACE THE TROLLEY CAR. IN FRONT OF CITY HALL IN 1890, THIS EARLY "SUMMER CAR" (WITHOUT WINDOWS) IS BOUND FOR PRICE HILL.

MOST HAND LANTERNS WERE MADE OF PRESSED STEEL OR TINPLATE. A FEW, OFTEN CALLED "PRESENTATION LANTERNS" BECAUSE THEY WERE RETIREMENT OR PROMOTION GIFTS, WERE OF BRASS. STYLE-CONSCIOUS TRAIN CREWS MIGHT ALSO USE A FANCY LANTERN AS A SHOW OF PRIDE.

trains to meet the ships that brought more than 8 million new Americans into the country between 1870 and 1900. Almost 789,000 immigrants arrived in 1882 alone, and most journeyed at least some distance by rail. The extensive reach of the railroad network meant that these new Americans could spread throughout the country, rather than concentrating in the eastern cities. Railroads, in effect, stirred the melting pot.

The steel highway improved the lives of millions of city dwellers. By the 1890s, the United States was becoming an urban nation, and railroads supplied cities and towns with food, fuel, building materials, and access to markets. The simple presence of railroads could bring a city economic prosperity. Railroads even helped shape the physical growth of cities and towns, as steam railroads and then electric street railways

BY THE 1860S, HORSE-DRAWN STREET RAILWAYS PROVIDED SERVICE IN MOST MAJOR CITIES. THEY WERE SLOW, OFTEN CROWDED, AND EXPENSIVE. BUT RIDING WAS BETTER THAN WALKING, AND THEY RAN ON PREDICTABLE ROUTES. THIS WAS THE BEGINNING OF URBAN MASS TRANSIT IN THE UNITED STATES.

THIS TELEGRAPH KEY COULD MEAN THE DIFFERENCE BETWEEN LIFE AND DEATH. RAILROADS WENT TO GREAT LENGTHS TO KEEP THEIR TELEGRAPH LINES FUNCTIONING.

facilitated growth along their lines and made suburban living feasible.

Mail, sorted enroute aboard Railway Post Office (RPO) Cars, permitted reliable and rapid communication. Railway express and the rise of mail-order merchants permitted people in the most remote rural areas to enjoy inexpensive consumer goods. Telegraphy and railroading had been inseparable since the beginning, and virtually everywhere there was a railroad, there was a telegraph wire.

In 1893, the United States celebrated the 400th anniversary of the "discovery" of the New World with a spectacular fair in Chicago. The Transportation Building at the "World's Columbian Exposition" featured railroad exhibits and equipment from around the world, but the most lavish displays were from Baldwin Locomotive Works, the Pullman Palace Car Company, and other American companies. The B&O erected a huge exhibit tracing the entire history of the railroad, while the Pennsylvania and New York Central railroads had separate exhibit buildings.

THE ADOLPHUS WAS ONE OF THE FINEST PRIVATE CARS TO GRACE THE RAILS IN THE NINETEENTH CENTURY. BUILT FOR ST. LOUIS BREWING MAGNATE ADOLPH BUSCH, IT WAS A FULLY EQUIPPED LUXURY HOTEL ON WHEELS. WEALTHY FAMILIES USED CARS LIKE THIS FOR EVERYTHING FROM TRAVEL TO RESORTS TO BUSINESS MEETINGS. THESE WERE THE PRIVATE JETS OF THEIR ERA.

The world's fair marks the high point of the railroad in American life. By the mid-1890s, almost the entire North American transport network was oriented around the 200,000 miles of track extending from the Atlantic to the Pacific and also connecting with substantial networks in the neighboring countries of Canada and Mexico.

By then, New York Central's *Empire State Express* had exceeded 100 miles per hour on its runs to Chicago, leaving no doubt about rail travel's potential for speed. As for comfort, Pullman cars of the day rivaled the finest hotels for the level of service and creature comforts pro-

WHETHER HOMEMADE OR STORE-BOUGHT, TOY TRAINS FIRED THE IMAGINATION OF BOYS—AND A FEW GIRLS— THROUGHOUT THE NINETEENTH CENTURY. IT DID NOT MATTER THAT THE CHICAGO, MILWAUKEE & ST. PAUL DID NOT HAVE A NO. 999.

IN 1873, THE PENNSYLVANIA RAILROAD COMPLETED THIS STATION IN WASHINGTON, D.C., ON THE SITE NOW OCCUPIED BY THE NATIONAL GALLERY OF ART. IN 1881, AN ASSASSIN SHOT PRESIDENT JAMES A. GARFIELD AS HE PASSED THROUGH THE BUILDING. THE STATION AND ITS TRACKS WERE REPLACED BY THE NEW UNION STATION IN 1907.

vided. Railroads offered convenience, taking travelers across the continent in less than a week—or down branch lines to the most remote Appalachian hamlet in a matter of days.

In the West, railroads helped open new territory to economic exploitation, and then played a large part in the creation of the first national parks. They also pioneered modern forms of hotels, resorts, and restaurants. As the nineteenth century ebbed, every aspect of society and culture was reflected in the railroad. When the Supreme Court ruled that racial segregation was legal, railroads in the South responded with "Jim Crow" cars having "separate, but equal," accommodations. There also were special Temperance Movement trains, as well as excursions promoting the vote for women.

By the turn of the century, tourists had become a major source of traffic for many railroads, especially those serving resort areas such as New York's Catskill Mountains. Trains had helped build industrial America; now they helped bosses and workers alike find recreation.

At 1,400 feet long, the Kaflle River Bridge in Rhode Island epitomized the state of railroad engineering in the late nineteenth century. Heavier, faster trains required substantial bridges. Inexpensive steel and new engineering designs permitted railroads to build impressive structures like this one. Many are still in service.

Women Working on the Railroad

For more than 150 years, women have been working on the railroads of America. As early as the 1830s, railroads employed women to clean cars and stations, cook in railroad eating houses, and do laundry. Before the Civil War, Andrew Carnegie (then an official on the Pennsylvania Railroad) began training women as railroad telegraphers, believing them more skilled than men at the task. After the war, railroads cautiously began hiring women as file clerks, "typewriters," and for other office tasks.

World War I marked the first time women were permitted to work as shop laborers and machinist helpers—traditionally male jobs. Some remained in those positions after the conflict, and severe World War II labor shortages gave American women in particular even greater access to better-paying "men's" work.

Since the 1970s, increasing numbers of women have excelled in every job from brakeman and laborer to railroad president.

Today, it is not unusual to find a woman at the throttle of an intermodal freight train or an Amtrak passenger train, and enlightened company policies—backed up by federal law—make any railroad job open to anyone who is qualified to do the work.

PHOTOGRAPHED IN 1942, THESE FEMALE WORKERS AT THE LONG ISLAND RAILROAD'S MORRIS PARK SHOPS HAVE REPLACED A SERVICE CREW THAT WAS PROBABLY ALL-MALE BEFORE WORLD WAR II. MANY WOMEN KEPT THESE JOBS AFTER THE WAR.

Americans celebrated the railroad in song, literature, and art. The fledgling motion-picture industry turned its hand-cranked cameras on speeding trains because they were the most exciting things on wheels. Virtually every form of entertainment traveled by rail, from the latest popular magazines to touring circuses and New York theater companies.

By 1900, the people of Canada, Mexico, and the United States had settled a vast continent that the best minds of Thomas Jefferson's day thought would take a thousand years to occupy. Largely because of railroads, it took only a few decades.

FOR SOME, THE REAL WEALTH TO BE TAKEN FROM THE WEST WAS IN THE FORM OF TIMBER FOR THE CONTINUING BUILDING BOOM. THIS WOOD-BURNING "CLIMAX" GEARED LOCOMOTIVE WAS INEXPENSIVE, POWERFUL, AND COULD HAUL LOGS EVEN ON POOR, TEMPORARY TRACK.

PERHAPS NOTHING IS SO SYMBOLIC OF THE LOCOMOTIVE ENGINEER AS THE LONG-SPOUT OIL CAN. WITH HUNDREDS OF MOVING PARTS NEEDING LUBRICATION, THIS WAS AN INDISPENSABLE TOOL. A SINGLE LOCOMOTIVE MIGHT USE SEVERAL QUARTS IN THE COURSE OF AN ORDINARY RUN.

Chapter 3

DAWN OF THE MODERN RAILROAD

By 1900, America's railroads were very nearly at their peak, both in terms of overall mileage and employment. In the 20 years leading up to World War I, however, the foundations of railroading would change drastically. New technology would be introduced, and the nation would go to war, during which time the railroads would be run by the government. Most significantly, the railroads would enter the age of government regulation.

THE PROFOUND CHANGES THAT CAME WITH THE TROLLEY INCLUDED INEXPENSIVE AND FREQUENT SERVICE TO NEW "STREETCAR SUBURBS," AMUSEMENT PARKS, AND BEACHES. IN SUMMER, OPEN-AIR "BREEZERS" LIKE THIS 1902 BRIGHTON BEACH CAR NO. 2048 OFFERED RESPITE FROM THE HUMIDITY OF THE ATLANTIC SEABOARD.

The dawn of the twentieth century was, for the most part, eagerly anticipated by America. There was much to celebrate. Things were going well for business, and that meant there was employment for almost everyone.

Railroads capitalized on the prosperity with colorful brochures promoting top-notch passenger trains. The West was glorified as the nation's wonderland, regularly being featured in railroad-commissioned paintings and in the pages of numerous magazines. Posters featuring dreamy damsels lured vacationers to exotic destinations like California, while fast "Limiteds" raced business travelers across the land.

The nation's railroads were still growing. By 1900, more than 195,000 miles of track were in service, and there were still another 16

years of expansion ahead. The biggest opportunities existed in the West and in the South, where large portions of the landscape were still lightly populated.

During the years preceding World War I, the Florida East Coast Railroad extended its rails all the way to Key West; the Union Pacific reached Los Angeles by crossing through the Utah, Nevada, and California deserts; the Western Pacific completed its line from Salt Lake City to Oakland, California; and the Chicago, Milwaukee, St. Paul & Pacific linked the Midwest to the West Coast.

It was around this time that the passenger train achieved levels of dependability, comfort, and speed that rail passengers would generally enjoy for the next 50 to 60 years. Trains became so reliable as to en-

SEASIDE PLAYGROUND MARGATE, NEW JERSEY, WAS PUT WITHIN EASY REACH OF NEW YORK BY THE ADVANCE OF SUBURBAN RAILROADS IN THE EARLY 1900S. "LUCY, THE MARGATE ELEPHANT," CONTAINING SHOPS, AN OBSERVATION DECK, AND A RESTAURANT, WAS A MAJOR ATTRACTION FOR URBAN FUN-SEEKERS.

THE RAILWAY MAIL SERVICE MOVED MAIL NIGHT AND DAY BY TRAIN, AND MAIL SORTING CREWS ON TRAINS WERE REQUIRED TO HANDLE MAIL EVEN IF THE TRAIN'S LIGHTING SYSTEM FAILED. WHEN IT HAPPENED, MORE THAN A DOZEN CANDLE LAMPS LIKE THIS ONE WOULD BE HUNG ON THE MAIL CAR WALLS AND THE WORK RESUMED.

courage entire generations of business travelers to schedule meetings in distant cities the next day, and the basic amenities of train travel— a comfortable lounge, impeccable dining car service, sleeping cars with restrooms and running water, and carpets through- out—were here to stay. Railroads even began to regularly operate their finer trains at speeds that even today's trav- elers would consider "fast"—80 to 100 miles per hour.

Nowhere was the railroad more evident than in the newsworthy events and popular culture of the day, which often featured colorful tales of railroading and railroaders. Take the story of Casey Jones, for instance. Although apparently due to Casey's own misjudgment, the famous wreck of his passenger train in 1900 at Vaughan, Mississippi—in which he perished—resulted in the deaths of no passengers. By sticking with his locomotive until it was too late to save himself, engineer Casey was able to slow the train appreciably,

BALTIMORE & OHIO'S MOST LUXURIOUS PASSENGER TRAIN OF THE 1890S, THE ROYAL BLUE, USED CHINA OF THIS PATTERN IN ITS DINING CARS.

THE ERA IN REVIEW

1898:
Spain and the United States go to war over Cuba's right to independence.

1900:
Casey Jones' famous train wreck occurs at Vaughn, Mississippi. Jones pays for his miscalculation with his life, but no passengers are killed, and the engineer becomes an American legend.

1901:
The federal government files suit against Northern Securities, a giant rail holding company, for restraint of trade.

1902:
Diesel power is on the rise, operating the entire Corliss Engine Works manufacturing operation. Street railways, meanwhile, carry five billion passengers nationwide.

1906:
Two-thirds of U.S. railroad mileage is controlled by a handful of rail magnates. Congress strengthens the regulatory power of the Interstate Commerce Commission.

1908:
Henry Ford introduces his Model T gas-powered automobile.

minimizing the collision's effects. The resultant publicity painted Casey as a hero; here was the story of a "brave engineer" who gave his life to save those of his passengers. The tale—and the popular song that soon followed—remain a permanent part of American folklore and history today.

ALTHOUGH THE TRADITIONAL STRIPED CAP HAS BECOME SYNONYMOUS WITH RAILROAD ENGINEERS, OTHER STYLES OF HEADGEAR WERE NOT UNCOMMON. THIS VERSION, BEARING A SOUTHERN PACIFIC HAT PLATE, HAS BEEN DATED TO SOMETIME BEFORE 1920.

With the rise of motion pictures and movie theaters, railroads and railroaders would enjoy a lengthy stay in the cinematic limelight. The success of the 1903 film *The Great Train Robbery*—a simple, fast-paced "shoot-'em-up" Western—guaranteed that more train-related movies would follow.

In 1905, a record-breaking dash by train, from Los Angeles to Chicago via the Santa Fe, was another railroading event that captured the nation's attention. The instigator, Walter Scott—popularly known as "Death Valley Scotty" and widely remembered for his colorful

THE ERA IN REVIEW

1909:
Milwaukee Road joins the ranks of transcontinental railroads.

1910:
Penn Station opens in New York City.

1914:
War breaks out in Europe.

1916:
America's peak year for railroad mileage—254,037—and employment—1,701,000. U.S. industrial activity picks up for the war effort.

1917:
The United States formally enters World War I. The federal government assumes control of American railroads as a wartime measure on December 28.

1918:
Armistice is signed on November 11. U.S. Railway Administration Director-General advocates five-year "test" of government control.

1919:
President Wilson announces that railroads will be returned to private control within a year.

Railroad Art

The western railroads, blessed with magnificent scenery, began commissioning painters to capture landscapes on canvas. Before the advent of color photography, paintings were necessary for printed materials such as calendars, brochures, menus, and posters. Artwork thus promoted the railroad's image as an arts patron while contributing to its advertising programs.

Thomas Moran, a well-known painter, had a key role in getting art programs started at the Northern Pacific and Atchison, Topeka & Santa Fe railroads.

Moran was a guest on an expedition to Wyoming's Yellowstone area in 1871 at the request of Jay Cooke and Company, NP financiers; Cooke's $500 advance permitted

THE FINANCIERS BACKING THE CONSTRUCTION OF THE NORTHERN PACIFIC RAILROAD SUBSIDIZED PAINTER THOMAS MORAN'S EARLY FORAYS INTO THE WEST. LATER, THEY USED MANY OF HIS PAINTINGS IN RAILROAD ADVERTISEMENTS.

Moran to make the trip and, ultimately, to paint his *Grand Canyon of the Yellowstone*, which today hangs in the Smithsonian Institution's National Museum of American Art in Washington, D.C. The railway reproduced the work as a lithograph and distributed thousands of copies.

William H. Bull, who came to California in 1893, carefully crafted bird's-eye views for the Southern Pacific. Maynard Dixon's work for Southern Pacific started in 1902, when he began working for *Sunset* magazine, then published by the SP passenger department.

Among the other major railroads that maintained art programs of appreciable size were the Denver & Rio Grande and Great Northern.

claims about his mining exploits—apparently hired the train purely for publicity's sake.

Periodicals, literature, and even the Post Office featured railroads in ways that could not escape public notice. Following its celebrated dash in 1893 at a top speed of 112.5 miles per hour, New York Central's famous locomotive, No. 999, had its likeness reproduced on a two-cent postage stamp. From accounts of cross-country rail travel in *Harper's Weekly* to Frank Norris's emotional, less-than-flattering fictional account of the struggle between farmers and the railroads in *The Octopus*, the nation's train system was constantly being observed and scrutinized.

Of course, there had to a be a downside, too. And indeed there was, in the form of a growing uneasiness among Americans about the ownership and management of the nation's biggest business—which the railroads had collectively become—being concentrated in the hands of a relative few. How much power was too much? Was government regulation or control necessary, or were market forces the best way to keep these empires in check? Widely talked about by citizens and politicians alike, and discussed in books such as *The Railroad Question*, these were issues that would not go away in the first decades of the twentieth century.

Before the turn of the century, railroads were engaged in an ongoing process of innovation, ex-

This "special ticket" for the Southern Pacific Railroad, issued in 1893, gave its bearer the right to travel on the company's trains "between all stations west of El Paso."

The level of basic comforts in standard mainline railroad cars rose quickly after 1890. Luxurious carpeting, inlaid woods, gas and electric lighting, plush upholstery, and fine dining on many trains added to the allure of a smooth round-trip journey to faraway places like the Rockies or the Grand Canyon.

pansion, and consolidation. Railroads shaped the nation, and were in turn shaped by it.

The new century was no different in a basic sense; the changes continued. But while some of the changes offered promise others seemed of less use, at least to the railroads. There were even innovations that, down the road, would pose competitive threats to railroads, though these were largely unrecognized at first.

Consider the telephone, for instance. In the early 1900s it was supplanting the telegraph on American railroads. The idea was the same—electrical impulses carried over wires—yet "telephony" represented a way to make these transmissions accessible to everyone. Previously, the station agent in many small towns was often the only person who had the "power" to translate telegraphic messages sent in Morse code.

AFTER 1900, THE PULLMAN COMPANY COULD BOAST THE GREATEST NUMBER OF SLEEPING CARS IN SERVICE. AS BUILDER OF ITS OWN CARS—AND ACQUIRER OF COMPETING COMPANIES' VEHICLES AS ITS SERVICE NETWORK GREW—THE PULLMAN NAME BECAME A HOUSEHOLD WORD.

The telephone held tremendous possibilities for business as well. It offered a way to communicate in real words, in real time—and at a moment's notice. Some observers speculated that there would be less need for traveling and face-to-face meetings in the future; there was even the possibility that telephones might prove useful in the home.

The internal-combustion engine also held promise for railroads. As early as 1890, a primitive 18-horsepower gasoline engine was used near Chicago to demonstrate the usefulness of self-propelled railcars. Just after the turn of the century, primitive gas-mechanical and gas-electric cars (the distinction being manifest in the transmissions) were built for such railroads as the Erie, the Pennsylvania, the Union Pacific, and the Southern Pacific.

As it turned out, self-propelled cars offered savings in the form of labor, but were generally quite troublesome to keep functioning prop-

THE BEAUTIFULLY PRESERVED INTERIOR OF A STRASBURG RAILROAD PARLOR CAR. BASED IN THE PENNSYLVANIA TOWN OF THAT NAME, THE HISTORIC LINE SURVIVES TODAY AS A SUCCESSFUL TOURIST RAILROAD.

BEFORE 1900, MOST RAILROAD CARS WERE BUILT PRIMARILY OF WOOD. AS ACCIDENTS INVOLVING WOODEN CARS INCREASED, COMPOSITE STEEL AND FULL-STEEL PASSENGER CARS BEGAN TO APPEAR. BY 1913, WHEN THE STEEL-BUILT PULLMAN SLEEPING CAR "FERNWOOD" WAS SIDESWIPED AND PHOTOGRAPHED BY HER OWNERS, THE OBVIOUS SAFETY QUALITIES OF STEEL WERE ABUNDANTLY CLEAR.

SPREAD PHOTO (NEXT PAGE): COLUMBIA RAILWAY NO. 20 IS FILLED WITH SCHOOLGIRLS ON A FOURTH OF JULY FIELD TRIP. WASHINGTON, D.C., AND NEW YORK CITY BOTH HAD IMPRESSIVE ELECTRIFIED STREETCAR SYSTEMS THAT FEATURED UNDER-STREET ELECTRIC CURRENT.

The "Safety First" Movement

*I*n an early and highly successful venture in worker participation, railroads turned to employee safety committees for help in reducing the costs of injuries and deaths. It fell to a Midwestern company, rather than a transcontinental carrier, to initiate the "Safety First" movement. In 1910, the Chicago & North Western appointed its longtime general claim agent, Ralph C. Richards, to head the Central Safety Committee. It was he who coined the "Safety First" slogan.

Within 30 days of the formation of the central group, Richards organized employees' committees in each of the C&NW's 17 operating divisions. At the end of the first 10 months, there were 54 fewer deaths and 1,559 fewer injuries than during the same period the previous year. In April of 1911, the railroad presented a congratulatory banner to its Sioux City Division for leading other divisions in the reduction of accidents.

Widespread publicity supported the safety campaign. The C&NW committee reported that 47 other roads—with 152,000 miles of track, or about 40 percent of the total in the United States—had adopted its "Safety First" practices by 1912. The National Safety Council was established the same year.

PULLMAN-STANDARD COMPANY WORKERS AND NURSES GATHER FOR A SPRINGTIME PARADE. DRIVES TO PROMOTE ON-THE-JOB INDUSTRIAL SAFETY FOR RAILROAD WORKERS BEGAN IN THE LATE YEARS OF THE NINETEENTH CENTURY.

*AT THEIR ANNUAL UNION
CONVENTIONS, STEAM
LOCOMOTIVE ENGINEERS
WORE HIGHLY ORNAMENTAL
INDENTIFICATION RIBBONS.
THEY WERE A MEASURE OF
ENGINEERS' PRESTIGE.*

*UNION PACIFIC'S
SUPERINTENDENT OF
MOTIVE POWER, WILLIAM
R. MCKEEN, WENT INTO
BUSINESS IN 1905 WITH HIS
DISTINCTIVE MCKEEN
MOTOR CAR. SOME 150
WERE BUILT, BUT ONLY ONE
ORIGINAL REMAINS TODAY
AT THE NEVADA STATE
RAILROAD MUSEUM.*

erly. The gasoline engine would turn out to be better suited to the personal automobile, which was also being developed at this time.

Then there was the diesel engine. In the early years of this century, the diesel—named for Rudolf Diesel, its German inventor—was already being put to work in a variety of industrial uses.

The Corliss Engine Works, considered the world's largest in 1902, ran its huge manufacturing plant entirely with diesel power. Brewer Adolphus Busch built the first diesel engine constructed in America for use at his brewery, eventually forming a new firm, Busch-Sultzer, to manufacture diesel engines for American and Canadian users. Even mighty American Locomotive Works, the nation's second-largest builder of steam locomotives, had tested the diesel with favorable results. Still, it would take American locomotive builders another quar-

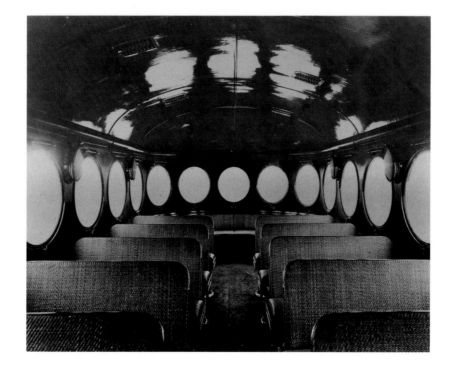

*FROM ABOUT 1880 TO
1900, PINTSCH CARBIDE
GAS LIGHTS WERE THE
LIGHTING OF CHOICE ON
MOST TRAINS. THE NEXT
WAVE OF PROGRESS WAS
ELECTRICAL TRAIN
LIGHTING, SEEN HERE
INSIDE A CHICAGO &
NORTH WESTERN BAGGAGE
CAR BUILT IN 1913. IN THIS
VIEW, BOTH GAS AND
ELECTRIC LIGHTS ARE
VISIBLE.*

ter of a century to begin a serious program of building and testing these prototype designs.

The railroad passenger benefitted greatly from technology's advance. For example, the introduction of steam heating got rid of the coal stove, always prone to uneven warming and unsafe in the event of collision. Following Edison's successful demonstration of the incandescent light bulb, electric lighting was introduced aboard passenger trains (although only on the finer trains; it would take until World War II for many railroads to fully convert to electricity for lighting). Tanks for fresh water would be introduced as well, allowing drinking and washing to be undertaken in good hygiene. And the all-steel passenger car's introduction in 1906 helped to assure greater safety in the event of a collision, at the same time reducing the likelihood of fire if such a misfortune did occur.

Electricity eventually provided clean, safe lighting aboard passenger cars, but a related event in Richmond, Virginia, in 1887 was almost immediately of concern to America's steam railroads. When inventor Frank J. Sprague successfully electrified that city's street railway system, the stage was set for the large-scale application of street railways to towns and cities of all sizes. Up to this time, only the

THIS CAST-IRON PAPERWEIGHT FROM THE MONON RAILROAD WAS AN ADVERTISING GIMMICK BASED ON THE ROUTE MAP OF THE CLEVELAND, INDIANAPOLIS & LOUISVILLE RAILROAD, WHICH WAS THOUGHT TO RESEMBLE THE OUTLINE OF AN ALLIGATOR.

FACING PAGE (LEFT): THIS UNIDENTIFIED RAILROAD DAY COACH OF 1913 WAS STYLISH AND UP-TO-DATE WITH RECLINING WALKOVER SEATS, CARPETING, SEPARATE WATERCLOSETS, AND GAS LIGHTING.

PENNSYLVANIA RAILROAD BEGAN ELECTRIFYING PORTIONS OF ITS TRACKAGE AROUND PHILADELPHIA AFTER 1910. ELECTRIC LOCOMOTIVES—KNOWN MORE COMMONLY IN THE INDUSTRY AS "MOTORS"— WERE ASSIGNED TO PASSENGER SERVICE. SHOWN HERE IS PENNSY'S NO. 3931.

Railroads and Depots

One aspect of rail development, that of building elaborate stations and terminals around the turn of the century, remains a solid and impressive achievement to this day.

St. Louis's Union Station, completed in 1894, had the distinction of being the "largest depot in the world" when it opened. Its 32 tracks served 18 railroads. Boston's South Station, opened in 1898, featured 28 tracks; it would go on to become the nation's busiest train terminal, with as many as 850 trains daily. Union Station in Washington, D.C., a classical masterpiece, opened in 1907. The city of Chicago, the nation's rail capital, was host to more than half a dozen major terminals.

But clearly New York City was home to the nation's two grandest train terminals—Penn Station and Grand Central—both on the island of Manhattan.

Penn Station came about as the result of the Pennsylvania Railroad's expansion into New York City from New Jersey. Completed at a cost of $114 million, the project entailed the purchase of 18 midtown acres and the digging of tunnels under both the Hudson and East rivers. When completed, it would be the world's largest through-station, with 21 tracks.

Rival New York Central's Grand Central Terminal was opened in 1912 just a few blocks away, replacing an older and smaller facility that had been outgrown by the railroad. Construction, begun in 1903, was a lengthy process; two subterranean levels of trackage were included in the station's design, and the construction had to work around continuing movement of trains into the old terminal.

OPENED FOR SERVICE IN 1908, NEW YORK'S GRACEFUL AND SPRAWLING PENNSYLVANIA STATION STOOD FOR ONLY 55 YEARS.

largest cities could support the necessary high ridership or large capital investments required for horse- or cable-propelled railway systems.

In a pre-automobile age, Sprague's success meant that city workers could now get to and from their jobs much more efficiently; it also meant that development was spurred to the edges of cities, a precursor to our modern-day pattern of suburban living.

Soon the new technology of the trolley car was being applied to elevated railways as well, allowing large cities such as New York, Chicago, and Boston to continue to grow rapidly. As the century turned, the boom was on. The electric railway industry mushroomed in size until by 1920 it was the fifth largest industry in the United States. In 1890, street railways carried two billion passengers; by 1902, the

IN THIS 1893 VIEW OF A DOWNTOWN STREETCORNER IN CINCINNATI, THREE FORMS OF URBAN RAILWAY ARE VISIBLE. AT LEFT, A CABLE-OPERATED CAR PULLS AROUND THE CURVE, WHILE AT CENTER, FOUR HORSECARS GO ABOUT THEIR USUAL BUSINESS. ABOVE ALL THIS ACTIVITY ARE ROWS OF ELECTRIC TROLLEY WIRES.

BETWEEN 1871 AND 1903, NEW YORK CITY HAD AN AMAZING SYSTEM OF FOUR ROUGHLY PARALLEL ELEVATED STEAM RAILWAYS OPERATING FROM THE HARLEM RIVER TO THE BATTERY. THE TRAINS TRAVELED AT AVERAGE SPEEDS OF 15 MPH. IN CONTRAST, HORSECARS MANAGED SPEEDS OF ONLY 4 TO 6 MPH.

number had risen to five billion, more than several times the number carried on the nation's steam railroads.

Another variation, the interurban electric railway, competed directly with steam railroads for the first two decades of the twentieth century. These interurbans, as they were called, followed major streets in urban areas, then set out—often paralleling existing railroads—across the countryside to serve nearby towns. Although the trip often was slower than the paralleling steam road's service, it was offered more frequently. Thus the interurban grew to its biggest proportion in regions that had scattered towns and suburbs surrounding a major metropolitan core—such as Los Angeles and Indianapolis—or had concentrated development along a population corridor, such as those connecting Chicago-Milwaukee, Cincinnati-Dayton, or Oakland-Sacramento-Chico (California).

RETIREMENT GIFTS FOR DECADES OF STEADY RAILROAD ENGINE SERVICE WERE OFTEN GOLD-DETAILED SHAVING MUGS, SUCH AS THIS ONE PRESENTED BY UNION CO-WORKERS TO READING RAILROAD ENGINEER E. BAKLEY. A TYPICAL READING PASSENGER "CAMELBACK" 4-4-0, PROBABLY THE ENGINE TO WHICH BAKELY MOST OFTEN WAS ASSIGNED, DECORATES THE MUG'S FACE.

HANGERS-ON CLUSTER AROUND THE BOILER OF A NEW YORK ELEVATED RAILROAD LOCOMOTIVE DURING THE 1890S ON A TRAIN BOUND FOR SOUTH FERRY STATION. THESE CLASS K FORNEY LOCOMOTIVES, ACQUIRED FROM ROME LOCOMOTIVE WORKS BEGINNING IN 1886, WERE CAPABLE OF SPEEDS OF 15 TO 25 MPH, THOUGH BURSTS OF 45 MPH WERE NOT UNKNOWN ON EXPRESS TRAINS.

The interurban turned out to be little more than a transitional step between sole reliance on the steam railroad for intercity transit and almost sole reliance on the personal automobile (which was still several decades in the future). Although a few interurban systems actually prospered—usually due to the fact that they also carried freight, in direct competition with steam railroads—few industries have grown so rapidly or declined so quickly, and no industry of its size ever had a more dismal financial record.

Not surprisingly, the interurbans began their precipitous decline on the eve of World War I—as the automobile was becoming available to all—and during the Depression the industry was virtually annihilated.

Competition is expected to be keen in a free-market society, but railroads prior to the turn of the century were engaged in a particularly cutthroat version. Railroad mileage was expanding, but particularly in the East and Midwest—where the railroad network by 1900 was densely packed—this new mileage was often built at the expense of competing lines. "The day of high rates has gone by; got to make money now on the *volume* of business" said W. H. Vanderbilt, eldest son of "Commodore" Vanderbilt and head of New York Central.

BEFORE ELECTRIC RAILROADS WERE DEVELOPED, EXCURSIONISTS TO CONEY ISLAND'S GRAND AMUSEMENT PARK WERE ACCUSTOMED TO RIDING ON SUBURBAN STEAM TRAINS SUCH AS THIS. COMBINATIONS OF OPEN-AIR AND ENCLOSED COACHES DRAWN BY BALDWIN LOCOMOTIVES WERE THE NORM IN WARMER MONTHS.

MANUFACTURED AROUND 1890, THIS SOUTHERN PACIFIC "VELOCIPEDE"—A TYPE OF HANDCAR—WAS STILL BEING USED BY RAILROAD PERSONNEL AS LATE AS THE 1940S.

Controlling costs was one way of helping make railroads more profitable, and the many improvements in technology around the turn of the century helped to accomplish just that. At the same time, the American railroad system was going through a period of consolidation that was unprecedented. By 1906, seven major interest groups controlled approximately two-thirds of all railroad mileage in the United States.

The Harriman lines—Union Pacific, Southern Pacific, and Illinois Central—comprised 25,000 miles; the Vanderbilt roads—New York Central and Chicago & North Western—22,000; the Hill roads—Great Northern, Northern Pacific, and the Chicago, Burlington & Quincy—21,000; the Pennsylvania group—the Pennsylvania Railroad, Baltimore

THIS CIRCA 1877 VIEW OF A NEW YORK ELEVATED RAILROAD TRAIN IS DISTINGUISHED BY THE DECOROUS STEAM DUMMY LOCOMOTIVE NO.18, BROOKLYN, BUILT BY BROOKS WORKS THAT YEAR. THESE UNUSUAL, COMPACT MACHINES HAD CENTRALLY LOCATED CYLINDERS AND A WATER TANK ATOP THE BOILER.

& Ohio, and Chesapeake & Ohio—20,000; the Morgan roads—Erie and Southern systems—18,000; the Gould roads—Missouri Pacific and several other southwestern systems—17,000; the Rock Island group—Chicago, Rock Island & Pacific system—15,000.

Consolidation, interestingly, went largely hand-in-hand with a trend toward less expansion. By 1910, the nation's railroads aggregated 240,293 miles; by 1916, the total reached 254,037—America's all-time record for railroad mileage.

Railroad employment grew as well, to a 1916 peak of 1.7 million persons, but the trend would be downhill from there. The era of the big-name "empire builders" was also coming to a close; the last, James J. Hill, died in 1916. Increasingly, business managers and bankers—rather than entrepreneurs—would assume the challenges of running

OAKLAND AND BERKELEY RAPID TRANSIT COMPANY, THE FIRST ELECTRIC LINE IN THE EAST SAN FRANCISCO BAY AREA, BEGAN BUSINESS IN THE 1890S. BACK THEN, CAR NO.10 HAD A LARGELY RURAL RUN BETWEEN THE TWO COMMUNITIES.

the nation's railroads. And difficult though it may be to comprehend today, a number of forces were at work to drastically alter the competitive picture—just as the railroads, it seemed, had reached some kind of equilibrium.

Those forces had actually been at work for some time. As early as 1871, railroad regulation had been enacted within individual states, in response to agitation by farmers for rate controls. The first significant federal regulation—the Interstate Commerce Act—followed in 1887; even then, the railway industry had little to fear, since "supervision is almost entirely nominal," wrote Attorney General Richard S. Olney in 1892.

The following year, President Benjamin Harrison signed the Railroad Safety Appliance Act into law, requiring air brakes (replacing manual ones cranked down "at speed" by brakemen atop swaying railroad cars) and automatic couplers (replacing the infamous "link and pin" variety that was responsible for the crushing of dozens of brakemen each year, and the loss of thousands of their fingers) to be phased in on most locomotives and cars around the turn of the century.

Although the Interstate Commerce Commission was

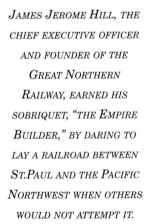

JAMES JEROME HILL, THE CHIEF EXECUTIVE OFFICER AND FOUNDER OF THE GREAT NORTHERN RAILWAY, EARNED HIS SOBRIQUET, "THE EMPIRE BUILDER," BY DARING TO LAY A RAILROAD BETWEEN ST. PAUL AND THE PACIFIC NORTHWEST WHEN OTHERS WOULD NOT ATTEMPT IT.

IN ORDER TO GAIN THE THROTTLE AND BOILER-TENDING POSITIONS ON A SPECIAL TRAIN, AN ENGINEER AND FIREMAN WOULD HAVE TO BID THROUGH THE SENIORITY SYSTEM. THE MEN WITH THE MOST YEARS OF SERVICE COULD HAVE FIRST PICK OF THE ASSIGNMENT, SUCH AS THESE TWO PROUD MEN SURELY DID ON A CHARTERED TRAIN FOR U.S. PRESIDENT WILSON IN 1919.

Photography, Postcards, and Promotion

Railroads frequently hired photographers at the turn of the century to promote travel and industrial development.

Noted western photographer William Henry Jackson left his studio in Denver in 1897 to become a partner in the Detroit Photographic Company. Before taking over duties of superintendent in 1903, he traveled across the United States, obtaining images for the company's booming postcard and stock photo business (several million prints were sold annually) and promoting sales. The company had U.S. rights to Photo-Chrome, a Swiss-developed process for reproducing color prints.

Jackson's visits included Washington, D.C.; Virginia; the Trans-Mississippi Exposition in Omaha; Chautauqua, New York; Boston; the Delaware Lackawanna & Western Railroad; California; the Memphis & New Orleans Railway; Canada; Florida; Nassau; Colorado; Yellowstone; the Adirondacks; and Georgian Bay.

Railroad travel publications also aided travel and industrial promotion. *Sunset* magazine, founded by Southern Pacific Railroad in 1898 and published by the railroad until 1914, took the lead in SP's efforts to promote tourism and economic development in the West.

Northern Pacific's annual *Wonderland* series, from 1883 to 1906, had much the same purpose. The series often focused on Yellowstone National Park, although writers also stressed the ranches, towns, and cities in "a region of wonderful phenomena, reached by the Northern Pacific Railroad."

The Detroit Publishing Company, under the direction of photographer William H. Jackson, created hundreds of railroad cards, such as this one featuring the Santa Fe Bridge over the Missouri River.

largely ineffectual prior to 1900, the onset of the Progressive Movement revived the issue of regulation. Most Americans were of the opinion that more stringent controls were needed to prevent abuses such as those perceived within the financial markets—and which on occasion had led to great collapses of railroad systems, as well as the resultant loss of investor fortunes. It was obvious that something needed to be done to restore the public's confidence.

In this light, President Theodore Roosevelt in 1901 directed his attorney general to file suit—under the provisions of the Sherman Anti-Trust Act—against Northern Securities, a giant holding company formed by railroad consolidationists Edward H. Harriman and James J. Hill. The company was outlawed in 1904, and later that year Roosevelt was reelected to a second term. Before the year was out, Roosevelt

ENGINEERS AND ROUNDHOUSE SHOPMEN USED LIGHTWEIGHT KEROSENE TORCHES SUCH AS THIS TO PROBE THE SHADOWS BENEATH STEAM LOCOMOTIVE BOILERS WHEN LOOKING FOR TROUBLE SPOTS AND LUBRICATION POINTS. THE TORCH BODY BEARS AN EMBOSSED SEAL WITH THE INITIALS OF THE WESTERN PACIFIC RAILROAD.

FACING PAGE (RIGHT): PRESIDENTIAL CANDIDATE THEODORE ROOSEVELT CAMPAIGNS IN MAINE IN 1904. BRASS-RAILED OBSERVATION CARS OF THIS TYPE ONCE ABOUNDED ON MAINLINE LIMITEDS AND EXPRESSES ACROSS THE NATION, PROVIDING A WINDY AND OFTEN MARVELOUS VIEW OF THE TRACKSIDE LANDSCAPE.

NORTHERN PACIFIC RAILWAY'S INAUGURAL NORTH COAST LIMITED WHIPS ALONG BEHIND A SCHENECTADY-BUILT TEN-WHEELER IN APRIL OF 1900. THE EIGHT-CAR TRAIN REMAINED, IN NAME, THE PREMIER PASSENGER HAULER OF THE NP UNTIL THE COMING OF AMTRAK IN 1971.

asked Congress to increase the powers of the I.C.C. This was done over-whelmingly with passage of the Hepburn Act, which empowered the commission to establish "just and reasonable" maximum rates.

"Within two years of [the Hepburn Act's] passage, more rate com-plaints—some 1,500—were made with the I.C.C. than had been filed in the two preceding decades," writes historian John F. Stover in his book *The Life and Decline of the American Railroad.* A related bill strength-ened the I.C.C.'s powers in 1910, requiring railroads to prove that any future rate hikes were reasonable and necessary. A related piece of leg-islation in 1913 provided for the regulatory agency to begin assessing the true value of each railroad, information that was needed if rates were to be established that would provide a fair return for investors.

Not unexpectedly, rate increases requested by the railroads were not always granted by the I.C.C. Rates between 1900 and 1916 dropped

ADULTS, LIKE CHILDREN, CAN BE EASILY CAPTIVATED BY STEAM LOCOMOTIVES. IT COMES AS NO SURPRISE THAT SOME INDIVIDUALS BUILT WORKING LIVE-STEAM MODELS OF ENGINES, SUCH AS THIS ONE, AS FAR BACK AS 1910.

Carrying The Nation's Burden

Although it was the passenger train that in large part defined the public's perception of the railroad, it was—and still is—the freight train that carried the raw materials and finished goods of an increasingly industrialized nation.

Interestingly, the railroads not only furnished the means of transport for this vital cargo, but also made a genuine effort to help farms and farmers flourish.

"As the American frontier closed, the railroad land agent was replaced by the agricultural agent, whose job was to stimulate farm production and so raise the tide of traffic," notes John H. White, Jr., in his book *The American Railroad Freight Car*. To that

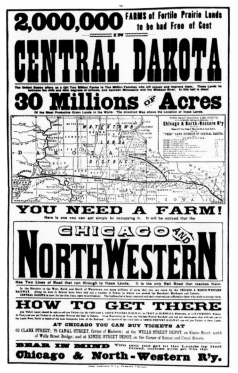

THIS BROADSIDE POSTER FROM THE 1880S DEPICTS THE MAINLINES OF THE CHICAGO & NORTH WESTERN AND THEIR PROXIMITY TO FREE LAND.

end, railroads set up touring exhibit trains, displaying the latest agricultural technology available to farmers. Often, farming experts were hired to accompany the exhibit and speak to assembled crowds.

This encouragement would occasionally surpass mere advice. Some railroads supplied farmers with replacement or substitute animals and plants following devastating years, while others planted farm plots to show off new types of crops that were available.

In 1911, the Great Northern Railroad even set up an exhibit in New York's Madison Square Garden to demonstrate the latest advances in wheat farming.

slightly, even though the nation's general price level increased by almost 30 percent.

Investment in railroads fell; maintenance standards went down; and new freight and passenger equipment was not ordered in sufficient quantities to keep up with the ongoing demands for replacement and modernization of railroad fleets. The nation had succeeded in regulating its railroads, but with unintended results.

On the eve of World War I, America's railroads were afloat in a sea of dramatic contrasts. On the one hand, the railroad's influence could still be felt in the towns and cities of America, and long-distance travel was still almost exclusively the domain of the passenger train.

And yet, in contrast to these healthy signs, wooden passenger cars were still in use on many railroads, as were outdated and underpowered locomotives. Freight-car fleets still were made up,

THE GOLDEN AGE OF THE EARLY 1900S AND THE OPENING OF THE SAN PEDRO, LOS ANGELES & SALT LAKE RAILROAD (WHICH WAS EVENTUALLY ACQUIRED BY UNION PACIFIC) WAS RECALLED BY A JANUARY 1955 CHARTER EXCURSION USING FORMER VIRGINIA & TRUCKEE RAILROAD TEN-WHEELER NO. 25 AND COACHES BORROWED FROM RKO MOTION PICTURE STUDIOS.

in large part, of older, lower-capacity (30-ton) cars, even though the increasing use of steel had made the 40-ton car a reality by now.

The outbreak of war in August of 1914 at first resulted in decreased American industrial activity. Rail ton-miles decreased four percent in 1914 and another four percent the following year. It was not until 1916 that the allied nations began to draw upon the economic resources of the United States. That year, ton-miles increased dramatically—32 percent—and soon the nation's railroads were feeling the strain. As the flow of traffic was mostly eastward, serious congestion was experienced in the yards, terminals, and ports of the Northeast and New England.

A car shortage developed as a result, primarily in the West and South. Car shortages were not unusual during peak periods of business prosperity, and a number had occurred before this time. Yet this

CONDUCTORS AND BRAKEMEN ON FREIGHT AND PASSENGER TRAINS ONCE RELIED EXCLUSIVELY ON HAND AND LAMP SIGNALS TO COMMUNICATE WITH EACH OTHER, THE ENGINE CREW, AND STATION AGENTS. THIS PULLMAN LANTERN WAS TYPICAL OF THE KEROSENE LANTERNS POPULAR BETWEEN THE 1880S AND 1900.

NEW YORK CENTRAL BEGAN ELECTRIFYING ITS TRAINS SHORTLY AFTER THE TURN OF THE CENTURY. IN THIS UNDATED VIEW, THE HOODED ELECTRIC THIRD RAIL, WHICH BROUGHT POWER TO TRAINS FOR EACH TRACK, IS CLEARLY VISIBLE. NEW YORK CENTRAL PREFERRED THIRD-RAIL CURRENT PICK-UP, USING OVERHEAD WIRE ONLY IN ITS HUDSON RIVER TUNNELS TO GRAND CENTRAL.

one would be different. Things went from bad to worse, and in January of 1917 the I.C.C. reported that, "The present conditions of car distribution throughout the United States have no parallel in our history... mills have shut down, prices have advanced, perishable articles of great value have been destroyed.... Transportation service has been thrown into unprecedented confusion."

By the time war was actually declared by the United States, in April of that year, the situation had grown intolerable. American railroads experienced their heaviest traffic in history during the preceding eight months, and the onset of war simply increased the burden. Yet the American spirit of individualism prevailed, and an executive committee called the Railroads' War Board was formed by industry leaders. This body succeeded in lessening car shortages and other problems. Unfortunately, the winter of 1917–1918 struck with a vengeance. That, plus a series of conflicting "priority shipment" orders from the federal government's own war agencies, finally brought things to a standstill.

On December 26, 1917, President Woodrow Wilson finally proclaimed: "I have excer-

THE EXPANSIVE TRAINSHED CONNECTED TO THE EQUALLY IMPRESSIVE TERMINAL HEADHOUSE AND CONCOURSE OF GRAND CENTRAL STATION IN NEW YORK WAS THE EQUIVALENT OF TODAY'S GREAT AIRPORTS. IN THIS 1913 SCENE, ONLY GAS-LIT COACHES, PARLORS, AND SLEEPERS ARE VISIBLE BENEATH ELECTRIC ARC-LIT PLATFORMS.

THIS COLORIZED COPY OF A WORLD WAR I-ERA PHOTO DEPICTS LIFE AT CAMP DIX, A MILITARY FACILITY IN SOUTHERN NEW JERSEY. VISITORS HEAD FOR THE CAMP'S RAILROAD DEPOT AFTER A VISIT WITH LOVED ONES.

FACING PAGE (RIGHT): DURING WORLD WAR I, RAILROADS ROSE TO THE CHALLENGE OF HAULING EVERYTHING IMAGINABLE TO KEEP THE COMMERCE OF THE NATION—AND THE WAR EFFORT—MOVING. SEEN HERE ARE MICHIGAN SOLDIERS PASSING THROUGH CINCINNATI.

cised the powers over the transportation system of the country, which were granted me by the act of Congress of last August, because it has become imperatively necessary for me to do so." He addressed Congress just a few days later, on January 4, 1918, telling all assembled that he had excercised this power "not because of any dereliction on their [the Railroads' War Board's] part, but only because there were some things which the government can do and private management cannot."

The new United States Railroad Administration, headed by William McAdoo, Wilson's former secretary of the treasury, went about its work with dispatch. Duplicated services were trimmed or eliminated; hefty wage increases were granted by the government to avert strikes; standardized locomotive and car designs were introduced; and

As each town's and city's boys marched off to war, the citizens joined them at inumerable railroad stations in a demonstration of national pride. Most men and their families thought they would end the war and be back home in a few months. They would all be sadly disappointed.

increases in freight rates and passenger fares were approved—but not enough to cover the increasing costs of providing service during those troubled years.

The reasons for the inability of railroads to meet the needs of war went back at least a quarter of a century, largely revolving around their inability to make a reasonable return on investment due to burdensome regulations. Maintenance had already been deferred on the nation's railroads prior to the war's onset; by the time the armistice was signed in 1918, incredible amounts of traffic had been moved by rail, yet relatively little maintenance had been performed. The railroads were worn out.

Ultimately, government operation of the railroads may have been satisfactory from an operational point of view, but it was a financial disaster. It also violated American

IN AN EARLY EXAMPLE OF INTERMODAL FREIGHT TRAFFIC, MILITARY TRANSPORT WAGONS HAVE BEEN LOADED ONTO SOUTHERN PACIFIC AND CENTRAL PACIFIC FLATCARS FOR SHIPMENT TO MARINE PORTS. THERE THEY WILL BE LIFTED INTO THE HOLDS OF WAITING SHIPS BOUND FOR THE EUROPEAN BATTLEFIELDS OF WORLD WAR I.

business ideology, and the general public by war's end was in the mood for a return to normalcy. Although a number of labor and other interests agitated for federal purchase and continuing control of railroads following the end of hostilities, this was not to be. The Transportation Act of 1920 returned the railroads to their owners as of March 1 of that year.

The Act greatly increased the power and scope of the I.C.C., while at the same time directed the Commission to prepare plans for the formal consolidation of railroads into a limited number of systems. Unfortunately, the Transportation Act seems largely to have ignored the fact that there were new forms of transportation on the horizon.

During the war, the U.S. government had demonstrated for the first time the potential for long-distance motorized freight transport, which had been necessary to supplement the overburdened railroads. Following the war, the United States was left with battered roads—much

THE PENNSYLVANIA HAMLET OF MAUCH CHUNK (LATER RENAMED AFTER SPORTS FIGURE JIM THORPE, A NATIVE SON) OFFERED A BUCOLIC SETTING AROUND THE TURN OF THE CENTURY. THE TOWN'S SUSQUEHANNA STREET, LINED WITH HOTELS, FACES ITS PRIMARY SOURCE OF COMMERCE, THE PENNSYLVANIA RAILROAD DEPOT AND TRACKS ALONG THE SUSQUEHANNA RIVER.

PHOTOGRAPHED DURING THE 1920S, NORFOLK & WESTERN'S POCAHONTAS GLIDES ALONG THE BANKS OF VIRGINIA'S NEW RIVER. NOTE THE SHARP LINES OF THE HAND-TENDED RAILROAD BED—A SOURCE OF PRIDE AMONG RAILROAD WORKERS.

Inferior Accommodation?

In the early years of regulation by the Interstate Commerce Commision, the Pullman Company, with its nationwide system of comfortable sleeping cars, was remarkably free from government control.

By 1913, only two railroads—the Great Northern and the Milwaukee Road—remained as large-scale non-Pullman operators, yet the I.C.C. was continuously kept at bay by Pullman's legal staff, which argued the company was first and foremost an "innkeeping" operation.

Around 1910, however, a setback was encountered by the company when a Minnesota traveler, Mr. George S.

"MAKING DOWN" AS MANY AS TWO-DOZEN BERTHS IN THE SPACE OF AN HOUR ABOARD A MOVING TRAIN REQUIRED SKILL AND TACT FROM PORTERS. THE COMPANIES HAD STRICT RULES FOR HOW EVERYTHING HAD TO BE DONE.

Loftus, succeeded in having the charge for upper berths on a Pullman lowered by 20 percent. Loftus had pestered the company for a number of years, insisting that uppers—which were avoided by most travelers—were inferior accommodations. In the end, the I.C.C. agreed with Loftus.

Pullman cars generally ran only half-filled, yet travelers often paid a small premium to have a lower berth. Otherwise, a climb up a ladder was required.

Silent movie stars Stan Laurel and Oliver Hardy perhaps best immortalized the trials of sleeping in an upper berth in their comedy feature *Berth Marks.*

like its railroads—and a huge postwar rebuilding program was begun with taxpayer dollars.

The railroads would enjoy no such rebuilding program. In some cases there would be years of haggling over the government's compensation for using the railroads (each was paid for the period of government control, but payments were based on pre-war freight rates). The entire saga of government control should have pointed to managed competition—not nationalization—as the answer to the woes of America's railroads, but it would take a good many more years for anything to be done in that direction.

THE SIGNATURE FEATURES OF PRAIRIE RAILROADING WERE TOWERING GRAIN ELEVATORS AND FLOUR MILLS AT TRACKSIDE. HERE, COLUMBIA SOUTHERN SERVES THE SANDOW FLOUR MILL IN A REMOTE AREA OF EASTERN OREGON DURING THE EARLY 1900S.

A RATCHET REAMER ALLOWED TRACKWORKERS TO DRILL HOLES IN STOUT TRACK AND BRIDGE TIMBERS, PLUS TELEGRAPH AND TELEPHONE POLES.

Landscaping Depots and City Planning

When railroads were building impressive stations across the United States in the 1890s and early 1900s, they hired landscape architects to carefully plan parks surrounding the structures.

The stations often were gateways, giving visitors their first and last impressions of communities. In an era when civic officials enthusiastically embraced the tenets of the city planning movement, the stations and grounds became a source of considerable civic pride.

During the 1880s, landscape architect Frederick Law Olmsted (best known for his work on New York's Central Park) collaborated with architect Henry Hobson Richardson on suburban stations for the Boston & Albany Railroad.

EVEN SMALL RAILROAD STATIONS WERE DEEMED WORTHY OF ORNAMENTATION AROUND THE TURN OF THE CENTURY. SHOWN HERE IS AN ITALIAN ROSE GARDEN AT DEPOT PARK IN EUGENE, OREGON.

In 1902, the Milwaukee Road put Chicagoan Annette E. McCrea, head of the Committee on Railroad Grounds of the American Park and Outdoor Art Association, in charge of "the work of beautifying the garden spots around its depots in Wisconsin" as the railroad was completing a major project to double-track its main line between Milwaukee and LaCrosse. She also obtained positions with the Chicago & North Western; Chicago, Burlington & Quincy; Illinois Central; and other railroads.

In the May 1904 issue of *Railroad Gazette*, McCrea proudly reported that she had "seen develop from tiny grass plats, grudgingly permitted by a few railroads, an almost universal system of parks surrounding the railroad stations throughout the country."

As the 1920s dawned, so too did a time of recovery, general optimism, and social experiment—especially with regard to the role of women in society. American railroaders could look back proudly at their accomplishments over the past two decades, even with the tarnish of wartime confusion and stifling government control. Yet the future held much less promise. A new era was dawning for the transportation systems of America, and railroads seemed likely to have a diminishing role.

Despite the less than favorable economic forecast, the 1920s would become the golden years for American railroading. The decade inspired a romantic image of the industry that persists to this very day.

HEAVY FORGED-STEEL TONGS SUCH AS THESE WERE USED BY TRACK LABORERS TO LIFT HEAVY, 8-FOOT-LONG RAILROAD CROSSTIES WHEN BUILDING OR REPAIRING TRACK.

ALTHOUGH CRUDE BY LATER STANDARDS, MECHANIZED ROAD-BUILDING EQUIPMENT SUCH AS THIS TRACTOR AND GRADER IN CALIFORNIA'S SIERRA MOUNTAINS PERMITTED THE RAPID CONSTRUCTION OF THOUSANDS OF MILES OF PUBLIC HIGHWAY—AT PUBLIC EXPENSE.

Chapter 4

THE CLASSIC ERA

The "Roaring Twenties" conjure many vivid images—bootleg liquor, flappers, Model T Fords. For railroading, already a century old, it was a decade of glamorous trains and record traffic. But nothing was truly as it seemed in the 1920s. Social upheaval, political shenanigans, and economic uncertainty rattled many Americans, setting the stage for the stock market crash of 1929 and the ensuing Great Depression.

AS A GREAT NORTHERN VICE PRESIDENT CEREMONIOUSLY THROWS THE SWITCH ON A COLD DAY IN 1929, A NEW ELECTRIC LOCOMOTIVE IS ABOUT TO TAKE THE FIRST TRAIN THROUGH THE CASCADE TUNNEL, LONGEST IN NORTH AMERICA.

AS A GREAT NORTHERN VICE PRESIDENT CEREMONIOUSLY THROWS THE SWITCH ON A COLD DAY IN 1929, A NEW ELECTRIC LOCOMOTIVE IS ABOUT TO TAKE THE FIRST TRAIN THROUGH THE CASCADE TUNNEL, LONGEST IN NORTH AMERICA.

Americans began the new decade war-weary, disillusioned that the brutal struggle seemed to have resolved nothing, and fearful of the "rising tide of Bolshevism." Two new constitutional amendments—one for women's suffrage, the other outlawing alcoholic beverages—revealed the well-intentioned, but somewhat befuddled, state of society at the time.

In hindsight, it seems ridiculous that it took so long to grant women full citizenship, but no more so than trying to legislate beer and whiskey out of existence. In the same fashion, the country seemed unable to think clearly about the transportation revolution unfolding in its midst. At exactly the same time that the government embarked on a course of unprecedented public spending for roads, waterways, and aviation, it was tightening the screws on a railroad industry battered by war and fettered by regulations.

Gone were the speculators and the great builders of the nineteenth century; in their places were able managers who operated their companies within the strictures of detailed, and often nonsensical, rules covering almost every aspect of railroading. By 1913, for example,

NO MATTER HOW SMALL THE RAILROAD OR HOW HUMBLE THE LOCOMOTIVE, ITS SMOKEBOX FRONT WAS ENTITLED TO WEAR A SHINY BRASS NUMBER PLATE. THE LIMA LOCOMOTIVE WORKS IN LIMA, OHIO, BUILT THE FAMOUS "SHAY" GEARED LOCOMOTIVES. COLLECTORS NOW PRIZE THEM AS TRUE RELICS OF THE GREAT AGE OF STEAM.

Congress and the Interstate Commerce Commission were so convinced that railroads were overvalued (rates were based on the value of invested capital) that they ordered a full accounting of every inch of every railroad in the land. It took more than five years of excruciatingly detailed fieldwork and years more of tabulation. The conclusion was that railroads were actually *under*capitalized—and had *not* been systematically cheating the public. Court cases and hearings to resolve the final "valuation" of the nation's railroad property dragged on throughout the 1920s.

For railroad employees, it was a time of uncertainty. The well-established unions representing the "running trades"—engineers, fire-

DURING THE SHOPCRAFT STRIKE OF 1922, WORKERS WAIT PEACEFULLY FOR NEGOTIATIONS TO REACH A CONCLUSION. THE GOVERNMENT CAME DOWN HARD IN FAVOR OF THE COMPANIES, AND THESE MEN AT SLATER, MISSOURI, ULTIMATELY CONCEDED TO THE RAILROAD'S TERMS.

men, brakemen, and conductors—and other skilled workers such as telegraphers were able to hold their own in the turbulent postwar economy. Other employees, including blacks, women who had temporarily taken "men's" jobs during the war, and those without union representation, suffered wage cuts or dismissal as the companies tried to cut expenses. The most dramatic confrontation was the Shopcraft Strike.

Throughout the war, there had been inflation and rising employment, but deflation, recession, and decreasing traffic beginning in the middle of 1920 led railroads to furlough workers and cut wages. When the shopcraft unions, representing machinists, electricians, and others who worked in the shops, went on strike in the summer of 1922, they had not counted on the anti-labor attitude of President Warren Harding and many railroad executives. Some companies hired replacement workers, and there was sporadic violence.

BEFORE THE USE OF AUTOMATIC GRADE-CROSSING EQUIPMENT, WATCHMEN AT THOUSANDS OF ROAD CROSSINGS THROUGHOUT THE COUNTRY USED HAND-HELD SIGNS LIKE THIS TO HALT TRAFFIC FOR PASSING TRAINS. OFTEN, CROSSING WATCHMEN WERE DISABLED RAILROADERS FROM OTHER CRAFTS WHO WERE ABLE TO FILL THESE JOBS.

THE ERA IN REVIEW

1920:
Congress passes the Esch-Cummins Act, returning railroads to private ownership and outlining a series of railroad mergers as the start of a national transportation policy.

1921:
The number of railroad passengers carried reaches an all-time high, then begins a modest, decade-long decline.

1922:
The AFL-affiliated craft unions withdraw from service in a wage dispute. The strike ends for some after two months; others never return.

1923:
Railroad presidents meet in New York and create a series of "Shippers Advisory Boards" to initiate programs designed to increase efficiency.

Canada's main railways, except the Canadian Pacific, are merged into the government-controlled Canadian National Railways.

1925:
The first commercially successful diesel-electric locomotive, Central Railroad of New Jersey's Switcher No. 1000, enters service.

Finally, after several months, the strike withered away as demoralized men returned to work on the companies' terms—or found other employment. Repercussions of the Shopcraft Strike—like the great strikes of 1877 and 1894—lasted for several years. Only after the passage of the Railway Labor Act in 1926 did relations between railroads and labor begin to improve somewhat. Some rail workers, most notably Pullman Porters, had to wait for the New Deal to settle their grievances.

If railroading before World War I still had a hint of the nineteenth century about it, railroading by the mid-1920s was distinctly modern. Locomotive and car designs based on the United States Railway Administration standards of 1918 would define railroading through the 1960s. Despite the fact that total rail mileage dropped slightly throughout the decade (largely through the abandonment of marginal or duplicate lines), railroads invested heavily in property and equipment.

THE MAN WHO WORE THIS HAT COULD BE MISTAKEN FOR NO ONE BUT A RAILROAD CONDUCTOR. HE WAS THE RANKING FIGURE OF AUTHORITY ABOARD HIS TRAIN.

THE ERA IN REVIEW

Armed with the latest technology and new theories about the construction of boilers and fireboxes, Lima Locomotive Works builds the "A-1," the first modern "Super Power" steam locomotive.

A. P. Randolph announces the formation of the Brotherhood of Sleeping Car Porters, a union for 12,000 Pullman employees and an early civil rights organization.

1926:
The railroad industry celebrates a century of service on the Mohawk and Hudson Railroad, later part of the New York Central.

Congress passes the Railway Labor Act, giving railroad employees the right to select union representation without fear of reprisals from management.

1927:
The first Centralized Traffic Control system goes into service—a great step forward in efficient train dispatching and railroad safety.

1929:
The collapse of the stock market signals the start of the Great Depression; railroad traffic drops immediately.

Even today, the period is widely considered to be the zenith of "classic" railroading. In 1920, the U.S. railroad network was still near its peak, with 253,000 miles of track operated by more than one-and-a-half million railroad men and women employed by at least 1,000 railroad companies.

Although somewhat erratic, the U.S. economy was vigorous, and railroads found it relatively easy to raise money on Wall Street for big projects. There were no great new lines to be built—the Milwaukee Road's 1916 Puget Sound extension, from the upper Midwest to Seattle, was the last major addition to the national system—but there was a great deal of "addition and betterment" work to be accomplished.

In Washington's Cascade Range, the Great Northern opened the Cascade Tunnel in 1929. To increase capacity and help reduce the hazard of asphyxiation, GN (like the Milwaukee Road) electrified portions of its mountainous lines. Elsewhere across the country, companies built cut-offs and generally "spent money to make money."

The steam locomotive had been around for more than a century, and its basic operating principles—involving thermodynamics, the factor of adhesion, and fuel efficiency—were well understood. But a new generation of designers, armed with new theoretical tools and increasingly sophisticated technology, sought to

TO MANY PEOPLE— INCLUDING THE MEN WHO RAN THEM—STEAM LOCOMOTIVES SEEMED TO HAVE PERSONALITY. THEY WERE OFTEN REFERRED TO AS "SHE," AND WHEN AT REST OR IN FULL STRIDE, THEY BREATHED AND SPOKE TO THE COUNTRYSIDE. TRULY, THEY RESEMBLED "IRON HORSES."

AS THE 1920S CLOSED, RAILROADS EXPERIMENTED WITH NEW TECHNOLOGIES SUCH AS MECHANICAL COOLING FOR PASSENGER CARS. IN SUMMER, TRAINS COULD BE UNCOMFORTABLY HOT AND PRONE TO CINDERS AND SOOT. THE FIRST AIR-CONDITIONED DINING CAR WAS THE B&O'S "MARTHA WASHINGTON," A FINE RESTAURANT ON WHEELS.

A.P. Randolph and the BSCP

Born in Florida in 1889, Asa Philip Randolph moved to New York with his family in 1911. He attended New York City College and became active in socialist and labor causes. Because of his work publishing *The Messenger*, a newspaper directed toward blacks and espousing a strong doctrine of civil rights and social justice, he was approached in 1925 to assist in forming a union of sleeping car porters. The Pullman Company was violently anti-union and had defeated five previous attempts on the part of the porters to organize.

In 1926, porters received a base monthly wage of $67.50 (for 400 hours of work) and were expected to make a living through tips. The men were held to rigid performance and service standards and were not permitted to sleep on duty—even though they might be on duty for days at a stretch.

The work of forming the Brotherhood of Sleeping Car Porters was difficult and continually hampered by institutional racism and the hostility of the company. The men had to meet in secret, facing dismissal if the Pullman Company learned of their affiliation. Finally in 1937, following New Deal legislation forcing the company to negotiate in good faith, the Brotherhood won formal recognition and negotiated a more satisfactory labor contract.

Randolph went on to become a major figure in the postwar Civil Rights movement. He died in 1979.

ASA PHILIP RANDOLPH IMPROVED THE LIVES AND WORKING CONDITIONS OF TENS OF THOUSANDS OF PULLMAN EMPLOYEES.

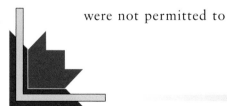

boost the power and efficiency of the steam locomotive. One result was what Lima Locomotive Works called "Super Power."

By increasing the size of the firebox well beyond what had previously been thought adequate for a given boiler size, Lima achieved a large locomotive capable of both high horsepower *and* high speed. Bigger wheel arrangements (4-6-4, 4-8-4, 2-10-4) and a variety of efficiency-boosting appliances (feed-water heaters, new firebox designs, and valve-gear improvements), helped define the basic principles of "Super Power." The famous Hudson 4-6-4 locomotives, built by the New York Central starting in 1927, exemplify the "big steam" of the 1920s.

Some improvements were less dramatic but equally important. Before the war, signal systems tended to rely on semaphores and mechanical interlockings—complex devices that prevented a signal from being displayed if the switches were not lined up properly. Partly because of the wartime leap in technology, railroads and signal compa-

A BIG BOILER, BIG WHEELS, AND BIG TENDER EQUALS POWER. THIS NYC HUDSON LOCOMOTIVE (4-6-4) COULD TAKE A 20-CAR PASSENGER TRAIN UP TO 90 MPH AND KEEP IT THERE FOR AS LONG AS THE WATER AND COAL HELD OUT. FREQUENTLY, IT EXCEEDED 100 MPH ALONG CENTRAL'S "WATER LEVEL ROUTE."

ASIDE FROM THE WATER GLASS FOR THE BOILER, NO INSTRUMENTS WERE AS IMPORTANT AS THE AIR-BRAKE GAUGES. THEY TOLD THE ENGINEER THAT THE SYSTEM WAS FUNCTIONING PROPERLY, AND THAT HE COULD INDEED STOP THE TRAIN. THIS DUPLEX SET CAN INDICATE FOUR DIFFERENT PRESSURES IN DIFFERENT PARTS OF THE SYSTEM AT ONCE.

nies were able to perfect new circuits and hardware to vastly increase the safety and capacity of existing lines. The introduction of reliable, high-visibility signal lights allowed railroads to begin the replacement of the high-maintenance mechanical semaphores. Another leap in safety came in 1922, when Congress legislated that all railroads with high-speed passenger trains (above 80 miles per hour) introduce an "Automatic Train Control" system designed to safely stop trains should the engineer miss a signal. That nearly 50 railroads were affected suggests the level of intensity at which the rail network was working.

For most employees, this was a good time to be "on the railroad." Some, like trackmen and carmen, still worked outside in all kinds of weather at physically demanding jobs. But brakemen no longer had to ride the tops of cars, and the 1917 Adamson Act had made the eight-hour day standard for railroad workers. The near-universal use of air brakes, automatic couplers, and safety appliances made the workplace vastly safer, while fundamental changes in the law made companies more aware of their liability for injuries.

The war had yet another long-lasting effect. Some of the temporary workers hired or promoted during the labor shortage managed to hold on to their jobs afterward, paving the way for increased partici-

BY THE 1920S, STEAM LOCOMOTIVES HAD ATTAINED THEIR MAXIMUM OVERALL SIZE, AS LARGER ENGINES SIMPLY WOULD NOT FIT ON THE RAILROAD. THIS B&O "BIG SIX" 2-10-2 COULD PULL 150 FREIGHT CARS ON LEVEL GROUND. ARTICULATED LOCOMOTIVES COULD BE EVEN LONGER, WITH YET ANOTHER SET OF DRIVING WHEELS.

A TRADITIONAL RAILROAD HAT SHOWS THE SIZE OF THIS ORDINARY RAILROAD SHOP TOOL. TRAINS WERE BIG, AND SOMETIMES IT TOOK A STURDY WRENCH, A LONG PIPE, AND A STRONG MAN TO WORK ON THEM. MANY SHOPS MADE THEIR OWN LARGE TOOLS, OFTEN A NECESSITY FOR THE UNIQUE MACHINERY FOUND ON STEAM LOCOMOTIVES.

pation in the railroad labor force by women, blacks, and other previously underrepresented minorities. Some railroads, like the B&O, showed remarkably enlightened labor policies; the railroad's Cooperative Plan of 1923 was quite similar to the "quality circles" and "total quality management" that many companies practice today. For the most part, railroad men and women enjoyed good wages, decent working conditions, and the respect of their neighbors. They were proud to be part of such a vast and well-functioning enterprise.

No single part of that network was greater in reach or more intricate than The Pullman Company. By this time it was the largest hotelier in the world, providing lodgings for as many as 40,000 people every night. Each of the 50 or so railroads offering Pullman service contracted with the company for the use of its sleeping cars, and in some cases, dining and lounge cars as well. Pullman staffed the sleepers with

FACING PAGE (LEFT):
PASSENGERS WITH THE INCLINATION—AND THE MONEY —TO ENJOY DINING CAR MEALS FOUND DELICIOUS FOOD, FLAWLESS SERVICE, AND OFTEN ORNATE SURROUNDINGS, AS EPITOMIZED BY THIS 1920S B&O "COLONIAL" DINING CAR. THESE WERE THE HEAVIEST AND MOST EXPENSIVE CARS ON THE RAILROAD—AND THEY NEVER MADE A PROFIT.

AS MANY AS 11 MEN MIGHT WORK IN A SPOTLESSLY CLEAN DINING CAR GALLEY LIKE THIS TO TURN OUT PREPARED-TO-ORDER FULL MEALS FOR 200 PASSENGERS: THREE COOKS, A DISH WASHER, A PANTRY MAN, AND SIX WAITERS. THEY MADE THEIR OWN BREAD, PIES, SAUCES, AND SPECIAL DISHES—AT 70 MPH.

THE NEW YORK CENTRAL EPITOMIZED "BIG" RAILROADING IN THE 1920S. THE COMPANY ADVERTISED ITS FOUR-TRACK MAINLINE AS "THE WATER LEVEL ROUTE" BECAUSE OF ITS EASY GRADES.

Dinner in the Diner

By the 1920s, dining cars were steel behemoths weighing upwards of 80 tons and carrying enough food, china, napery, and staff to serve several hundred people.

They were expensive to operate and consistently lost money. Furthermore, the cars might only serve a small segment of the total train's passengers, as most were unwilling to pay $1.00 to $1.75 for a multicourse hotel-style dinner. Yet no self-respecting railroad would operate a major passenger train without a state-of-the-art dining car and the requisite crew of 10 to 12 men. Why?

Pride, perhaps, or the fact that the public *knew* that a first-rate railroad had first-rate food. Even though they operated at a loss, dining cars catered to well-heeled passengers and provided a necessary level of comfort on longer journeys. They were "loss leaders," intended to provide the same level of cuisine as the best hotel dining rooms. Most railroads offered regional fare, such as southern cooking on the B&O, Seaboard, and

southern railroads, or wild game on the cars of western lines.

Crews in the East and South tended to be black males, but elsewhere, men (and a few women) of all ethnicities served on dining car staffs. The life was hard and the schedule brutal, but the jobs paid well and were considered to be good ones to have in the service industry.

DURING THE CLASSIC ERA, THE PULLMAN COMPANY USED THIS "TREE OF LIFE" PATTERN WITH THE COMPANY NAME PROUDLY DISPLAYED BOTH AS ADVERTISING AND TO DISCOURAGE PILFERAGE.

black porters trained in the exacting service that was the company's hallmark.

Pullman travel cost more than coach fare, but in the days before interstate highways, it was the safest and most comfortable way to go. One could board a Pullman car in Key West, Florida, and with a few changes of cars arrive in northwestern Canada without ever leaving the watchful eye of the Pullman Company. Americans toured the mountains of Mexico by Pullman, and they chartered private cars for everything from "wilderness" camping trips to political campaigning.

Of course, there was train travel, and there was glamorous train travel. While the traveling salesman ("drummer" to his contemporaries) boarding the standard 12-section, one-drawing-room sleeper in Butte, Montana, would have encountered substantially the same service as even the most famous passengers, some trains were simply better than others. The Pennsylvania and New York Central railroads competed for the cream of the New York-Chicago passenger business. Movie stars, tycoons, politicians, and the royalty of American culture rode the *Broadway Limited* and the *Twentieth Century Limited* on the finest equipment and fastest schedules available anywhere. Everyone transferred in Chicago, and passengers for "the Coast" had a choice of luxury trains

EVEN AFTER WORLD WAR I, CALIFORNIA REMAINED A SPARSELY SETTLED PARADISE-IN-WAITING. THE UNION PACIFIC AND OTHER RAILROADS WORKED HARD TO CONVINCE THE REST OF THE COUNTRY THAT THE BEST WAY TO GET THERE WAS BY TRAIN.

THESE DINING AND PULLMAN CARS PARKED AT BALTIMORE'S MT. ROYAL STATION WAIT TO BE PICKED UP BY A NEW YORK-BOUND TRAIN FOR THE OVERNIGHT RUN. THEY REPRESENT THE "STANDARD" FORM OF THE AMERICAN PASSENGER CAR, CALLING TO MIND THE PULLMAN COMPANY SLOGAN: SAFETY, SPEED, AND COMFORT.

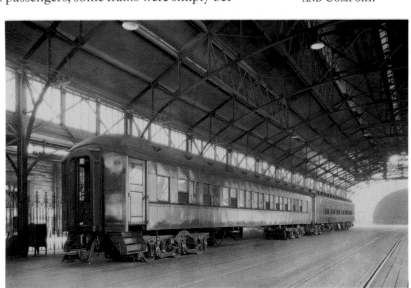

P.18673.
L.4329.
9-9-15. JP.V.V.

such as Santa Fe's *California Limited* and Great Northern's *Empire Builder*.

Railroad publicity men staged all kinds of events to attract passengers and to capitalize on whatever famous passengers might happen to be aboard. Reporters covered the arrival of trains at L.A.'s Union Passenger Terminal the way newspapers in New York treated the arrival of the *Queen Elizabeth* sailing from England. The trip was still long—at least three days to cross the continent—but it was far from uncomfortable. The finer trains had maids, valets, barbershops, and, of course, dining cars serving high-quality meals. Observation cars with open platforms permitted an exhilarating view of the scenery, while ample lounge and smoking spaces reduced the sense of being confined. Some trains had radios and libraries; others featured directed social activities and even rolling gymnasiums.

THE OPEN PLATFORM WAS THE TRAIN'S "BACK PORCH": A PLACE TO WATCH THE SCENERY GO BY, GET SOME FRESH AIR, OR ENJOY A CIGAR. THERE IS NO SUCH PLACE ON TODAY'S LIABILITY-CONSCIOUS PASSENGER RAILROADS.

THE B&O'S COLUMBIAN FERRIED TRAVELERS BETWEEN WASHINGTON AND NEW YORK IN HANDSOME DARK-GREEN CARS STAFFED BY ATTENTIVE CREWS. EACH CAR MIGHT WEIGH UP TO 60 TONS, WHICH MEANT A SMOOTH, STEADY RIDE. PHOTOGRAPHED IN 1931, THIS WAS THE FIRST FULLY AIR-CONDITIONED TRAIN.

The Railroader's Watch

Time had always been important on the railroad, but it was not until the introduction of Railroad Standard Time in 1884 that the companies themselves began to closely regulate the quality and accuracy of the timepieces carried by their employees.

As the standards evolved, so did the distinctive form of the railroad pocket watch. It had to have an open face, Arabic numerals, and a separate second-dial. The time was set by removing the crystal and moving a small lever to prevent accidental alteration of the correct time.

To be "railroad grade," the watch had to have no fewer than 21 jewels (small pieces of precious stones used as almost frictionless bearings for the moving parts) and be "corrected" for six positions, meaning that it would remain accurate no matter how it was oriented.

The American watch industry created a wonder of technology: a chronometer small enough to fit in a pocket. While they were made on an assembly-line basis, each watch took thousands of steps and a great deal of care to manufacture. Yet because so many railroad men were required to own them, they were widely available and surprisingly inexpensive.

Perhaps best known of the classic watches is the Hamilton 992-B, developed in the 1920s and worn by tens of thousands of train and engine crews. Railroaders still depend on watches such as these, and many people collect them. The picturesque ritual of the crew comparing the times on their watches was not for show. In those days on the railroad, a minute really counted for something.

FEW TIMEPIECES ARE AS DISTINCTIVE AS TRADITIONAL RAILROAD WATCHES LIKE THIS 1917 WALTHAM.

Some aspects of travel were still beyond the railroad's control. Showers were a great luxury, and going for several days in the cinder-rich environment of the railroad could be a trial. Air conditioning on trains did not become a practical reality until the 1930s, so summer travel could be hot, humid, and dusty all at once. In the late 1920s, the Pennsylvania and Santa Fe railroads set up a rail-air-rail relay that whisked passengers from New York to Los Angeles in 48 hours. Unfortunately, it wasn't long before all-air transcontinental service siphoned much of the most glamorous traffic from the rails. Nevertheless, the "standard" Pullman car—along with its counterpart, the steel day coach—defined travel for millions of North Americans throughout the decade.

IN A SCENE RE-CREATED THOUSANDS OF TIMES ACROSS THE LAND, THE RAILROAD HELPS DEFINE THE CENTER OF TOWN. HERE AT BRIDGEPORT, OHIO, TWO RAILROADS AND A ROAD INTERSECT—THUS THE ELEVATED WATCHMAN'S SHANTY ON THE RIGHT.

Their gateway to the world was the train station. Like the shopping malls of today, the train station, whether it was a country depot or a neoclassical palace in a big city, was central to any journey. In most stations of any consequence, you could buy a ticket to anywhere, have lunch, send a message via Western Union (the 1920s version of the Internet), and often get a shave, shower, and shoe shine.

Most stations appeared during the burst of railway construction between 1890 and 1910, but some major examples went up after World War I. Cleveland's impressive Terminal Tower, a combination train station and 52-story office building, took from 1923 to 1930 to complete. In 1925, the new Union Station in Chicago was dedicated; Amtrak and Metra trains use the renovated facility today. The Pennsylvania Railroad commenced building its monumental Thirtieth Street Station in Philadelphia in 1927. Two years later, work began on Cincinnati Union

THE STRAW HATS REVEAL THAT IT'S SUMMER AT PENNSYLVANIA STATION IN NEW YORK. TENS OF THOUSANDS OF PEOPLE MIGHT PASS THROUGH IN A SINGLE DAY, EVEN MORE DURING HOLIDAYS. MAJOR STATIONS LIKE THIS WERE LIKE SMALL CITIES WHERE HUNDREDS OF RAILROADERS TOILED AROUND THE CLOCK TO MAKE THE TRAINS RUN.

BUILT TO HOUSE THE RAILROAD EMPIRE OF CLEVELAND'S VAN SWERINGEN BROTHERS, TERMINAL TOWER WAS A COMBINATION RAILROAD STATION AND OFFICE BUILDING. AFTER A THOROUGH RESTORATION, IT REMAINS A STRIKING EXAMPLE OF MONUMENTAL RAILROAD ARCHITECTURE.

Terminal, a magnificent Art-Deco palace replacing a half-dozen outmoded passenger facilities. Large and small stations throughout the country received facelifts, reflecting the sincere—but mistaken—conviction that rail travel was a fixture in American life.

In fact, railroading seemed to be everywhere. Railroad advertising had long been a part of the visual culture of the U.S. and Canada, but by the mid-1920s, the railroad industry had something else to celebrate: It was 100 years old.

Several railroads vied for the title of America's "first" or "oldest" railroad; the New Haven, New York Central, Pennsylvania, and Delaware & Hudson railroads all had sincere claims, since all had corporate roots dating back to the mid-1820s. The Baltimore & Ohio made the most convincing claim, however, with the added advantage that it had operated continuously under its original charter since February of 1827. Many railroads constructed replicas of their first locomotives, and railroad history exhibitions appeared with increasing frequency, especially throughout the East.

The centenary celebrations highlighted a little-noticed fact. Whereas railroads had always tried to create a favorable public image

PENNSYLVANIA STATION IN NEW YORK WAS A GATEWAY TO ONE OF THE GREATEST CITIES ON EARTH, AND THE PENNSYLVANIA RAILROAD SPARED NO EXPENSE IN MAKING IT IMPRESSIVE. SHOWN HERE IS JUST ONE CORNER OF THE MAIN ROOM.

AS THE 1920S WANED, HIGH STYLE CAME TO THE DINING CAR AS EVEN TRADITION-MINDED RAILROADS BEGAN USING SILVERWARE WITH ART DECO OR MODERNE LINES. OFTEN THE HEAVY, TRIPLE-PLATED HOTEL-GRADE WARE WAS MARKED WITH THE RAILROAD'S LOGO OR INITIALS. THIS WATER PITCHER IS FROM THE SOUTHERN RAILWAY.

of themselves, and had always advertised to attract traffic, it was during the 1920s that the railfan hobby emerged as a legitimate pastime. Surely there had been railfans before then, and to this day there are people interested in railroading who do not see themselves as true railroad enthusiasts. But in the 1920s, men—and a few women—began to organize clubs and excursion groups simply to enjoy railroading. The major model clubs and national railfan and history organizations would get their start in the 1930s, but this period saw the pioneers establish the foundations for what would eventually become a substantial hobby and an important advocate for the continuing preservation of railroading's heritage.

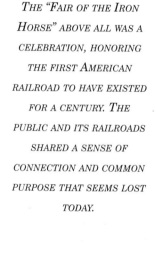

TOY TRAINS SUCH AS THIS DORFAN NO. 51 HELPED MAKE RAILFANS AND RAILROADERS OF SEVERAL GENERATIONS OF AMERICAN BOYS (BUT SELDOM GIRLS). THEY ALSO LAUNCHED TWO GREAT HOBBIES: TOY TRAIN COLLECTING AND MODEL RAILROADING.

THE "FAIR OF THE IRON HORSE" ABOVE ALL WAS A CELEBRATION, HONORING THE FIRST AMERICAN RAILROAD TO HAVE EXISTED FOR A CENTURY. THE PUBLIC AND ITS RAILROADS SHARED A SENSE OF CONNECTION AND COMMON PURPOSE THAT SEEMS LOST TODAY.

Meanwhile, trains continued to be an important part of American culture. The pull-toy and wind-up trains of the prewar era gave way to standard-gauge electric trains that more closely approximated the prototypes. Lionel, American Flyer, and other "tinplate" manufacturers introduced new types of electric trains with even more fidelity. A small, but slowly growing, number of enthusiasts attempted to make scale models of trains as a way to simulate real railroading.

In some parts of the country, trains became a Christmas tradition. In Baltimore, for example, firemen began setting up elaborate model-train displays in firehouses each year, encouraging public visits.

The Fair of the Iron Horse

The B&O, which for years had represented itself as the country's first common carrier railroad, celebrated its centenary in 1927 with a huge railroad exhibit and pageant outside Baltimore. More than a thousand employees spent the better part of a year preparing for the fair. They rebuilt the B&O's collection of historic locomotives, crafted comprehensive exhibits on all aspects of railroading, prepared an elaborate historical pageant that was presented daily, and built a magnificent setting at which to host the railroad's "birthday party."

Approximately one-and-a-half million people enjoyed the "Fair of the Iron Horse" during its three-week run in September. The Transportation Building alone was a tenth-of-a-mile long. The parking lot held 9,000 cars, and special trains brought people from as far away as Pittsburgh and Philadelphia. Admission was free, and the railroad was careful to conduct the entire affair with dignity and consideration for its guests.

This was no cheap promotional gimmick. The B&O intended to keep the buildings open as the country's first public railroad museum, but the Depression intervened. The collection went into storage, until it was reinstalled in historic buildings at the company's Mt. Clare Shops in Baltimore in 1953. The fair, and the subsequent B&O Transportation Museum, provided the precedent for almost every major railroad museum and railroad fair to follow.

WHEN THE B&O CELEBRATED ITS CENTENARY IN BALTIMORE IN 1927, THIS LETTER OPENER WAS ONE OF MANY ITEMS AVAILABLE AS A SOUVENIR OF THE EVENT.

And just as railroads reached out to the public with advertising of all kinds, images of railroading graced all kinds of products ranging from S. S. Pierce's "Overland" cigars (with a handsome passenger train on the lid of the box) to Campbell's Soup and Coca-Cola.

North Americans also saw trains in the silent films that were packing moving-picture houses all over the country. The *Perils of Pauline* adventures were one example of long-running serial films in which trains were central to the plot. The drama and daring rescues possible with racing trains were irresistible to directors. Some films centered on the complex and visually fascinating workings of the railroad itself. Others used trains and tracks as backdrops for love stories, westerns, crime and mystery plots, and assorted cinematic heroics.

One of the classics of this period is an early talkie entitled *Danger Lights*. The plot involves a love trian-

THERE WAS NO BETTER WAY FOR A RAILROAD TO ILLUSTRATE PROGRESS THAN TO CREATE A WORKING REPLICA OF ITS FIRST LOCOMOTIVE. SHOWN HERE IS THE "DeWITT CLINTON" OF THE MOHAWK & HUDSON RAILROAD, LATER THE NEW YORK CENTRAL.

gle, but the real stars are the Milwaukee Road trains and the dramatic race to save the Division Superintendent's life. The dialogue reveals what Hollywood thought railroaders thought about themselves. At one point, the main character says: "We're railroad men...we gotta keep the schedule. That's our religion—that's our life."

Even if the railroad was not everyone's "life," it made their lives possible. In the years when central heating meant a coal furnace in the basement, that coal came from distant mines by rail. Similarly, the radio advertisements for Nabisco crackers and other emerging national brands of food and other products were predicated on the fact that boxcars could deliver consumer goods to stores in the most remote corners of the continent. And with an irony lost on railroaders of the day, trains hauled the raw materials for the roads, automobiles, and air-

By 1925, the Pullman car was a place of quiet formality and restrained decor. The carbody was all steel and rode smoothly upon six-wheel trucks. Each section "made down" into an upper and lower berth, with heavy curtains for privacy.

So many people rode the legendary Twentieth Century Limited on the New York Central from the Big Apple to the Windy City that it often ran in multiple sections. By morning, these folks will be in Chicago.

Songs of the Railroad

Music in the 1920s reflected America's continuing fascination with railroading. The growing popularity and falling price of 78 rpm recordings made music available to everyone, which meant that jazz, blues, and popular music would be preserved along with more "respectable" works.

Black musicians frequently mimicked train sounds with voice or instrument, basing hundreds of jazz pieces, shuffles, instrumentals, and marches on the rhythms of the rails. Hillbilly music—exemplified by the likes of Jimmie Rodgers, the "Singing Brakeman"—included everything from traditional ballads like "The Little Red Caboose Behind the Train" to fast-paced violin and banjo pieces suggestive of steam locomotives.

Railroad work songs and train wreck songs—like the plaintive "Engine 143" or the catchy "Wreck of the Old 97"—became major hits and helped found the genre of country & western music.

The railroad was a hook in countless songs. In the 1927 ditty "Hello Swanee," the singer implores, "Please, Mr. Conductor, don't give me air; Please, Mr. Conductor, I haven't got the fare." Everyone back then knew what "give me the air" meant: As the air brakes stopped the train, the ticketless passenger was unceremoniously shown the door.

STYLED AS THE "SINGING BRAKEMAN," JIMMIE RODGERS HAD INDEED RAILROADED FOR A WHILE. BUT HIS GIFTS TO AMERICA WERE HIS SONGS. "BLUE YODEL," "IN THE JAILHOUSE NOW," AND "ANY OLD TIME" HELPED DEFINE COUNTRY & WESTERN MUSIC.

planes that would wreak havoc upon the industry—and nearly cripple it—over the decades to come.

The 1920s represent a period in which the government and the railroads settled into a highly regulated working relationship, even while new competitors arose as real threats. Railroad companies, for instance, could only compete on the basis of service; rates were strictly controlled, and underpricing another carrier was illegal. The Interstate Commerce Commission oversaw almost every facet of the railroad business, and its officials were continually busy with complaints ranging from the highly technical to the absurd. Thousands of railroad clerks kept a mind-numbing array of statistics so that the government could "protect" the American people.

To the north, the newly formed Canadian National Railway was itself a Crown corporation, owned by the Canadian government. Its rival, Canadian Pacific, was a private corporation, but both were closely regulated, as were the nationalized railroads of Mexico beginning in the late 1920s. Such close attention would have worked fine had it not been for the competition.

During World War I, so much war traffic clogged the railroads that a young Army officer by the name of Dwight Eisen-

STEEL SWITCH LOCKS HELPED PREVENT TAMPERING WITH RAILROAD TRACKS AND EQUIPMENT. THE "SWITCH KEY" WAS A BADGE OF HONOR FOR MANY RAILROADERS, FOR IT MEANT THEY HAD THE TRUST OF THE COMPANY. HARDWARE LIKE THIS WAS RARELY PRETTY, BUT IT WAS INDISPENSABLE TO THE SAFE OPERATION OF THE RAILROAD.

YARDS LIKE THIS PENNSYLVANIA RAILROAD FACILITY IN NEW YORK CITY SORTED IMMENSE QUANTITIES OF INBOUND AND OUTBOUND FREIGHT. ESSENTIAL TO AMERICAN BUSINESS, RAILROADS MADE IT POSSIBLE TO HAVE ONE TRULY NATIONAL MARKET ACROSS THE COUNTRY.

THE CANADIAN NATIONAL RAILWAY WAS A PIONEER IN THE USE OF "OIL-ELECTRIC" (DIESEL) LOCOMOTIVES. BY 1928, THE TECHNOLOGY HAD BEEN PERFECTED AND A FEW DOZEN WERE IN SERVICE IN THE UNITED STATES AND CANADA. TEN YEARS WOULD PASS BEFORE TRULY PRACTICAL ROAD LOCOMOTIVES BECAME WIDELY AVAILABLE.

hower was ordered to attempt the cross-country transport of vital materials by road. His trucks pounded the fragile pavement between Maryland and California to dust, but he proved a point: Roads were effective for long-distance travel. After the war, as more people bought automobiles and wanted to "see America," popular support for a network of all-weather highways became irresistible. Tens of thousands of miles of new road went down each year as roads first linked metropolitan areas, then started off for more distant points.

At the same time, the Army Corps of Engineers stepped up its programs to improve rivers and canals, which greatly benefitted the barge lines in direct competition with railroads. The Post Office began letting air mail contracts in 1918, and transcontinental air mail routes

were well established by 1925. That formed the basis for the civil aviation industry, which used publicly funded facilities and accumulated a yearly total of 73,000,000 passenger miles by 1930. Perhaps most worrisome to the railroads were the diversions to roads. Passengers began deserting passenger trains for automobiles in earnest, and buses competed directly on some routes.

Worse yet, for the price of a truck and a tankful of gasoline (at 18 cents a gallon), anyone could be in the freight business, with the road provided free of charge. The railroads were not opposed to good roads or lively competition. They were, however, very much aware that the playing field was not level. They could not fairly compete with other forms of trans-

THE ENGINEER'S STEAM GAUGE TOLD HIM HOW MUCH POWER HE HAD TO WORK WITH—AND HOW WELL THE FIREMAN WAS DOING HIS JOB. EVERY LOCOMOTIVE CARRIED ONE.

THE STURDY LEATHER AND CANVAS RAILWAY MAIL BAG TOOK THIS SHAPE SO THAT THE MAIL COULD BE HUNG FROM A "CRANE" AT A STATION. A HOOK ATTACHED TO THE SIDE OF THE MOVING RAILWAY POST OFFICE CAR WOULD SNATCH IT "ON THE FLY" AS THE MAIL CLERK DROPPED OFF THE BAG CONTAINING MAIL FOR THAT LOCATION. SELDOM DID EITHER MISS.

NORFOLK & WESTERN HAD THE CAPITAL TO INVEST IN THE VERY BEST EQUIPMENT. THE RAILROAD BECAME A "CONVEYOR BELT" FOR FREIGHT AND COAL, USING THE BIGGEST POWER ON THE BEST TRACK THE INDUSTRY COULD PROVIDE.

portation that were both lightly regulated (if at all), and at the same time were heavily subsidized by the government. That theme would echo throughout the railroad industry for 50 years before Congress finally addressed the situation.

The railroad industry was not without fault. Had it been more astute in its assessments, it might have raised more powerful objections sooner, perhaps helping to shape national transportation policy to a greater degree. But on the whole, the 1920s were good years, and the industry grew comfortable, if not complacent.

Collectively, railroads spent nearly $7 billion for improvements and boosted efficiency tremendously. There were also new technologies, such as the diesel locomotive (introduced commercially in 1925), lightweight car construction, and new types of air-brake systems that

AT FIRST, TRUCKS MERELY SUPPLEMENTED RAILROADS. THROUGH THE 1920S, AS TRUCKS GOT LARGER AND HIGHWAYS GOT BETTER, THEY BEGAN SIPHONING OFF PREMIUM FREIGHT. TRUCKS COULD BE CHEAPER, FASTER, AND MORE VERSATILE THAN TRAINS, BUT THAT WAS LARGELY BECAUSE THE GOVERNMENT PROVIDED THE ROADS FOR FREE.

REGULAR COMMUTING TO WORK BY TRAIN ORIGINATED BEFORE THE CIVIL WAR, BECOMING MORE COMMON IN THE LATE NINETEENTH CENTURY. WHITE PLAINS, NEW YORK, WAS THE QUINTESSENTIAL RAILROAD SUBURB. A PARADE OF COMMUTER TRAINS CARRIED WHITE-COLLAR WORKERS IN AND OUT OF "THE CITY."

promised great economies—someday. Railroads were in no great hurry to fix a system that worked well, even if it had a more than a healthy amount of excess "fat."

As early as 1926, Harvard professor William Z. Ripley, a respected expert on railroad finance and business, warned of the "honeyfugling, hornswoggling, and skulduggery" he saw on Wall Street and in corporate board rooms. Not all of American business was as conservative as the railroads, and after years of speculation, fraud, and self-delusion, the stock market began to wobble in early 1929. The country had just elected Herbert Hoover president; he was a good man, following two ineffectual presidents, but despite his reassurances that the econ-

Through the Rockies: The Moffat Tunnel

In 1927, the Denver & Salt Lake Railroad (later merged with the Denver & Rio Grande Western) completed the Moffat Tunnel in Colorado. The six-mile bore eliminated the treacherous main line over Rollins Pass, providing a shorter route from the Midwest to the Salt Lake basin.

In the nineteenth century, Denver had been bypassed by the Union Pacific, the first transcontinental railroad. While it grew to become the great city of the Rocky Mountain West, it had only roundabout lines westward across the mountains.

After lengthy court battles and bruising political fights, David Moffat was able to begin construction of the tunnel that bears his name. For three years, miners labored far beneath the blazing summer sun and frigid winter storms to carve a mainline railroad tunnel, through mostly solid rock, at an elevation of more than 9,200 feet above sea level. When the miners broke through in February of 1927, they had managed to drive two working faces 32,800 feet through the Continental Divide—and meet dead-on in the middle of the mountain.

THE MOFFAT TUNNEL, COMPLETED IN 1927, STILL SERVES AS A MAIN EAST-WEST TRUNK ROUTE.

Denver feted the men, holding a great parade and entertaining them at the Cosmopolitan Hotel. This was a symbolic triumph, for the 38-mile Dotsero Cutoff linking the line west of the tunnel with the railroad to Salt Lake City would not be finished until 1934. But it opened the way for a far easier crossing of the Rockies. The Moffat Tunnel today carries both Amtrak and freight trains.

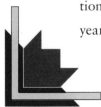

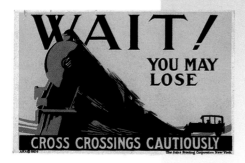

omy was sound, 13 million shares of stock changed hands on October 24, 1929, the day that became known around the world as "Black Thursday."

Over the next few weeks, the economy began a slide that would last two years and obliterate hundreds of millions of dollars of wealth. Railroad traffic dropped immediately, and the companies found themselves desperately attempting to reduce expenses while they, too, tried to see the market's bottom. Canada was not to be spared; before it was over, one out of every two adult Canadian males would be unemployed.

After a pleasant few years of boom, North America's seemingly invincible railroad industry faced an unprecedented bust. There was nothing to do but ride it out as best they could.

FACING PAGE (LEFT):
AUTOMOBILES
REPRESENTED NOT ONLY
ECONOMIC COMPETITION
FOR RAILROADS, THEY
COULD BE REAL HAZARDS,
TOO, AS PEOPLE SOMETIMES
TRIED TO RACE TRAINS TO
THE CROSSING.

THE BOSTON & MAINE'S
YANKEE FLYER, NORTH OF
BOSTON IN 1926, APPEARS
TO BE MOVING AT A GOOD
CLIP. RAILROADING WAS
ONE OF THE MOST LABOR-
AND CAPITAL-INTENSIVE
INDUSTRIES IN THE UNITED
STATES. THIS WAS THE
GOLDEN AGE: BIG
LOCOMOTIVES, NICE
TRAINS, GOOD TRACK, AND A
PRIDE IN RAILROADING THAT
MADE IT ALL WORK.

Chapter 5

HARD TIMES AHEAD

The period between 1930 and 1945 was a time of contrast and change. The railroad industry, shrunken by economic crisis and competition from the automobile, developed new ways to lower costs and attract passengers. Meanwhile, diesel locomotives began to replace steam engines as the nation prepared for war. Literally everything moved by rail during the conflict, leaving the railroads exalted but exhausted as they approached the postwar era.

The railroad industry entered the 1930s in a state of deep pessimism. While most business and government leaders proclaimed that the national economy was in good condition, unemployment had risen from 1.5 million in late 1929 to an estimated 4 million by the spring of 1930.

Railroads had not come through the 1920s in very good condition. Nationalization during World War I left the major railroads worn out, and reinvestment was hampered in the capital markets, which favored more lucrative—and speculative—outlets for investment. Railroads also suffered the effects of restrictive governmental regulation, public investment in competing transportation systems, and the loss of passenger business to the automobile. The national economic collapse that began in 1929 only sharpened the predicament faced by railroads since 1920.

Unemployment had risen to nearly 5 million by January of 1931. The Depression reached a low point in mid-1932, with unemployment

FACING PAGE (RIGHT): AS THE 1930S PASSED, THE AUTOMOBILE AND THE BUS BEGAN TO CUT HEAVILY INTO THE RAILROAD INDUSTRY. PEOPLE WERE TRAVELING LESS, AND WHEN THEY DID GO, THE NEW, FEDERALLY SUBSIDIZED HIGHWAYS AND BACKROADS WERE OFTEN THE PATH OF CHOICE. THE TIME WAS RIPE FOR CHANGES IN RAILROAD PASSENGER SERVICE.

THE PESSIMISTIC YEARS OF THE 1930S WERE AS TERRIBLE FOR BUSINESSES—INCLUDING THE RAILROADS—AS THEY WERE FOR THE PUBLIC. LARGE NUMBERS OF MEN TOOK TO THE RAILS, SEARCHING FOR JOBS, FREELOADING AS HOBOES, OR JUST RUNNING FROM THE MISERIES OF LIFE.

standing at 12 million, the overall economy having contracted by 40 percent, and industry producing at half of 1929 levels. Railroad employment fell by 42 percent during the same period. Employees who weren't furloughed had to bump fellow workers with lower seniority or accept demotion in order to keep working. Increased freight tariffs were granted in 1931 to shore-up falling revenues. This proved to be a disaster, as shippers diverted traffic to lower-cost trucks. In January of 1932, railroad management and labor agreed to a 10 percent reduction in wages for one year. The net income of railroads plummeted from $977 million in 1929 to a *loss* of $122 million in 1932; the industry would not be profitable again until 1937.

Capital investments were cut, and maintenance was deferred to the greatest extent possible. Locomotive sales plummeted during the

BEFORE AIR CONDITIONING, WHEN FANS STIRRED THE SUMMER AIR OF OFFICES, PAPERWEIGHTS SUCH AS THIS WERE BOTH FUNCTIONAL AND A REMINDER THAT "THE BUSINESS OF AMERICA WAS BUSINESS."

THE ERA IN REVIEW

1930:
The Santa Fe Railway suffers the worst traffic losses in its history as the Midwest is transformed by drought into a "Dust Bowl."

1931:
In May, B&O's Columbian, the first completely air-conditioned passenger train, is put into service between New York and Washington.

1932:
Depression-era hardship causes industry leaders to lower railroad wages by 10 percent for one year. Despite that concession, the net income of railroads plummets to a loss of $122 million.

1933:
Roosevelt is inaugurated: He promises quick recovery as the United States enters "The 100 Days."

1934:
Union Pacific's M-10000 streamliner does a coast-to-coast run in 57 hours.

1935:
The Railroad Retirement Act of 1934 is declared unconstitutional.

The streamlined Challenger, running between Omaha and Los Angeles, introduces such luxuries as air-

early 1930s, and most railroads had long "dead lines" of locomotives collecting dust in storage yards.

Unused engines and cars tied up substantial amounts of capital, had costs associated with bond interest, and weren't earning any money to pay these costs. One third of the nation's railroads went into bankruptcy during this period, and the cruel realities of railroad economics spelled the demise of many companies in the 1930s.

The "New Deal" of President Franklin Roosevelt sought to stabilize the economy in a number of ways. The Reconstruction Finance Corporation had been chartered during the Hoover administration to loan money to essential businesses, including banks and railroads, but had accomplished little before 1934. Despite Roosevelt's skepticism about the economic benefit of federal public works spending, his new Public Works Administration funded

By 1934, the Lima Locomotive Works in Ohio was turning out some of the finest steam locomotives ever built. Each proudly carried the distinctive, red diamond builder's plate on each side of the smokebox.

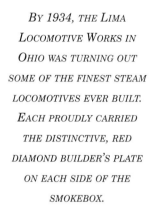

THE ERA IN REVIEW

conditioning, free pillows, and attendants trained as nurses.

1936:
Santa Fe's Super Chief, America's first all-Pullman diesel-powered streamliner, begins twice-a-week service between Chicago and Los Angeles. Running time is less than 40 hours.

1939:
In September, a war emergency is declared in the United States.

1941:
Japan attacks Pearl Harbor on December 7. Congress declares war.

1942:
Gasoline rationing is imposed, and travelers flock to passenger trains;

Northern Pacific responds by trying to discourage civilian travel.

1944:
The last Southern Pacific cab-forward locomotive is delivered.

1945:
In August, the United States drops atomic bombs on Hiroshima and Nagasaki. Japan surrenders.

schools, courthouses, hospitals, highways, bridges and other transportation improvements. Though thousands of miles of highways were built, the largest railroad project of the era was the RFC/PWA-financed electrification of the Pennsylvania Railroad between New York City and Washington, D.C.

The Pennsylvania Railroad began to experiment with electrification in 1895 and by 1906 had electrified its Long Island Railroad and West Jersey & Seashore Railroad subsidiaries. Electric power pulled as many as 1,000 trains a day under the Hudson River to New York City's Pennsylvania Station, opened in 1910. Suburban lines around Philadelphia were electrified before World War I, and there was serious discussion about adopting electric power for mainline freight and passenger trains.

A number of steam railroads tried electric traction during this period. The technology was new and intriguing, and electric locomotives

WHEN PENNSYLVANIA RAILROAD EMBARKED ON A MASSIVE ELECTRIFICATION OF ITS BUSY TRACKAGE BETWEEN NEW YORK AND WASHINGTON, D.C., DURING THE GREAT DEPRESSION, IT ALSO SET ABOUT DEVELOPING SUITABLE HIGH-HORSEPOWER ELECTRIC LOCOMOTIVES.

promised operating advantages over steam locomotives. They were faster, easier on track, cost only one-third as much to maintain, would last twice as long, could run in either direction, and never had to be removed from service for monthly boiler washes. Electricity also eliminated smoke and cinders, fuel and water stops, roundhouses, and turntables.

The Baltimore & Ohio, New Haven, New York Central, Boston & Maine, Milwaukee, Great Northern, Virginian, and Norfolk & Western railroads all developed substantial mainline electrification projects, but the Pennsylvania's plan was to be the biggest of them all. In late 1928, the railroad announced its intent to electrify 1,300 miles of track over the 325-mile route between New York City and Wilmington, Delaware. This ambitious scheme was expanded a year later with a plan to extend the electrified territory past Washington, D.C., to Potomac Yard north of Alexandria, Virginia.

The timing of this second announcement coincided with the start of the Great Depression. There were serious concerns about the wisdom of attempting such a project in the face of the national economic collapse, but the Pennsylvania saw great future benefits from electrification and decided to continue. The railroad had sufficient capital resources to get work under way and carry the project through 1931, when financing for any railroad project—even the "Standard Railroad of the World"—dried up. A $27.5 million loan was received from the Reconstruction Finance Corporation to continue the work. Another loan,

THE B&O's LOGO FEATURING THE NATION'S CAPITOL DOME WAS FIRST DEVELOPED IN THE 1890S AS AN APPEAL TO THE PATRIOTIC FERVOR OF AMERICANS WISHING TO SEE WASHINGTON, D.C. THIS VERSION OF THE COMPANY ICON HIGHLIGHTED THE SERVICES OF THE NEWLY AIR-CONDITIONED CAPITOL LIMITED OF 1934.

UNDOUBTEDLY THE MOST SUCCESSFUL AND ENDURING ELECTRIC LOCOMOTIVES IN AMERICA, THE PENNSYLVANIA'S GG-1S WERE THE MOTIVE-POWER BACKBONE OF THE "STANDARD RAILROAD OF THE WORLD" FOR MORE THAN 50 YEARS, EVEN OUTLASTING THE RAILROAD THAT BUILT THEM.

The PCC Car

*M*ost of the 75,000 streetcars running around the United States in the 1920s were old and tired, and it seemed the way to revitalize the industry was to design a new type of streetcar—one that would replace the boxy and rattling old traditional streetcars and bring the image of modern comfort and design to the street railroad industry.

A planning group formed late in 1929 to study the problem. Representatives of railroads and the manufacturing industry collaborated to evaluate everything about the streetcar, from controllers and brakes to the shape of seats and exterior appearance. Their new design, named the PCC (after the President's Conference Committee) Car, was modern in ap-

No. 1149 TYPIFIES THE EARLIEST TWO-MAN STREETCAR OPERATION; THE CONDUCTOR TOOK UP FARES WHILE THE MOTORMAN KEPT BOTH HANDS FULL WINDING UP THE CONTROLLER AND OPERATING THE MANUAL BRAKES. THE CLEVER "ECLIPSE" FENDERS WERE FOLDING GRATES MEANT TO SCOOP UP CARELESS PEDESTRIANS THAT GOT IN THE CAR'S WAY.

pearance and featured innovations that made it lighter, smoother riding, more comfortable, and more durable than earlier cars.

The first was placed in service in Brooklyn during early 1936, and lines in Baltimore and Chicago soon placed orders. Almost 5,000 PCC cars were built, most of them ending up in perhaps 30 cities across North America.

The PCC did not save the street railroad industry, but it helped slow the inevitable decline. The PCC car's durability and relatively low maintenance cost allowed several transit operations to survive during the postwar period, and these venerable streetcars can still be seen serving transit riders in Philadelphia, Boston, Pittsburgh, Newark, and Toronto.

for $80 million, was provided by the Public Works Administration to finance the Washington, D.C., section.

The great project was complete by 1940, giving the Pennsylvania Railroad the largest—and the last—electrified common-carrier mainline railroad in the nation. The result was a 20 percent increase in operating efficiency, which would pay substantial dividends during World War II, when traffic on the electrified lines reached an all-time high.

The Pennsylvania Railroad's electrification was one of the few truly bright spots on the railroad landscape during the Depression. A more general trend was for railroads to cut service on lightly used lines and abandon routes that had no hope of recovery. Inroads from automobiles and trucks made the situation worse, but a number of smaller lines, though uneconomical to operate, were able

PENNSYLVANIA RAILROAD'S ELECTRIFICATION OF ITS "BROAD-WAY" LINE, SERVING WASHINGTON, BALTIMORE, PHILADELPHIA, AND NEW YORK, BROUGHT DROVES OF WEEKDAY COMMUTERS TO ITS MULTIPLE-UNIT ELECTRIC TRAINS. WEEKEND PASSENGERS TRAVELED TO STORES, AMUSEMENT PARKS, AND BEACHES.

EVERY DINING CAR ON THE PENNSYLVANIA RAILROAD CARRIED SUGAR BOWLS LIKE THIS ONE IN THE 1930S.

to hang on because they represented the only reliable means of reaching isolated parts of the West. Other small railroads made ends meet with federal mail contract subsidies.

The Depression magnified the effects of competition from other modes of travel. For the first 50 years of its existence, the steam railroad enjoyed an unchallenged position as the principal form of public transportation. Two alternative propulsion tech-

As horseless carriages gave way to reliable automobiles like this 1925 Chevrolet, nearly everyone wanted to buy one. All-season paved roads increased in number and, as a result, short-haul business for steam railroads, streetcar systems, and electric interurbans began to drop.

The introduction by Ford of its first light-duty pickup truck as an optional body for the 1925 Model T Runabout proved a bellwether for the automotive industry. Suddenly, less-than-carload traffic could be carried far less expensively by road than by rail.

nologies became commercially viable during the 1890s, shaking and then toppling the steam railroads' preeminent position. The first of these was development of electric street and interurban railroads; the second was the rise of the automobile.

Henry Ford did not *invent* the automobile or the assembly line, but he had a Populist conviction that private automobiles were a democratic force, and he developed ways to make and sell them in the millions. In what

A TYPICAL SEAL FOUND IN BAGGAGE CARS DURING THE 1930S. THE SEALING WAX REVEALS THAT THIS ONE WAS USED BY SOUTHERN PACIFIC EMPLOYEES BASED IN SAN JOSE, CALIFORNIA.

has been described as possibly the most expensive litigation in American history, he fought an eight-year battle with the licensees of George Selden, who had been issued a patent on the automobile in 1895. The 1911 decision confirmed that literally anybody, Ford included, had the right to build automobiles.

Ford's Model T cost more than $900 when it was introduced in 1908, dropping to $345 by 1916 and $280 in 1927, when production stopped after more than 15 million cars had been produced. Not only had Ford made the automobile a mass commodity, he and others created a new economy based on the installment financing of newly invented consumer products. The manufacture of automobiles surpassed all other industries by 1926 and was described by Alfred P. Sloan of

THE VEHICLE THAT CHANGED THE THOUGHT AND TRANSPORTATION PATTERNS OF AMERICANS AS SURELY AS RAILROADS HAD ALTERED PERSONAL TRAVEL IN THE 1830S WAS THE FORD MODEL T. INEXPENSIVE AND TRUSTWORTHY, COUPES LIKE THIS 1919 MODEL ALLOWED TRAVELERS TO GO WHEREVER AND WHENEVER THEY PLEASED.

General Motors as "... the greatest revolution in transportation since the railway." Indeed, it was. By 1930, one in every five Americans owned an automobile, and the consequences to the railroad industry would be profound.

The new automobile culture increased the government's role in public works development. There were only 161,000 miles of surfaced roads in the nation in 1905. The total jumped to 521,000 miles in 1925 and 1,721,000 miles in 1945. Nearly all of this investment was made by the government.

This governmental involvement reflected a shift in public attitudes toward transportation. Prior to the rise of the automobile, it was taken for granted that public transportation would be provided by private companies, and most specifically by the railroads. This was an obligation assumed by the railroads in their capacity as a "natural monopoly." Railroads could develop and expand as economic need dictated, and investors would assume the risks and the benefits. The role of government was to ensure that the public's interests were served, and the railroads were expected to accept this regulation in exchange for business opportunities.

Railroads had long been viewed—with varying degrees of accuracy—as being abusive in the exercise of their

MEN AND WOMEN FROM ALL WALKS OF LIFE COLLECT RAILROAD MEMORABILIA LIKE THIS PRR COVERED CREAM PITCHER. SOME PEOPLE ENJOY THE AESTHETIC QUALITIES OF "RAILROADIANA"; OTHERS HAVE A FONDNESS FOR A PARTICULAR RAILROAD.

FLEXIBLE LOUNGE SEATING ON THE PULLMAN COMPANY'S "MARYLAND CLUB" CAR PROVIDED STATE-OF-THE-ART COMFORT FOR FIRST-CLASS PASSENGERS.

FACING PAGE (RIGHT):
IN SPITE OF THE HARD ECONOMIC TIMES, THE NATION'S MAJOR RAILROADS STILL OPERATED A FEW OPULENT TRAINS. SHOWN HERE IS THE "CREEK CLUB," A PULLMAN LOUNGE CAR OF THE 1930S.

power and gradually came under oppressive regulation by state and federal authorities. Grangers, Progressives, and any number of other "reformers" took advantage of the railroad industry as a convenient political target.

The automobile arrived as a practical consumer item at the same moment the nation and its political leadership were looking for an alternative to the railroad. The Good Roads movement channeled government monies into highway construction on a larger scale than ever before. More roads led to a larger market for cars, which increased political pressure to build even more and better roads, and so it went until a new public works philosophy became established.

The job of the government shifted from regulation to the actual provision of services—specifically, the building and maintenance of roads. Indeed, the social philosophy of transportation itself moved from public transportation being something available to anyone who could afford it to that of a personal right that should be provided to all by the government.

THE PULLMAN COMPANY PHOTOGRAPHED ITS LOUNGE-OBSERVATION CAR "MARYLAND CLUB" IN 1934 TO SHOW THE LEVELS OF COMFORT THAT AWAITED PASSENGERS.

DIRECT COMPARISONS ARE DIFFICULT, BUT THIS 4-8-2 STEAM LOCOMOTIVE WAS A MATCH FOR THE DIESEL LOCOMOTIVES OF ITS DAY. SOON, HOWEVER, IMPROVED DIESEL-ELECTRICS TURNED THE TIDE.

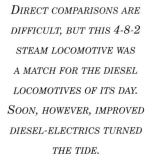

The Great Depression created an environment in which additional types of transportation began to receive permanent government support. Airlines, barge operators, and even pipelines were subsidized by federal investments, leaving the railroads in the unique and unenviable position of being subjected to greater regulation than any competing transportation mode, but without any resulting benefits. This,

The Vanishing Shortline

Depression-era road development pushed all-weather highways into formerly inaccessible territories. This allowed mail delivery to be shifted to trucks, condemning parallel railroads to abandonment. At the same time, the value of scrap iron was increasing, buoyed by purchases from Japan and a rearming United States.

Unable to compete with trucks, and with their passenger business lost to automobiles and buses, some shortline railroads found themselves worth more as scrap than as operating railroad companies. It was an ironic paradox: Railroads that had survived the Depression were killed off in the recovery.

Dozens of shortlines were abandoned and torn up for salvage during the Depression. In Nevada alone, the Randsburg Railway was abandoned in 1933, parts of the Nevada Copper Belt lost service in 1933 and 1935, the Nevada Central Railway was abandoned in early 1938, as was part of the Nevada & California Railway, followed by the Eureka & Palisade Railroad a few months later.

Service on the Virginia City line of the fabled Virginia & Truckee Railroad was discontinued in 1939, and the Tonopah & Tidewater stopped operating in mid-1940. The rails that weren't torn up immediately disappeared during wartime scrap drives.

Amtrak's "Autotrain" service is just the latest incarnation of an old idea. In this 1947 view, an automobile is loaded into a specially equipped Chesapeake & Ohio baggage car.

in essence, is "the railroad problem" that began to take form during the late 19th century and remains with us even today.

During the 1920s, some railroad designers became conscious of the developing public interest in the automobile and the fledgling commercial aviation industry. They sought to make the American railroad more contemporary, looking to modern, design-inspired trains in Europe as examples. Otto Kuhler took it upon himself to modernize the steam locomotive, and he published drawings in 1928 that resulted in his appointment as an industrial designer for the American Locomotive Company.

By the early 1930s, a competition was under way among the railroads and carbuilders to discover the best—and most marketable—way to combine the technical innovations of streamlining, internal combustion power, and lightweight construction. Over the next few years, a series of streamlined—and air-conditioned—motor trains were produced to test and demonstrate these concepts.

First of the new "streamliners" was the Union Pacific's Pullman-built M-10000, announced in 1933. Made entirely of aluminum alloy, its three articulated cars weighed less than a single conventional sleeping car and could accommodate 110 passengers. Powered by distillate—a low-grade petroleum fuel—the train was inaugurated in February 1934 as a harbinger of things to come.

RIDING HARD ON THE MARKERS OF PROTOTYPE STREAMLINER M-10000, UNION PACIFIC'S M-10001 CITY OF DENVER PROVIDED STREAMLINED OVERNIGHT SLEEPING-CAR SERVICE FOR THE FIRST TIME ANYWHERE IN THE UNITED STATES.

FACING PAGE (RIGHT): THE WONDER OF WONDERS, CHICAGO, BURLINGTON & QUINCY'S ORIGINAL ZEPHYR WAS LIKE NOTHING EVER CREATED WHEN IT TOOK TO THE RAILS IN 1934. THE TRAIN TRANSFORMED ITS BUILDER, THE EDWARD G. BUDD MANUFACTURING COMPANY, INTO AN INDUSTRY LEADER, SETTING THE STAGE FOR GREATER ZEPHYRS TO COME.

In the age of the automobile and the airplane, railroads strove mightily to convey the sense that they, too, were "Ahead of the Times."

The Budd Company of Philadelphia produced the *Zephyr* for the Chicago, Burlington & Quincy two months later. The *Zephyr's* engine was fueled with diesel oil, which proved to be much superior to distillate and established the pattern for subsequent diesel-electric locomotives. Pullman built another motor train in 1936 for the Illinois Central's St. Louis-Chicago *Green Diamond*, and others for Union Pacific, while Budd began producing streamliners for the Burlington line.

The Union Pacific christened its trains the *Cities*, while the Burlington had various kinds of *Zephyrs*. Trains like the *City of Portland* and the *Twin Zephyrs* influenced public attitudes about passenger travel, creating a demand for even more comfortable and flexible streamline service.

Although striking in appearance, articulated motor trains had serious limitations. The cars were permanently coupled together, making it extremely difficult to adjust capacity in order to meet demand. If the power car needed repair, the entire train was out of service, and the great length of some trains taxed yards and terminal facilities. The solution was to apply the materials and construction techniques used in the motor trains to individual locomotive-hauled cars.

Pullman built a pair of aluminum observation cars in 1933, and the Milwaukee Road started to build lightweight coaches the next year. Budd turned away from articulated motor trains in 1936 and began to produce individual cars to its distinctive fluted stainless-steel design. Aluminum and lightweight high-tensile-strength steel alloys allowed the new cars to weigh as little as 37 tons—although 50 tons was more customary—compared with 85 tons or more for conventional, or "heavyweight," cars. The new cars could be pulled by conventional lo-

Besides the regular trade press, a number of magazines catered to the reading tastes of railroad employees and enthusiasts. Railroad Stories *contained fiction, industry news, and plenty of innocent pulp journalism.*

The Zephyr's Daring Dash

Most famous of the motor trains was the *Zephyr*, named after the Greek god of the west wind. It was a complete, compact, self-propelled three-car train, clad in gleaming stainless steel and looking every bit like the train of the future.

Christened in April of 1934, the diminutive train toured the East and Midwest while plans were laid for a spectacular promotional stunt. The stubby little *Zephyr* was to make the 1,015-mile trip from Denver to Chicago in a dawn-to-dusk dash of 14 hours—12 hours under the fastest regular service. The trip got off 65 minutes late on May 26, 1934. The shovel-nose streamliner reached a top speed of 112 miles per hour as it hurtled across the Plains. Its progress, closely followed by the press, was announced to visitors at Chicago's Century of Progress Exposition.

The train broke a timing tape in Chicago at 7:10 p.m.—13 hours, 4 minutes, and 58 seconds after it left Denver—and rolled onto the stage at the climax of the "Wings of a Century" pageant at the exposition. There, with Lake Michigan as a backdrop, the *Zephyr* signaled the end of the Steam Age, claiming the future for the diesel-electric streamline train.

FOLLOWING ZEPHYR'S RECORD-SHATTERING SPEED RUN FROM CHICAGO TO DENVER, THE TRAIN WENT ON A NATIONAL PROMOTIONAL TOUR. ARRIVING IN OAKLAND, CALIFORNIA, THE TRAIN IS MOBBED BY CURIOSITY SEEKERS.

comotives and offered greater adaptability than the motor trains, while effecting a considerable weight savings over conventional equipment.

Integral to the lightweight car concept was mechanical air conditioning and air circulation. No more would the comfort of passengers be dependent on outside air temperature, and cinders were permanently banished from clothes and bedding.

Railroads that were reluctant to invest in motor trains saw potential in the new lightweight cars, and it wasn't long before they began to plan new, high-capacity streamline trains. Many of these would be pulled by diesel-electric locomotives, marking a nearly complete break with the tradition of heavyweight cars being pulled by steam locomotives.

AN ELDERLY 4-6-2, STREAMLINED BY THE LEHIGH VALLEY RAILROAD, LEADS THE BLACK DIAMOND TRAIN THROUGH THE MOUNTAINS OF PENNSYLVANIA CIRCA 1940. THE SOMEWHAT UNORTHODOX LINES OF THE LOCOMOTIVE'S PROFILE WERE THE WORK OF INDUSTRIAL DESIGNER OTTO KUHLER.

THE MILWAUKEE ROAD'S CRACK HIAWATHA TRAINS WERE HOMEGROWN STREAMLINERS. THE COWLING ON THE LOCOMOTIVE SUGGESTED SPEED AND MADE IT RESEMBLE A DIESEL LOCOMOTIVE. THESE TRAINS ROUTINELY HIT 100 MPH.

Pullman-Standard, Budd, and American Car & Foundry were the principal commercial builders of new cars. Seeking less costly alternatives, some railroads rebuilt older cars in the streamline style or constructed their own lightweight equipment. The Milwaukee Road built distinctive lightweight cars in the Milwaukee Shops and in May 1935 introduced the *Hiawatha*, the first steam-powered streamliner, which it preferred to call a "speedliner." Not to be outdone, the Baltimore & Ohio "streamstyled" heavyweight cars for its 1938 *Capitol Limited*.

COMMERCIAL ARTIST
LESLIE RAGAN WAS
COMMISSIONED BY NEW
YORK CENTRAL TO PAINT A
SERIES OF ADVERTISING
ILLUSTRATIONS. THIS ONE
PORTRAYS A STREAMLINED
J-3A "HUDSON."

New cars and streamlined diesel-electric locomotives transformed the passenger train and established new standards for passenger comfort and amenities. The great names of the early streamline era still resonate: the *Coast Daylight*, the *Rocky Mountain Rocket*, the *City of San Francisco* and *City of Los Angeles*, the *Hiawatha*, the *400*, and dozens more. First-class "name" trains captured the public imagination.

New York Central billed *TheTwentieth Century Limited*, operating between New York and Chicago, as "the most famous train in the world," and indeed it was. The New York *Evening World* effused that the train was "so magnificent that it should never be printed save in capital letters." Re-equipped as an all-bedroom streamliner in mid-1938, the train was a picture of stately refinement in shades of silver and grey as it sped on its 16-hour run. Industrial designer Henry Dreyfuss integrated every detail of the train, from the locomotive (whose bullet-pointed nose was split by a scimitar-shaped flange) to the china in the dining car.

West from Chicago, the Atchison, Topeka & Santa Fe Railway's *Super Chief* combined stainless steel and elegance in America's first all-Pullman diesel-powered streamliner. Making the trip to Los Angeles in 39½ hours twice a week, the *Super Chief* was the flagship of the

THE LABOR SHORTAGES CAUSED BY WORLD WAR II MADE A FEW PREVIOUSLY ALL-MALE RAILROAD JOBS AVAILABLE TO WOMEN. ELIZABETH A. JOHNS IS WORKING ON THE PENNSYLVANIA RAILROAD'S "PAOLI LOCAL" OUT OF PHILADELPHIA IN 1943.

EVEN AS A PAPERWEIGHT, HENRY DREYFUSS'S RENDERING OF THE 4-6-4 "HUDSON" SUGGESTS SPEED AND POWER.

Santa Fe and a favorite of the Hollywood crowd and their publicists. Like other first-class, extra-fare trains, the *Super Chief* reflected the growing importance of design and style to the traveling public. Just getting there wasn't good enough any more; one had to get there in style.

Few could afford a ticket on one of the new first-class streamliners, and coach train service continued to erode under pressure from buses and cars. Thousands of dispossessed rode the trains nevertheless, hopping freights as economic hobos. Though illegal and dangerous, the practice was often ignored by sympathetic railroaders, and at other times brutally suppressed by railroad police and local sheriffs.

Those among the impoverished whose pride, respect for the law, or practicality prevented them from catching a freight train swarmed onto the highways in old cars and trucks, searching for a better life. It may be argued that the railroads' emphasis on speed, comfort, and luxury for the fortunate few alienated a substantial segment of the market and drove less affluent travelers permanently into the culture of the automobile.

As important as lightweight cars to the creation of the modern streamline train was the introduction of a successful diesel locomotive for mainline use. Gasoline, naphtha, and distillate engines had been tried in motorcars and small locomotives with limited success. Most had mechanical

CHICAGO, BURLINGTON & QUINCY RAILROAD'S PIONEER ZEPHYR, SEEN HERE IN REGULAR SERVICE, HELPED PUT AN END TO THE STEAM AGE BY SHOWING THE SUPERIORITY OF DIESEL-ELECTRIC STREAMLINE TRAINS.

SOME RAILROAD CHINA WAS UNIVERSALLY REGARDED AS BEAUTIFUL, OR AT LEAST AS CLASSIC AND ATTRACTIVE. FOR SOME CHINA, THERE ARE DIFFERENCES OF OPINION. THE MILWAUKEE ROAD'S 1937 PATTERN "TRAVELLER" FEATURED A PINE TREE AND FLYING GOOSE MOTIF IN PINK.

End of the Interurban

Substantial areas of the United States and several regions of Canada were served by networks of interurban railroads. A special type of electric railroad that connected cities or urban areas, interurban lines were generally built to heavier standards than street railroads and were intended to compete directly with steam railroads.

Interurban mileage grew from seven miles in 1890 to a peak of 15,580 miles in 1916. An extensive system of interurban lines flourished in Ohio and central Indiana, where the terrain is relatively flat and towns are fairly close together, but interurban railroad development was not confined to the Midwest. The nation's largest system, with 700 route miles, was the Pacific Electric Railway, which shaped the development of the Los Angeles region. Forty states and five Canadian provinces had interurban lines, making them the largest single competitor to steam railroads prior to the advent of the automobile.

Construction of new interurban mileage plummeted after World War I, stopping entirely by 1927. Abandonments averaged 650 miles per year during the 1930s. World War II temporarily halted the decline as demands on every type of railroad reached record levels, but there were only 2,680 miles left in 1943. Nearly all were gone within a decade.

ELECTRIC INTERURBAN RAILROADS COUNTED ON A STEADY DIET OF LESS-THAN-CARLOAD EXPRESS FREIGHT AND PASSENGERS TO REMAIN PROFITABLE. MANY LINES WERE BUILT AND RUN AT A DEFICIT, HOWEVER, AND THE ADVANCES OF THE AUTOMOTIVE AGE KILLED NEARLY ALL OF THEM BEFORE WORLD WAR II.

In 1939, Electro-Motive Corporation quietly slipped its first fully standardized diesel switching locomotive, the SW-1, into railroad yards and industrial works all across the country. The SW-1 was the progenitor of all subsequent EMD SW switchers built through the early 1970s.

The locomotive that introduced diesel-electric power to many railroads was the humble switching engine, such as this early 1940s General Motors model SW-1.

drivetrains—much like a truck—which weren't well suited to railroad service. The General Electric Company developed an electric transmission system that had the engine drive a generator. The resulting electricity could be easily controlled and used to power motors on the axles, like those fitted to electric streetcars. This system was applied to gas-electric motorcars and, later, to small locomotives.

GE built three unsuccessful diesel-electric locomotives in 1918, and in 1925 began to furnish electrical equipment for Alco diesel-electric switchers. These were moderately successful and pointed the way to the production of several hundred diesel-electric switchers prior to 1940. Developing a diesel powerplant capable of surviving the rigors of mainline service was another matter, and it was here that the upstart manufacturer Electro-Motive Corporation had the edge.

EMC had been purchased by General Motors in 1930, as was the Winton Engine Co. Winton perfected a practical two-cycle diesel engine light enough for service on a road locomotive by 1932, and these

Facing page (right): In the days before television, newly elected President Franklin D. Roosevelt and his wife Eleanor (seen at the far left) took to the nation's rails in 1934 and 1935 to promote the economic recovery promised in his ground-breaking "New Deal" politics.

Wreck of the San Francisco

Deliberate train-wrecking has been an uncommon occurrence in the United States. Until the 1995 Amtrak derailment in Arizona, the nation's best known and most intractable act of railroad sabotage was the derailment of the streamliner *City of San Francisco* on the Southern Pacific Railroad near Harney, Nevada.

At about 10:32 P.M. on August 12, 1939, westbound train No. 101, consisting of 14 cars carrying 149 passengers, approached a bridge over the Humboldt River. Sometime earlier that day, someone had removed the splice bars at a rail joint 165 feet east of the bridge. The rails were pried out of alignment and deliberately re-spiked nearly five inches out of gauge.

The train derailed at 60 miles an hour. The locomotives and the first two cars made it across the bridge, grinding to a stop 865 feet past the gap. The next two cars demolished the bridge and ended up under three others in a mass of wreckage on the riverbed, with the eighth car sticking out of the ravine. Six more cars stayed upright, although three of them had derailed. Twenty-four people died in a scene of horror and devastation.

A nationwide investigation located a number of suspects, but no one was ever charged with the crime.

THE SLEEPING CAR "CHINATOWN" LIES ACROSS THE TWISTED REMAINS OF OTHER RAILROAD CARS AND THE BRIDGE THAT CAME DOWN AROUND THEM IN THE 1939 SABOTAGE-CAUSED WRECK OF SOUTHERN PACIFIC'S CITY OF SAN FRANCISCO.

LOCOMOTIVES AND ROLLING STOCK WERE SHOWN AT THE CENTURY OF PROGRESS EXHIBITION STAGED IN CHICAGO BETWEEN 1933 AND 1934. UNION PACIFIC'S M-10000 IS AT FAR LEFT, WHILE B&O'S RELIQUARIANS AND THE CAPITOL LIMITED SHARE CENTER TRACKS. THE DELAWARE & HUDSON SENT ONE OF ITS 4-6-2S AND THE 7-TON STOURBRIDGE LION, BUILT IN 1828.

companies experimented with ways of matching diesel engines and electric transmission for mainline purposes. EMC furnished the propulsion equipment for the *Zephyr* and most other motor trains of the era. This experience allowed EMC to develop a design for full-size passenger locomotives, which were placed into production in 1937. The E-series passenger locomotives dominated the market and pulled most of the pre-war diesel streamliners.

EMC had also commenced the manufacture of switching locomotives in 1936, and had a road freight locomotive, the FT, in production by 1939. Diesel production exceeded steam locomotive production for the first time in 1938.

In January of 1941, with the technologies of EMC and Winton developed to the point that their products were proving to be of substantial commercial value, the two subsidiaries were consolidated and

merged into the General Motors Corporation as the Electro-Motive Division. EMD's FT freight locomotives were the only diesel-electric freight locomotives allowed to be commercially manufactured during World War II under War Production Board restrictions. This helped establish market preeminence and meant that the competitors—all of them established steam locomotive manufacturers—were building an obsolete product.

The nation looked on uneasily as the clouds of war gathered over Europe and Asia. Countering the prevailing isolationist mood, President Roosevelt proposed increased military appropriations in 1938 and the creation of a two-ocean navy. The concept of national defense and the need to rearm gained impetus with the declaration of a limited war emergency on September 8, 1939. The export of scrap iron was halted a year later, and an unlimited national emergency was declared on May 27, 1941. Though not officially at war, the nation was definitely on a war footing.

Railroad traffic increased as the armed forces rebuilt. A freight car shortage occurred in late 1939 for the first time since 1921, and the railroads worked steadily to put long-dormant cars and locomotives back in service. Determined to avoid the chaos that resulted from government seizure during World War I, an

IN A VIRTUAL WAR OF ADVERTISING, PENNSYLVANIA RAILROAD MET NEW YORK CENTRAL'S ANNUAL EXAMPLES OF SERVICE ILLUSTRATIONS WITH WORKS BY ITS OWN ARTIST, GRIFF TELLER. DURING THE HEIGHT OF WORLD WAR II, TELLER PRODUCED THIS SCENE OF PATRIOTIC HYPERBOLE.

FACING PAGE (RIGHT): ON JULY 30, 1942, WORKERS OF THE PRESSED STEEL CAR COMPANY EXAMINE A LOAD OF ARMY TANKS FABRICATED BY THE FIRM AS PART OF ITS CONTRIBUTION TO THE WAR EFFORT.

Office of Defense Transportation was created to exercise general control over the railroads and ensure that national transportation priorities were met.

World War II would prove to be the zenith of public rail transportation. More people and materials than ever before had to travel, and nearly everything moved by rail. Demand increased spectacularly. In 1940, steam railroads handled 378,343 million ton-miles: about 62 percent of all freight. This nearly doubled by 1944 to 745,829 ton-miles, representing 70 percent of all freight transported in the United States. Passenger miles increased at an even greater rate during the same period, from 23,816 million passenger miles to 95,663 million pas-

DURING THE GREAT DEPRESSION AND SUBSEQUENT WAR YEARS, RAILROADS SOMETIMES EXHIBITED EXUBERANT TASTES IN RAILROAD CAR FURNISHINGS. THIS LOUNGE CAR ASHTRAY WAS INTENDED TO TILT WITH THE MOTION OF THE CAR.

Cincinnati Union Terminal

The Cincinnati Union Terminal opened on March 31, 1933, during the Depression. Located a mile and a half from the central city, the project made extravagant use of open space and featured an illuminated cascading fountain, plantings, an entry esplanade, and a semi-circular driveway.

Most striking was the main concourse, featuring a 116-foot-high semicircular dome clad in Indiana limestone. Projecting over the 16 through-tracks behind the concourse was the awesome, 410-foot red-marble waiting room, capable of handling the passengers of as many as 200 trains a day.

That day, of course, never came. Service dropped during the Depression, and fewer than 100 trains marked daily comings and goings during the postwar era. The arrival of Amtrak in 1971 meant only one train each way served the depot. Amtrak soon moved to less costly facilities.

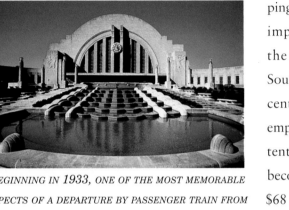

BEGINNING IN 1933, ONE OF THE MOST MEMORABLE ASPECTS OF A DEPARTURE BY PASSENGER TRAIN FROM CINCINNATI WAS THIS VIEW OF THE TRIUMPHAL ART DECO FACADE OF THE CITY'S UNION TERMINAL.

The once-grand terminal became a shopping center, later losing its imposing concourse to the expansion of the Southern Railway's adjacent yards. Forlorn and empty, it attracted the attention of civic leaders, becoming the focus of a $68 million project that transformed it into a museum center.

The terminal reopened in 1990 as home to Cincinnati's Museum of Natural History & Science, History Museum, Historical Society Library, and an Omnimax theater. In 1991, it became a stop for Amtrak's Chicago-Washington-New York *Cardinal*.

senger miles. In 1944, the peak war year, more than 75 percent of all commercial passengers traveled by rail, as did an astonishing 97 percent of military passengers.

World War II actually delayed the conversion from steam to diesel locomotives. Steam locomotive builders recognized that the existing technology had been almost fully developed by the late 1930s, and they were willing to concede the superior characteristics of diesel-electric locomotives. Most believed that the conversion from steam to diesel was inevitable, but would occur over an extended period of time as steam locomotives came to the end of their economic lives and were replaced.

It was suggested that some roads would never buy diesels because of their commitment to coal, and that smaller lines would be years in

THOUGH WOMEN LABORED IN ALL SORTS OF MEN'S JOBS AS THEIR HUSBANDS, SONS, AND BROTHERS WENT OFF TO WAR, MEN TOOK THEIR JOBS BACK IF THEY SURVIVED TO RETURN. STILL, RAILROADING WOULD NO LONGER BE EXCLUSIVELY A MAN'S DOMAIN.

THE RAILROAD MANUFACTURERS' WAR EFFORTS WERE MONUMENTAL. CONVERTED FOR THE DURATION OF HOSTILITIES INTO MATERIEL AND AMMUNITION MAKERS, FIRMS LIKE BALDWIN LOCOMOTIVE WORKS IN EDDYSTONE, PENNSYLVANIA, PRODUCED ARTILLERY AND RELATED ARMAMENT WITH MUCH OF THE SAME MACHINERY USED TO BUILD ITS STEAM LOCOMOTIVES.

THIS SCENE AT PHILADELPHIA BRINGS HOME THE JOY THAT WAS FELT BY EVERYONE WHEN OUR TROOPS RETURNED FROM WORLD WAR II. LIKE THE MEN, THE RAILROADS HAD PERFORMED HEROICALLY, MOVING BILLIONS OF TONS OF FREIGHT, MATERIEL, AND PASSENGERS.

Railroad Retirement

The assignment, furlough, and recall of most railroad employees was based on seniority. When work became scarce, employees with the least seniority were the first to be laid-off. The majority of railroaders were covered by pension plans, but private pension payments could be reduced if revenues were down, and many had been cut drastically by 1932.

This practice created a conflict between older employees, who preferred the certainty of a paycheck to an unreliable pension, and younger employees, who saw opportunity for increased job security if superannuated workers could be induced to retire by guaranteeing them a decent pension.

Railroad workers formed an association to agitate for government action. Labor proposed

RUNNING A LARGE STEAM LOCOMOTIVE REQUIRED PHYSICAL STAMINA, GOOD JUDGMENT, AND AN ALMOST INTUITIVE SENSE AS TO THE BEHAVIOR OF THE ENGINE AND TRAIN. THIS MAN PROBABLY SPENT MANY YEARS EARNING THE RIGHT TO PULL A THROTTLE.

its own plan in response, eventually compromising with the workers to produce the Railroad Retirement Act of 1934. This legislation anticipated the Social Security Act of 1935, which covered most other employees, and was tailored to address the specific concerns of railroad workers.

The 1934 Act was soon found unconstitutional, but President Roosevelt intervened to push for a lasting compromise. This pressure resulted in the Railroad Retirement and Carrier Taxing Acts of 1937, which made railroad employees the only private-sector workers outside the Social Security system to have a separate, federally administered pension plan. More than 95,000 elderly and disabled railroad employees applied for pension benefits by the end of 1937.

converting because of the availability of low-cost second-hand steam locomotives. The conversion would be gradual and orderly, permitting the manufacturers to invest in new production facilities. The principal builders—Baldwin, Alco, Lima—expected to compete against one another for locomotive orders long into the future.

The reality was quite different. Despite the higher cost—a diesel-electric locomotive cost two and one-half times as much as a comparable steam locomotive—most railroads were eager to change over as quickly as possible. Wartime production restrictions limited the numbers and types of diesel locomotives that could be produced, so even though they wanted diesels, the railroads, strapped for motive power, had to continue buying steam locomotives.

More than 4,000 locomotives were built for domestic use during the war. The most memorable year was 1944, distinguished by production of the last and best examples of several remarkable steam locomotive designs, including the Union Pacific 4-8-8-4

INSPIRED BY THE STYLING OF BRITISH LOCOMOTIVES, THE B&O CREATED THE EXPERIMENTAL "LORD BALTIMORE" IN 1935. THE ENGINE HAD MANY NOVEL FEATURES AND WAS FAST, BUT IT COULD NOT COMPETE AGAINST THE DIESEL-ELECTRIC.

Big Boys and 4-6-6-4 Challengers, Santa Fe's 4-8-4 Northerns, Baltimore & Ohio's 2-8-8-4s, and Southern Pacific's 4-8-8-2 cab-forwards. The War Production Board restricted the designing of new steam locomotives, establishing production criteria that were intended to make locomotives more useful during wartime. This resulted in Southern Pacific's 4460-class engines having smaller drivers than their prewar sisters, and the design being copied for the Western Pacific and Central of Georgia. Even the proud Pennsylvania found itself building locomotives derived from a Chesapeake & Ohio design.

Despite restrictions, there were also brave attempts to improve the steam locomotive. The Pennsylvania Railroad was the leader in this direction, developing a direct-drive steam turbine locomotive, two different four-cylinder locomotives, and the shark-

Conductors were required to wear regulation uniforms. Usually, they were sturdy, well-tailored suits of heavy blue or black wool. Polished buttons and company insignia gave them a formal, almost military, look.

During the war, millions of young men who had never been away from home were loaded into "main trains" for transfer to steamships headed for the European or Pacific battle theaters. For tens of thousands, it would be a one-way ride.

PASSENGERS WISHING TO SLEEP ABOARD TRAINS IN BEDS WOULD BOOK AN EXTRA-FARE TICKET WITH THE PULLMAN COMPANY IN ADDITION TO PAYING THE RAILROAD ITS BASIC COACH FARE. THIS TRIPLE BERTH IS UNUSUAL, DOUBLE BUNKS BEING THE NORM.

nosed T-1 4-4-4-4s. These efforts did little to stem the tide of dieselization: 608 diesel-electric locomotives were built in 1944, compared with 491 steam locomotives. The first Class 1 railroad to fully dieselize was the New York, Susquehanna & Western, which replaced 29 steam locomotives with 16 Alco diesel-electrics between 1942 and the summer of 1945.

The war's end brought the gradual elimination of travel restrictions, but it took months for the railroads to complete their wartime work and return to a peacetime footing. Millions of soldiers, sailors, and aviators had to be processed through discharge centers and returned home in the months following V-J Day—nearly every one of them traveling by train. Restrictions imposed in the closing months of the war, such as the removal of sleeping cars from runs of less than 450 miles, eased the problems of military travel but increased the burden faced by civilians.

BY THE BEGINNING OF THE 1950S, UNION PACIFIC HAD CREATED A STYLISH FLEET OF STREAMLINERS AND DOMELINERS SERVING ALL MAINLINE POINTS ON ITS SYSTEM. THE DOMELINER CHALLENGER HAD ITS OFFICIAL PORTRAIT TAKEN IN RAINBOW CANYON, WEST OF CALIENTE, NEVADA.

Rise of the Railfan

The appearance of streamline trains and diesels coincided with the extinction of many smaller railroads. These events prompted an increased appreciation of railroad history and a desire to preserve at least a few of the old locomotives and cars that were otherwise going to scrap.

Railroads attracted a loyal following of enthusiasts. Widespread availability of economical cameras allowed railroad hobbyists to easily capture their favorite subject in photographs, and the exchange of pictures, timetables, and other information led to the creation of formal railroad hobby clubs. The first of the national groups was the Railway & Locomotive Historical Society, founded in Boston in 1921. Other groups of "railfans" gathered in different parts of the country.

Enthusiasts would ride and photograph soon-to-be-defunct railroads and gather to share their experiences. By 1937 there was sufficient interest to charter entire railroads for the enjoyment of railroad buffs. Taking the concept of preservation to the next step, railfans started to acquire old locomotives, cars, and streetcars to keep them from going to the scrapper, setting the stage for the creation of several railroad museums after World War II.

STREAMLINED TRAINS HAVE BECOME CULTURAL ARTIFACTS. SANTA FE'S SOLE REMAINING "WARBONNET" F-UNITS ARE ON DISPLAY AT THE CALIFORNIA STATE RAILROAD MUSEUM IN SACRAMENTO, WHILE THE PRESERVED CALIFORNIA ZEPHYR DOME COACH IS A PRIVATELY OWNED CAR AVAILABLE FOR CHARTER SERVICE.

The sheer necessity of the service provided by railroads meant that their wartime work wouldn't be completed for months, while competing modes of transportation could respond to peacetime civilian demands quickly. The greatest troop movement of the entire war occurred on August 3–4, 1945, when Army returnees departed from Camp Kilmer, New Jersey, to various destinations around the country. More than 20,000 soldiers packed onto 31 trains, requiring 331 Pullmans, 100 coaches, and 41 kitchen cars. That same week, more than 250,000 servicemen and women were transported in organized troop movements requiring 726 Pullman cars and 512 coaches. The Army maintained its priority for Pullman cars well into 1946. By comparison, gas rationing ended quickly after the war, and even the airlines had gotten their planes back from the government by the end of 1945.

Peace meant that the nation could turn its attention to fulfilling expectations that originated during the 1920s and '30s, but were deferred by the Depression and the war. The prewar world's fairs popularized the vision of a modern consumer-oriented future embodying innovations in transportation and communication. This end could now be pursued by incorporating wartime developments in jet aviation, electronics, and synthetic materials. The railroads, tired but triumphant after serving as a bulwark of the war effort, needed to reinvest in order to preserve a place for themselves in the nation's transportation future.

THE BURLINGTON'S FLEET OF ZEPHYR TRAINS WERE SOMETIMES CALLED "VEST POCKET STREAMLINERS." THEY REPLACED MUCH LARGER TRAINS AND WERE MUCH MORE ECONOMICAL TO OPERATE.

Chapter 6

CLASSIC RAILROADING TAKES AN ENCORE

The railroad industry in post-World War II America was swimming against the tide of change. Both in terms of aesthetics and operating practices, the period between 1945 and 1960 was the beginning of the end for traditional railroading. This 15-year period saw the ultimate flowering of steam in high-horsepower locomotives, but it also brought the first generation of diesels that would ultimately replace them.

WEARING EYE-CATCHING CHOCOLATE, ORANGE, AND YELLOW STRIPES WITH A GREEN DIAMOND LOGO, ILLINOIS CENTRAL'S STREAMLINERS WERE GREAT FAVORITES OF TRAVELERS. SHOWN BELOW IS THE CITY OF MIAMI, STARTING ITS JOURNEY SOUTH FROM DOWNTOWN CHICAGO.

When World War II ended, America's railroads were exalted but exhausted. The volume of men, machines, and supplies that had been moved during the conflict was unquestionably a triumph for the industry and a significant factor in the Allied victory. But it had come at a price.

Locomotives and rolling stock were worn out from being pressed beyond their limits moving troops and materiel while continuing to meet unprecedented civilian travel needs. Railroad research and development, to say nothing of nonessential production, had been put on hold. For a generation of American males, the operative image of passenger railroading involved a troop train, not the *Twentieth Century Limited*.

PRIZED AS COLLECTIBLES TODAY, SOUVENIR MATCHBOOKS WERE AN INEXPENSIVE WAY FOR RAILROADS TO PROMOTE THEIR IDENTITIES.

FACING PAGE (RIGHT): THE CAB OF THE MODERN STEAM LOCOMOTIVE WAS A HOT AND OFTEN DIRTY PLACE. THAT, PLUS THE INHERENT COMPLEXITY OF STEAM LOCOMOTIVES AND THEIR GREAT THIRST FOR WATER, DOOMED THE BREED WHEN CONTRASTED WITH THE QUIET MIGHT AND RELATIVELY INEXPENSIVE OPERATION FOUND IN DIESEL-ELECTRICS.

THE GREATEST WEAKNESS OF STEAM POWER WAS ITS NEED FOR LABOR-INTENSIVE CARE. HORDES OF WORKERS WERE NEEDED TO KEEP THE TRAINS RUNNING SAFELY.

After the war, however, the railroads lost no time in moving to counter these problems. Diesels had proven their worth before and during the war, and there was little doubt that their role was about to rev up dramatically as worn-out equipment was replaced.

The immediate postwar years were a time of optimism and renewal for Americans. New prospects appeared, as well as new conveniences, and the railroads confidently saw themselves as part of this resurgence. Despite precipitous declines in both passenger and freight traffic in the Depression-ridden 1930s, the railroads' posture remained expansive and upbeat.

Perhaps the most visible and dramatic action taken by America's railroads in the immediate postwar years was the placement of massive orders for new streamliners by virtually all of the nation's Class 1 carriers. All three of the major carbuilders—the Edward G. Budd Manufacturing Company (which in 1946 would become part of The Budd

THE ERA IN REVIEW

1945:
New York, Susquehanna & Western becomes the first Class 1 railroad to embrace diesel technology. Other railroads are quick to follow.

The Chicago, Burlington & Quincy Railroad debuts Silver Dome, the first dome car, on its popular Chicago-Twin Cities Twin Zephyr.

1947:
General Motors' four-car, all-dome Train of Tomorrow, *a product of its highly competitive Electro-Motive Division, is unveiled at Soldier Field in Chicago on May 28.*

Alton Railroad becomes part of the Gulf, Mobile & Ohio.

1948:
Santa Fe's Chicago-to-Los Angeles Super Chief, *successfully inaugurated in 1936 and streamlined in 1937, begins daily service.*

New York Central fields the all-new Twentieth Century Limited; rival Pennsylvania Railroad counters with a new Broadway Limited.

Company), the Pullman-Standard Manufacturing Company, and American Car & Foundry—were swamped by the demand, so much so that the delivery window could be as long as five years.

Planning for new trains—and even some orders for equipment—had been suspended when the United States entered the war in 1941. The wartime focus was squarely on utility. "Non-revenue" cars such as lounges were banned, for instance, and Pullman runs under 450 miles were cancelled.

When peace came, rail luxury was resurrected with a vengeance. Not surprisingly, traditionally pro-passenger railroads took the lead. New York Central ordered more than 700 cars, reequipping its fabled flagship, the *Twentieth Century Limited*, along with the balance of its "Great Steel Fleet," as the railroad called its imposing roster of long-distance passenger trains. This extraordinary order, shared by Pullman and Budd, encompassed coaches, diners, tavern-lounges, parlor-ob-

PENNSYLVANIA RAILROAD FULLY REEQUIPPED ITS BROADWAY LIMITEDS IN 1948, ADDING TWIN BLUNT-END OBSERVATION LOUNGE CARS.

THE ERA IN REVIEW

1949:
Burlington, Rio Grande, and Western Pacific launch the Vista-Dome California Zephyr *between Chicago and Oakland, California; however, for the first time in history, airline passenger-miles exceed those of the Pullman Company.*

1950:
President Truman orders U.S. troops to the aid of South Korea.

1953:
Norfolk & Western's Roanoke Shops build the last steam locomotive in the United States, an 0-8-0 switcher.

1955:
Santa Fe is an early convert to diesel technology, partly due to the scarcity of water on its desert lines.

1959:
When an 0-6-0 switcher drops its fires at Camden, New Jersey, the Pennsylvania Railroad is dieselized.

1960:
Grand Trunk Western pulls its Northerns out of local service in Michigan, putting an end to regularly scheduled passenger steam service in the United States.

servation cars, mail cars, baggage cars, and sleepers, most arriving in 1948 and 1949.

All of these cars were in the "lightweight" streamliner mode; construction of "heavyweight" or "standard" cars of riveted steel was over by this time. Budd products were all built of stainless steel using a patented "shotwelding" process—spot welding with a powerful "shot" of electric current. Pullman and ACF cars were generally fabricated of Cor-Ten steel, a durable alloy marketed by United States Steel beginning in 1934. More than two-thirds of all lightweight cars built would be of Cor-Ten, with stainless steel second and aluminum a distant third (though many of Union Pacific's lightweights used this metal). Stainless steel and aluminum cost approximately ten times more than Cor-Ten.

New York Central's vast postwar order for passenger cars included more than 250 Pullmans in configurations typical of the period. More than half were what railroaders call "ten and sixes," meaning that they contained ten roomettes and six double bedrooms. Some had roomettes only, 22 in number, and others were configured with six double bedrooms and a buffet-lounge at one end.

Like virtually all sleepers, heavyweights and light-weights alike, these cars carried names—evocative names to be sure, but also useful, since they were assigned in series and thus served to

IN THE LATE 1930S, THE
NEW YORK CENTRAL AND
PENNSYLVANIA RAILROADS
HIRED INDUSTRIAL
DESIGNERS TO CREATE A
NEW LOOK FOR THEIR
PREMIER PASSENGER
TRAINS. THIS COACH FROM
THE CENTRAL'S
TWENTIETH CENTURY
LIMITED EPITOMIZES THE
CLEAN LINES AND
"MODERNE" STYLE OF THE
STREAMLINE ERA.

identify car types. (The only major railroads that chose not to name their lightweight sleepers were the Southern Pacific and, later, the Northern Pacific.)

Central's Pullman-Standard-built 10/6s were named in the "River" series: "Agawam River," "Kalamazoo River," "Chateauguay River," and so on—97 cars in all. Budd's 10/6s were "Valley" cars, while its 22-roomette cars were in the "Harbor" series. Pullman-Standard's were named "Sandusky Bay," "Thunder Bay," and so on. Of the hundreds of cars that arrived to upgrade NYC's passenger services, two were clearly the crown jewels: "Hickory Creek" and "Sandy Creek," the deep-windowed sleeper-observation lounges for the *Twentieth Century Limited*.

Sailing along with the "Great Steel Fleet" were the colorful new streamliners of other railroads. Competitor Pennsylvania Railroad upgraded its "Fleet of Modernism," including its illustrious *Broadway Limited*. Delaware, Lackawanna & Western launched a New York

The Twentieth Century Limited's *deep-windowed* observation cars *"*Hickory Creek*" and "*Coffee Creek*" featured a raised* Lookout Lounge *with bar service and five double-bedrooms. The updated trains favored a wealthy business clientele.*

City-Buffalo train with an old name: *Phoebe Snow*, the "maid all in white" who had touted the virtues of the line's clean-burning locomotives, fired with Pennsylvania anthracite coal.

Meanwhile, Atlantic Coast Line and Seaboard Air Line buffed up their New York City-to-Florida trains, ACL's *Champions* and SAL's *Silver Meteor* and all-new *Silver Star*. Illinois Central inaugurated the *City of New Orleans* (which decades later would be made famous in song) from Chicago and updated its all-Pullman *Panama Limited* on the same route. Southern Railway and partners fielded a new *Crescent* between New York and New Orleans and the *Royal Palm* between the Midwest and Florida. Norfolk & Western introduced a pair of Cincinnati-Norfolk streamliners, the daylight *Powhatan Arrow* and overnight *Pocahontas*.

The Louisville & Nashville line was off the blocks quickly, in late 1946, with its Cincinnati-New Orleans *Humming Bird* and St. Louis-Atlanta *Georgian* with partner Nashville, Chattanooga & St. Louis. (In 1950, Wabash would enter the bird sweepstakes with its *Blue Bird*.)

Monon's postwar streamliners were unique. While other railroads turned to the major builders, this modest Midwestern carrier made a deal with the U.S. Army to buy a bunch of almost new hospital cars made surplus by peace

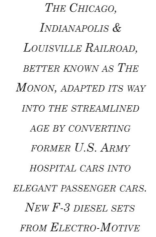

THE CHICAGO, INDIANAPOLIS & LOUISVILLE RAILROAD, BETTER KNOWN AS THE MONON, ADAPTED ITS WAY INTO THE STREAMLINED AGE BY CONVERTING FORMER U.S. ARMY HOSPITAL CARS INTO ELEGANT PASSENGER CARS. NEW F-3 DIESEL SETS FROM ELECTRO-MOTIVE PROVIDED THE POWER.

BUILT IN 1885, CHICAGO'S OLDEST OPERATING DEPOT BEFORE THE COMING OF AMTRAK WAS DEARBORN STREET STATION, SEEN HERE IN THE 1950S. C&WI'S RS-1 NO. 253 SWITCHES AN ERIE TRAIN, WHILE MONON'S HOOSIER PREPARES TO DEPART BEHIND F-3 NO. 84-B.

Sleeping on the Streamliners

The 10-roomette/6-double-bedroom cars that were predominant in the New York Central's postwar Pullman order would be the "plain-vanilla" sleepers of the lightweight era, surviving as part of Amtrak's "Heritage Fleet" into the 1990s.

The roomette was a cleverly contrived single room with a full-sized bed; a toilet discreetly hidden under a commode that doubled as a footrest; a washbasin that folded out of the wall; plus closet, mirrors, hooks, a luggage rack, fan, and a variety of useful lights, including the blue night-light that was traditional aboard Pullmans. Roomettes were essentially a product of the lightweight era, while double bedrooms (with upper and lower berths) had become common in the 1930s, when many hundreds of heavyweight

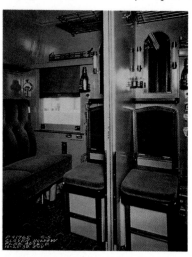

THE INTERIOR OF THE HEAVYWEIGHT SLEEPER "CLOVER HOLLOW" HAS BEEN UPDATED BY THE PULLMAN COMPANY WITH A HANDFUL OF STREAMLINER APPOINTMENTS. FIRST-CLASS PASSENGERS WOULD HAVE NOTICED LIGHTER COLORS AND SOFTER UPHOLSTERY ON THE COUCH, AMONG OTHER DETAILS.

Pullmans had been rebuilt, air-conditioned, and modernized.

Notably absent in the Central's order were any "open section" accommodations: the curtained upper and lower berths that were the dominant sleeping style aboard heavyweight Pullmans. Though popular in Canada even today, they were a relative rarity in postwar America.

A budget sleeping option that in part replaced them was the "Siesta Coach" introduced by Budd in 1953. These thrifty cars, called "Slumbercoaches" by the purchasing railroads—including Burlington, Northern Pacific, and Baltimore & Ohio—carried 40 passengers in 24 single and 8 double rooms. New York Central had similar "Sleepercoaches," converted from 22-roomette cars.

and—with the help of industrial designer Raymond Loewy—turned them into handsome red-and-gray streamliners, complete with baggage-mail cars, coaches, dining-tavern cars, and flat-end parlor-observation cars. Thus equipped, the *Hoosier* and *Tippecanoe* streamliners entered service between Chicago and Indianapolis, while the *Thoroughbred* ran between Chicago and Louisville.

Western railroads invested heavily. Great Northern got in ahead of all the rest, with its reequipped *Empire Builder,* inaugurated in early 1947 to operate between Chicago and the Pacific Northwest, and competitor Milwaukee Road came along about six months later with its *Olympian Hiawatha*, featuring unique glass-turreted "Skytop" obser-

WHEN THE DOME CAR IDEA TOOK HOLD IN THE LATE 1940S, NEARLY EVERY WESTERN AND MIDWESTERN RAILROAD PLACED ORDERS FOR THEM. A GOOD MANY OF THESE GLASS-TOPPED CARS HAD STYLISH LOUNGES, AS EXEMPLIFIED BY THIS UNION PACIFIC DOMELINER ON THE CITY OF ST. LOUIS.

THE SLEEK, BOAT-TAILED DOME LOUNGE OBSERVATION CAR "SILVER SKY" BRINGS UP THE MARKERS ON THE END OF THE RIO GRANDE ZEPHYR AT GRANBY, COLORADO.

vation cars (offered on the road's Chicago-Twin Cities *Hiawathas* as well). Northern Pacific, also vying for passengers between Chicago and the Northwest, upgraded its lightweight *North Coast Limited*. New on Southern Pacific were a streamlined Oakland-Portland *Shasta Daylight* (in the lovely red and orange colors introduced before the war) and the Los Angeles-New Orleans *Sunset Limited*.

Union Pacific enhanced its Overland Route fleet serving Chicago, St. Louis, Denver, Los Angeles, San Francisco, and Portland (with partners Chicago & North Western, Southern Pacific, and Wabash). The Santa Fe *Chiefs*—and in particular, the all-Pullman, extra-fare *Super Chief* between Chicago and Los Angeles—received a massive infusion of new equipment.

Chicago, Burlington & Quincy was a streamliner pioneer, having introduced its three-car, fluted-stainless-steel *Zephyr* in 1934. (Along with UP's *Streamliner*, which debuted a week or so earlier, Burlington's little train, later called the *Pioneer Zephyr*, kicked off the lightweight era.) By the time World War II broke out, Burlington had significantly expanded its "Zephyr" fleet, a process the company continued immediately after Japan's surrender.

THE FIRST STREAMLINED SUPER CHIEF WAS CALLED "THE TRAIN OF THE STARS" BECAUSE OF ITS PATRONAGE BY THE HOLLYWOOD MOVIE AND BROADWAY STAGE ELITE.

FACING PAGE (LEFT): SANTA FE'S SAN FRANCISCO CHIEF GLIDES ATOP MUIR TRESTLE OUTSIDE MARTINEZ, A SHORT DISTANCE FROM ITS RICHMOND, CALIFORNIA, TERMINAL.

INDUSTRIAL DESIGNER BROOKS STEVENS WAS HIRED BY THE MILWAUKEE ROAD TO CRAFT DISTINCTION INTO ITS LAST GREAT TRAIN, THE OLYMPIAN HIAWATHA OF 1949. STEVENS' SOLUTION WAS THE "SKYTOP" OBSERVATION LOUNGE CAR, A UNIQUE SLEEPER-SOLARIUM LOUNGE-OBSERVATION CAR.

FROM THE VERY
BEGINNING, CARD-PLAYING
WAS A FAVORITE PASTIME OF
PASSENGERS. SOME
RAILROADS GAVE DECKS OF
CARDS AWAY AS
PROMOTIONS. OTHERS SOLD
THEM ONBOARD AS A
CONVENIENCE.

In September of 1945, Burlington ordered an identical pair of trains from Budd (its exclusive supplier in the lightweight era) that two years later would enter service between Chicago and the Twin Cities as the *Twin Zephyrs*. These trains were notable in that each contained four Vista-Dome cars for sightseeing— undoubtedly the most exciting innovation in postwar passenger railroading. In July of 1945, just months before the *Twin Zephyrs* order, Burlington had introduced its *Silver Dome*, the prototype Vista-Dome, converted in the railroad's Aurora (Illinois) Shops from a Budd coach.

The dome-car brainstorm had come a year earlier to Cyrus R. Osborn, a General Motors vice president and general manager of its Electro-Motive Division, builder of diesel locomotives. The inspiration occurred while he was riding in the cab of one of his company's products through Colorado's Glenwood Canyon. It struck Osborn that passengers would gladly "pay $500 for the fireman's seat" with the

DINING BENEATH A PENTHOUSE OF GLASS WAS A COME-ON FEW COULD RESIST, YET ONLY THE UNION PACIFIC BOUGHT CARS BASED ON THIS PRECURSOR FROM THE TRAIN OF TOMORROW. GENERAL MOTORS HIRED HOLLYWOOD STARS PHIL HARRIS AND WIFE ALICE FAYE TO PROMOTE THE SWANK WONDERS OF THE WHOLE IDEA.

THIS STUDIO-ALTERED VIEW OF GENERAL MOTORS' TRAIN OF TOMORROW DEMONSTRATOR SHOWS WHY DOME CARS WOULD PROVE ENDURINGLY POPULAR. UNION PACIFIC LATER PURCHASED THE TRAIN WITH ITS EMD E-7A LOCOMOTIVE.

FOR 21 YEARS, THE LEGENDARY CALIFORNIA ZEPHYR OFFERED THE BEST ROUTING THROUGH WESTERN CANYONS AND MOUNTAIN FORESTS, PLUS SPLENDID FOOD AND FRIENDLY TRAIN CREWS THAT EMBODIED PUBLIC SERVICE. THIS VIEW OF THE EASTBOUND CZ WAS TAKEN AT ALTAMONT PASS, CALIFORNIA.

views it afforded. Osborn sketched the dome idea and General Motors eventually built it, in the four-car, all-dome prototype *Train of Tomorrow*, which debuted in 1947.

This little demonstration train consisted of a round-end observation-lounge, sleeper, diner, and chair car, all topped with glass-enclosed observatories. Each of these types would be replicated for some of the 16 railroads (virtually all of them in the West, since clearances on most eastern lines prohibited dome operation) that would come to own a grand total of 236 dome cars by the time the last one was built in 1958.

Probably the greatest dome train of all was the Chicago-San Francisco *California Zephyr*, operated by Burlington in partnership with

the Denver & Rio Grande Western and Western Pacific. This handsome Budd-built train was ordered in 1945, just a month after the *Twin Zephyr*, but didn't enter service until 1949, so extensive (67 cars, for six trainsets), complex, and elegant was the equipment ordered. With five domes and a schedule designed to transit both the Colorado Rockies and California's Feather River Canyon in daylight, the CZ, as it was known to its intimates, made good its publicists' claims by becoming the "most talked about train in America."

Perhaps the most bizarre episode in the postwar passenger boom involved the Chesapeake & Ohio Railroad and its impetuous chairman, Robert R. Young. Though the route of the coal-hauling C&O was relatively short on population areas and thus passenger potential, in the mid-1940s Young ordered a total of 351 cars to modernize its passenger service. This included 46 cars from Budd to inaugurate the *Chessie*, an all-new daytime streamliner to run between Washington and Cincinnati (with connecting sections to Newport News, Virginia, and Louisville, Kentucky). The equipment for this luxuri-

FROM THE START, THE CALIFORNIA ZEPHYR WAS MORE LIKE A CRUISE SHIP THAN A TYPICAL PASSENGER TRAIN. TIMED FOR VIEWING THE REGAL VISTAS OF THE WEST BY DAYLIGHT, THIS LAST OF THE ORIGINAL ZEPHYRS WAS A SUAVE TRAIN THAT COULD NOT EASILY BE DUPLICATED TODAY.

CONTINUING THE DECORATIVE DIRECTION PIONEERED BY THE SANTA FE IN ITS FIRST STREAMLINED SUPER CHIEF, THE FULLY REEQUIPPED TRAIN OF 1951 CARRIED OUT A SOUTHWESTERN AMERICAN INDIAN THEME. THE STYLISTIC APPOINTMENTS IN THE LOUNGE OF THE "PLEASURE DOME" CAR SEEN HERE WERE PURE 1950S CHIC.

Joe Stalin's Locomotives

While the diesel population soared and steam plummeted in the postwar years through 1960, the number of electric locomotives remained relatively constant at about 2 percent of a slightly shrinking total. The count included the "Little Joes," a small fleet of locomotives named for Soviet leader Joseph Stalin, that ran on the Milwaukee Road and the Chicago, South Shore & South Bend line.

In March of 1946, the Russian government had ordered 20 5,500-horsepower electric locomotives from General Electric. These powerful locomotives, bidirectional and double-ended, were handsomely sleek with streamlined carbodies. Prior to delivery, however, the Cold War froze deeper, and in 1948 an embargo was placed on strategic shipments—including these locomotives. By then, 14 had been completed in Russia's

A CHICAGO, SOUTH SHORE & SOUTH BEND 2-C-C-2 FREIGHT MOTOR AT MICHIGAN CITY, INDIANA, ORIGINALLY INTENDED FOR SERVICE IN THE STALINIST SOVIET UNION.

five-foot gauge; the half-dozen still in progress were rolled out in U. S. standard gauge. Then GE set about finding a buyer.

They found three. The Paulista Railroad in Brazil took five. CSS&SB, a Chicago-area interurban, took three. In 1950, the Milwaukee Road took the remaining dozen (nine of them converted from broad gauge) for use on its Rocky Mountain electrification through Montana and Idaho.

The Cold War thus was a boon for the Milwaukee Road, delaying for 25 years the demise of its electrified services. The "Joes," modified in 1958 so they could be run in multiples with diesels, proved stalwart, though even they could not prevent the inevitable, and in 1974 the Milwaukee's wires came down. CSS&SB's "Joes" lasted a few years longer, and Brazil's soldiered on into the '90s.

ous train, which had two dome cars and a lounge car featuring a fish tank, was delivered in August of 1948.

By then, however, a downturn in business conditions and disappointing ridership on both C&O and competitor Baltimore & Ohio caused the *Chessie* to be rethought—and abandoned before it was even inaugurated. All but four of the 46 *Chessie* cars were sold off, and by 1951 only 130 cars from among Young's 351-car order remained in C&O service, many having been diverted before they were ever delivered. (Southern Pacific and Rock Island had been responsible for a similarly stillborn train, the *Golden Rocket*, on the Golden State Route between Chicago and Los Angeles. This tri-weekly luxury service was set to debut in 1947, but the operators pulled the plug, setting a sad precedent for the *Chessie*.)

The 1952 "Superdomes" of The Milwaukee Road required onboard dedicated HVAC powerplants for cooling, but the vistas from these ten cars built for Twin Cities Hiawatha and Olympian Hiawatha service were fantastic. Santa Fe, Great Northern, and Southern Pacific would soon secure similar cars.

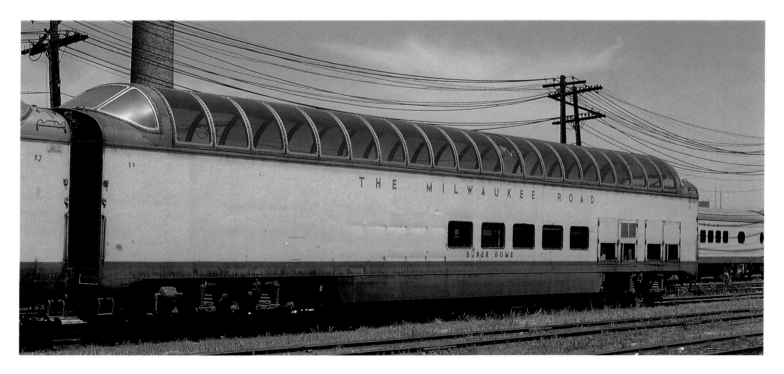

C&O's controversial Young was not shy about publicity. One occasion that garnered plenty of it was a 1956 magazine ad he instigated with a banner headline that screamed, "A Hog Can Cross America Without Changing Trains—But YOU Can't!" A pig lolled contentedly in the door of a stock car, while a distraught family —labeled "John Q. Traveler"—watched the train roll by.

Indeed, the United States had never had a true transcontinental, coast-to-coast train (and wouldn't until 1993, when Amtrak extended its Los Angeles-New Orleans *Sunset Limited* to Jacksonville and Miami). In the ad, Young prodded the industry, saying that C&O "stands ready" to join with other carriers in providing such service.

THE MOST LAVISH COACH TRAINS ASSEMBLED FOR THE SOUTHERN PACIFIC WERE THE DIESELIZED SHASTA DAYLIGHTS, WHICH OPERATED BETWEEN OAKLAND, CALIFORNIA, AND PORTLAND, OREGON. COMPLETED IN 1949, THEY WERE SCHEDULED FOR DAYTIME TRAVEL TO ALLOW THE BEST VIEWS OF MOUNT SHASTA, THEIR 14,162- FOOT NAMESAKE.

FACING PAGE (RIGHT): SEAMLESS FORM, COLOR, AND REDUCED WEIGHT WERE FUNDAMENTAL ASPECTS OF THE STREAMLINER YEARS. BY THE CLOSE OF THE 1940S, THE STYLING OF THESE TRAINS WAS APPROACHING FULL FLOWER. SHOWN HERE IS BALTIMORE & OHIO'S NEWLY BUILT COLUMBIAN.

THE FABLED TWENTIETH CENTURY LIMITED, PHOTOGRAPHED IN 1951 AT NEW YORK'S MOTT HAVEN YARDS IN THE BRONX.

Steam Versus Diesel

Though in the end it was no contest, the steam-versus-diesel debate raged heatedly for some 20 years, but never hotter than in the days immediately after World War II.

On steam's side was tradition—plus the fact that steam locomotives were much less expensive to build than diesels. There the economic edge ended, however, as diesels were far cheaper to operate. Fuel costs were less, for openers, but that was just the beginning. Typically, steam spent far too little time on the road and far too much in the shops and engine terminals being serviced and inspected.

New York Central tried to get a handle on this in the fall of 1946 by placing six of its Nia-

PERHAPS NO OTHER SINGLE CLASS OF LOCOMOTIVE WAS AS FAMOUS AS THE NEW YORK CENTRAL'S "HUDSON" (4-6-4) PASSENGER ENGINES. OVER THREE DECADES, THEY ESTABLISHED ENVIABLE REPUTATIONS HAULING FAST, HEAVY TRAINS ALL OVER THE SYSTEM. SADLY, NONE WERE SET ASIDE FOR PRESERVATION.

garas in a controlled test program, operating head-to-head with diesels between Chicago and Harmon. By fitting monthly boiler washes and daily inspection and repairs into brief turnarounds, the Central was able to get an impressive, diesel-competitive 27,221 miles per month out of the Niagaras.

But it was the Norfolk & Western that most effectively modernized its steam-servicing procedures, particularly at its mammoth Shaffers Crossing facility in Roanoke, Virginia. N&W stuck by its guns longer than any other United States railroad, believing that modern steam power, when creatively operated could overcome diesels' natural advantages. In the end, it couldn't.

Though a transcontinental train would have to wait nearly four decades, through-service had been planned even before the war and was inaugurated in March of 1956. Trains traveled from New York and Washington to San Francisco and Los Angeles. The participants were the New York Central, Pennsylvania Railroad, and Baltimore & Ohio in the East and, in the West, the Santa Fe, Southern Pacific, Rock Island, Chicago & North Western, Union Pacific, Southern Pacific, Burlington, Rio Grande, and Western Pacific. The cars were interchanged at Chicago.

During this era, Chicago remained the great railroad center it had always been, with no fewer than six major, main-line train stations: Union Station (serving the Pennsylvania Railroad, Milwaukee Road, Burlington, and Gulf, Mobile & Ohio), LaSalle Street Station (New York Central, Nickel Plate, Rock Island), Dearborn (Santa Fe, Erie, Grand Trunk, Chicago & Eastern Illinois, Wabash, and

ANNOUNCING THE PRESENCE OF A MOST SPECIAL TRAIN, THIS GLOWING DRUMHEAD SIGN DIRECTED PASSENGERS TO THEIR CARS ON TRACK NO. 5 AT CHICAGO'S DEARBORN STATION. FOLLOWING TRADITION, THE TRAIN'S OBSERVATION CAR ALSO CARRIED A SIMILAR NIGHTLIT TAILSIGN.

DEARBORN STREET STATION SERVED AS THE TERMINAL FOR A NUMBER OF RAILROADS ENTERING CHICAGO, AMONG THEM THE CHICAGO, ROCK ISLAND & PACIFIC. SOME 20 YEARS BEFORE THE ROCK ISLAND'S DEMISE, ONE OF ITS SMARTLY ATTIRED ROCKETS MAKES READY FOR DEPARTURE WESTBOUND.

Monon), Grand Central (Baltimore & Ohio, Chesapeake & Ohio, Soo Line), Central (Illinois Central), and the Chicago & North Western Passenger Terminal. Countless thousands of passengers poured through these grand stations, bound for hundreds of cities from coast to coast.

Chicago's depot diversity, while architecturally and operationally rich, complicated transfers of passengers, luggage—and, later, through-cars that were sleepers. Parmalee Transfer was the company dedicated to shuffling people and their belongings among the stations. The Pullmans, too, had to switch tracks, a complicated operation that involved four stations. Though performed expeditiously, the switching involved layovers for servicing, which kept the through-car option from being entirely successful. Passengers could stay aboard during switching maneuvers, or they could detrain to see the sights of Chicago.

These through-services were part of the railroads' postwar passenger revival, which by 1948 was in full swing. Some 2,500 new cars were in service, enough to assemble 250 new streamlined trainsets, with another 2,000 cars on order. Putting this in perspective, and highlighting the vastness of rail passenger operations of the era, is another revealing statistic: In 1950, lightweight cars, pre- and postwar, accounted for only 15 percent of the country's total operating fleet. Though long out of production, the old riveted

The Chicago Railroad Fair

Held on the lakeshore site of the 1934 Century of Progress Exposition (where Burlington's brand-new *Zephyr* had made a dramatic entrance at the conclusion of a non-stop sprint from Denver), the Chicago Railroad Fair was testimony to the lingering centrality of trains in the public mind in the immediate post-war years.

The fair celebrated the centennial of railroading's arrival in Chicago. Thirty-seven railroads participated, from the Atchison, Topeka & Santa Fe to the Wabash. Highlights included exhibits of locomotives and cars, a chance to ride behind steam on the narrow-gauge "Deadwood Central," and various theme-park-type attractions, such as an Indian village sponsored by Santa Fe.

The centerpiece was the "Wheels a-Rolling" pageant, presented in a dozen scenes. Though Scene One chronicled the National Road, Pony Express, Overland Trail, and early "horseless carriages," trains took center stage as the pageant recreated the Golden Spike ceremony and other important events in railroad history, at the same time paying homage to the Harvey Houses, the *Pioneer Zephyr*, and other icons of railroad lore.

The closing scene included automobiles and trucks. Had they known what the future held, the railroads might not have been so magnanimous.

THE CHICAGO RAILROAD FAIR OF 1948 AND 1949 WAS A PUBLIC CELEBRATION OF THE HERITAGE AND REBIRTH OF AMERICAN RAILROADING.

heavyweights still ruled the roost, maintaining an almost exclusive hold on local and suburban services.

In 1948 and again in 1949, the Chicago Railroad Fair provided an admirable showcase for innovations in passenger service and other aspects of railroading. Dieselization and streamlining, two parts of the equation that equaled modernization, went hand in hand, and diesels were much in evidence in the Railroad Fair's equipment displays. Fairbanks-Morse was represented by a 1,500-horsepower road switcher and a streamlined passenger unit powering Milwaukee Road's *Hiawatha*. The Electro-Motive Division (EMD) of General Motors brought its *Train of Tomorrow* with its sleek E7 diesel, along with an A-B-B-A set of streamlined F3 freight diesels.

These F3s were an improved version of the FT that the division had introduced in 1939 and sent barnstorming—84,000 miles over 20 railroads—with the mission of making diesel believers of hardened

SERVICE ABOARD MOST DINING CARS WAS PATTERNED AFTER THE FINEST BIG-CITY HOTELS. THAT MEANT USING HEAVY, BUT GRACEFUL, HOTEL-GRADE KITCHENWARE, SUCH AS THIS C&O WATER PITCHER.

A STAR ATTRACTION AT THE CHICAGO RAILROAD FAIR WAS CHICAGO, BURLINGTON & QUINCY'S ORIGINAL ZEPHYR OF 1934. THE TRAIN ARRIVED AT THE FAIR A BIT MODIFIED AND WEARING THE NAME PIONEEER ZEPHYR IN REFERENCE TO ITS TRAILBLAZER STATUS.

NOTED FOR THEIR ABILITIES TO LUG AT LOW, SUSTAINED SPEEDS, BALDWIN-LIMA-HAMILTON'S VO AND S-SERIES SWITCHERS WERE UNMATCHED. HOWEVER, BALDWIN'S ARRIVAL AT STANDARDIZED DIESELS CAME FAR TOO LATE TO COMPETE AGAINST GENERAL MOTORS AND ALCO. ERIE MINING COMPANY'S NO. 7246 POSES AT HOYT LAKES, MINNESOTA.

steam-seasoned skeptics. The demonstrator FTs were remarkably successful, considering the daunting nature of their task, and 1,172 FTs (and similarly powered though somewhat improved F2s) were produced before, during, and immediately after the war.

While steam locomotives were endlessly individualized—from task to task and from railroad to railroad—EMD's salesmen staked their reputation on the utility of a standard product: one size fits all. This allowed locomotive-builders to adopt the production-line approach long since perfected by the automobile companies.

Basically, diesels of the "first generation"—those that performed the herculean and not uniformly appreciated task of vanquishing the steam locomotive—fell into three categories: yard switchers, road

THE SWEEPING CHANGES OF FUNCTION AND FORM BETWEEN THE 1850S AND 1950S ARE BROUGHT HOME IN THIS SCENE OF PASSENGERS AND ONLOOKERS WAITING FOR ONE OF BALTIMORE & OHIO'S LIMITEDS TO STOP AT THE SILVER SPRING, MARYLAND, DEPOT.

switchers, and "cab units," the streamlined locomotives that were originally the norm on the main lines. Yard switching was the diesel's first-calling, one that, by the 1940s, was widely accepted. Sleek diesels hauling passenger trains also became an accepted, if somewhat rare, phenomenon in the late 1930s.

But it was the line-haul application to freight pioneered by the FTs that would shake the industry during and after the war. Freight, according to conventional railroad wisdom, was the inviolate domain of steam. EMD's FT and successors proved otherwise.

Produced from 1945 to 1953, the F3s and F7s were a bit more powerful than the FTs (1,500 versus 1,350 horsepower per unit) and embodied myriad improvements that surfaced while FTs were running their wheels off in wartime service. The F3s, F7s, and F9s (a 1,750-horsepower version marketed from 1954 to 1957) eventually numbered 5,856 units. That's standardization. It's also market dominance.

Competitors, including steam-building giants American Locomotive Company and Baldwin, scrambled to get into the act. Both had been testing the waters of diesel-locomotive-building since the 1920s, but neither had done much more than that. Steam died hard, and these two companies, along with the Lima Locomotive Works, represented the "big three" of steam. As an offspring of automaker General Motors, EMD was less encumbered by tradition.

TRAINMEN ABOARD PASSENGER TRAINS KEPT THIS "TOOL BOX" HANDY IN CASE THEY HAD TO SIGNAL OTHER TRAINS. IT INCLUDED A RED FLAG, RED FUSEES (RAILROAD FLARES), AND EXPLOSIVE "TORPEDOES" THAT COULD BE ATTACHED TO THE RAIL TO BE DETONATED AS A WARNING TO PASSING TRAINS.

ALCO PA'S ON A PASSENGER SPECIAL AT COLLIERS, NEW YORK, MEET A FREIGHT BEHIND GENERAL ELECTRIC DIESELS, ALL IN DELAWARE & HUDSON'S FINE COLORS OF THE 1970S.

In the freight-locomotive marketplace, EMD had a signficant advantage in addition to its wholehearted commitment to internal combustion (which Alco and Baldwin understandably lacked until long after the writing was on the wall). In 1943, EMD had been ordered by the War Production Board to resume manufacture of the FT and was simultaneously prohibited from building switchers or passenger locomotives. Alco and Baldwin were assigned switchers as their niche. By the time the war ended and these strictures were lifted, these two former steam greats were hopelessly behind in freight-locomotive technology and visibility.

Alco did have some success marketing its FA/FB cab units, designed primarily for freight service, in competition with EMD's evolv-

ing succession of F-units. Alco's distinctively flat-faced locomotives had their devotees, but the 1,354 eventually sold represented but a fifth of the total tally racked up by EMD's Fs. Baldwin's equivalent products—popularly known as "Babyfaces" and "Sharknoses" in reference to their designers' variations on EMD's classic "Bulldog" snouts—sold but 265. Fairbanks-Morse, a railroad supply that built locomotives from 1944 to 1963, had a similar product popularly known as the "C-Liner." Total sales: 123.

THE GRANDFATHER OF LOCOMOTIVE BUILDERS, BALDWIN, RESPONDED TO THE EMD F-UNIT AND ALCO'S FA SERIES OF DIESELS WITH ITS RF-16 AND BP-20 "SHARKNOSE" LOCOMOTIVES. BALDWIN'S CONSERVATISM IN LOCOMOTIVE DESIGN AND PRODUCTION KEPT THE COMPANY FROM OFFERING STANDARDIZED DIESELS CAPABLE OF PERFORMING WELL IN A VARIETY OF SERVICES.

WHEN LOCOMOTIVE BUILDER BALDWIN BEGAN TO REFINE ITS NEW LINE OF FREIGHT AND PASSENGER DIESELS, IT ELECTED TO EMULATE THE DISTINCTIVE PROFILE OF ITS EARLIER PENNSY T-1 STEAM LOCOMOTIVES. THE SHARPLY ANGULAR DIESELS QUICKLY EARNED THE COLLOQUIAL NAME "SHARKNOSES," AS APTLY DEMONSTRATED BY PENNSYLVANIA'S BP-20 PASSENGER UNIT NO. 5773.

EMD, Alco, Baldwin, and FM had passenger counterparts to these freight diesels. In all cases they were stretched versions (with plenty of room in the carbodies for two diesel engines rather than one, plus heat-supplying steam generators and boilers), riding on six-wheel rather than four-wheel trucks for better tracking at high speeds. Market-share among the builders roughly paralleled the freight-unit breakdown.

Electro-Motive was not interested in customization, nor in having the purchasing railroads telling them how to make their mousetrap, so to speak. The company staunchly resisted requests for modifications, feeling that it knew best, at the same time recognizing that standardization was the key to financial success. The very fact that diesels were by definition building blocks—each F3, for instance, being a 1,500-horsepower unit that could be operated alone or in lash-ups of two, three, four, or even five or more—allowed endless customization. The former steam builders, on the other hand, lacked this clarity of vision on diesel standardization. As a result, Alco and (particularly) Baldwin tended to get unproductively mired down in special orders.

Erie Railroad turned to both Alco and EMD for passenger and freight diesel power. This photo captures a single Alco PA leading a local passenger train through rural upstate New York before the merger that created Erie-Lackawanna.

Short-lived Visions of the Future

*I*n the depths of the Depression, railroading lifted travelers' spirits with a bevy of pocket streamliners—fast, flashy, undersized, articulated trainsets like Burlington's *Zephyr* and Union Pacific's *Streamliner*.

Twenty years later, in the mid-1950s, another flurry of futuristic, high-speed, undersized, articulated trains arrived on the scene. These came and went without significant impact, victims of unreliability and cramped accommodations.

"Train-X" had been unveiled as far back as the Chicago Railroad Fair in 1948, where—at the behest of gadfly Robert Young—a full-sized model of a coach had been displayed by Chesapeake & Ohio. By 1956, when the first Train-X (built by Pullman-Standard, with a locomotive by Baldwin) was delivered, Young was at New York Central,

UNDER THE MCGINNIS ADMINISTRATION OF THE COMBINED BOSTON & MAINE, MAINE CENTRAL, AND NEW HAVEN RAILROADS, NUMEROUS EXPERIMENTS WERE TRIED IN THE NAME OF ECONOMY AND PROGRESS. MCGINNIS ORDERED AN AMERICAN FORM OF THE SPANISH "TALGO" PASSENGER TRAIN FOR SERVICE ON THE B&M.

so the train went there too. New Haven's Patrick McGinnis, a Young crony, also bought a set.

In addition, McGinnis ordered a "Talgo," one of three trainsets for U. S. railroads built by American Car & Foundry in cooperation with Patentes Talgo S.A. of Spain. ACF built a Talgo demonstator in 1949, plus trainsets that went to Spain to launch a fleet very much alive today.

The third of the 1950s experimentals was the General Motors "Aerotrain," two trainsets of modified GM bus bodies powered by automotive-looking EMD diesel locomotives. After a year or so of touring and testing—with long-term stints on the Pennsylvania, New York Central, and Union Pacific—the Aerotrains were sold to the Rock Island, where they ran for some eight years in suburban service before being given to museums.

In any case, the diesels certainly were coming, with EMD leading the charge. Raw numbers tell the story. In 1944, America's Class 1 railroads rostered 39,881 steam engines, which accounted for 91 percent of total motive power; 3,049 diesels, or 7 percent; and 863 electric units, 2 percent. By 1955, just over a decade later, the numbers had more or less flip-flopped: 24,786 diesels (79 percent), 5,982 steamers (19 percent), and 627 electrics (2 percent). By 1960 the case was closed: diesels 28,278 (97), electrics 492 (2 percent), and steam 261 (1 percent). The steam era was history.

Steam didn't go down without a fight, however. It was tried and true motive power, not without its virtues, and certainly not without its supporters—given that the business of railroading has typically been filled with hidebound traditionalists. Steam locomotive production had continued apace through the war, and a number of lines continued to order (and in a few cases, build) steam for a few years afterward. This final incarnation of steam took a relative high-tech form,

DINING CAR CHINA WAS ANOTHER MEDIUM THROUGH WHICH TO ADVERTISE. THE "400" OF THE C&NW REFERRED TO THE FACT THAT ITS CRACK TRAINS COVERED THE 410 MILES BETWEEN CHICAGO AND MINNEAPOLIS-ST. PAUL IN JUST 400 MINUTES, WITH INTERMEDIATE STOPS.

GENERAL MOTORS' EXPERIMENTAL AEROTRAINS TOURED THE NATION IN THE EARLY YEARS OF THE 1950S. DESPITE FUTURISTIC STYLING, THE PUBLIC'S ACCURATE PERCEPTION OF POOR RIDE QUALITY, CRAMPED SEATING, AND OTHER PROBLEMS BROUGHT THE UNUSUAL TRAINS QUICK AND QUIET RETIREMENTS.

exemplified by Lima's "Super-Power" locomotives and by comparable products from Baldwin and Alco. They featured higher boiler pressure, feedwater heaters (heating water on the way to the boiler), roller bearings on engine and tender, mechanical and pressure lubricating, one-piece cast-steel bed frames, superheaters (heating steam passing to the cylinders), and often boosters on trailing trucks to provide a little added power for starting heavy trains.

Coal-hauler Chesapeake & Ohio was an unusually good steam customer, purchasing a number of locomotives after the war (but all to previously established designs). Lima delivered 20 and Alco 30 of the 2-8-4s (called "Kanawhas," not "Berkshires," on C&O), and Lima delivered five 4-8-4s ("Greenbriers," since C&O was too Southern to roster a "Northern"). Lima supplied 2-6-6-6 "Alleghenies" and Baldwin, its 2-6-6-2s—the last of which, No. 1309, arrived in September 1949, concluding Baldwin's long history as a builder of steam for domestic use. Number 779, the last of 10 Berkshire's that Lima delivered to Nickel Plate in 1949, wrote *finis* for that builder. Alco's last steamer was also a Berkshire, for Pittsburgh & Lake Erie. (The 27 4-8-4 "Niagaras" that Alco had built for New York Central from 1945–46 represented one of the last successful American steam-locomotive designs.)

SOUTHERN PACIFIC'S DAYLIGHT TRAINS PROVIDED FAST, FREQUENT SERVICE BETWEEN LOS ANGELES AND SAN FRANCISCO. BAGGAGE STICKERS LIKE THIS FROM THE EARLY 1950S ADVERTISED THE RAILROAD AND SERVED AS STATUS SYMBOLS FOR AT LEAST SOME RAILROAD PASSENGERS.

NORFOLK & WESTERN CREATED 14 COAL-BURNING SUPER 4-8-4 PASSENGER LOCOMOTIVES AT ITS ROANOKE SHOPS BY 1950. ARGUABLY THE MOST SUCCESSFUL AND MODERN STEAM POWER EVER BUILT, THE CLASS J ENGINES COULD HANDLE HEAVY TRAINS IN THE MOUNTAINS OR RACE ACROSS THE FLATLANDS AT TREMENDOUS SPEEDS.

Only a few railroads had the size, expertise, and facilities to build their own locomotives in the modern era: CB&Q at West Burlington, Illinois Central at Paducah, Great Northern at Hillyard, Frisco at Pine Bluff, and Canadian Pacific at Montreal. Reading built 30 T1 Northerns from 1945–47, and 10 G3 Pacifics— both notable in being new designs that were fielded late. But in homemade steam, Pennsylvania and Norfolk & Western were preeminent by far. Pennsy's Juniata Shops in Altoona turned out nearly 7,000 locomotives in a wide variety of classes—ending, in 1946, with 25 streamlined, shark-nosed T1 4-4-4-4 duplexes for passenger service (Baldwin built another 25) and 25 Q2 4-4-6-4s. Neither class was wholly successful.

But when it came to steam in the twilight years, the Norfolk & Western—a coal road, like C&O, that invested in burning what it hauled—stood alone. N&W's Roanoke Shops was the birthplace for some of the most advanced and powerful locomotives ever built: Y6

The final Norfolk & Western Class J 4-8-4 to operate was No. 611. Built in 1950 while diesels reigned supreme throughout America, this mighty locomotive held the internal combustion intruders at bay until the early 1960s. No. 611 enjoyed another 14 years in the limelight before NS shut down its steam program.

2-8-8-2s for coal drags and general merchandise, Class A 2-6-6-4s for fast freight (and just about anything else), J 4-8-4s for passengers, and S1 0-8-0s for switching. These were major players in steam's final chapter.

The sleek, powerful Js were unusual in being designed as streamlined locomotives (though some built in wartime ran temporarily without shrouds, to save metal); the last trio among the 14 that were built rolled out of Roanoke Shops in 1950, the same year Class A construction ended—and even then, N&W wasn't finished. Y6s were assembled into 1952. The honor of being the last steam locomotive ever built in America fell to an S1 switcher the following year.

One of steam's greatest charms was at the same time its greatest weakness. To function, the steam locomotive required a substantial coterie of attendants and an elaborate physical structure of support. Many of traditional railroadings' most cherished icons—the water

THE RAPID DISAPPEARANCE OF STEAM LOCOMOTIVES AND STANDARD TRAINS FROM THE AMERICAN LANDSCAPE LEFT IMAGES SUCH AS THIS, OF A HOMEWARD-BOUND READING COMPANY "IRON HORSE RAMBLE" DOUBLEHEADER GILDED IN THE SUNSET'S GLOW.

tower, the coaling dock, the turntable, the roundhouse—existed to fuss over the steam engine. Workers known as "hostlers" were kept busy coaling, watering, and lubricating locomotives between runs, and tending their fires—building, cleaning, dropping, and banking. In the roundhouses, workers performed routine inspections at regular, mandated intervals and made relatively minor "running repairs." In backshops, heavy overhauls and rebuilding occupied boilermakers, machinists, and members of various other crafts.

Fortunately, these final days of steam are well-documented, since they came at a time when the enthusiasm for trains (and particularly steam) was an established and growing hobby, and when quality cameras were common enough to be in the hands of many talented and dedicated fans. Plenty of fine photographers captured a plethora of images, most of them informative, some deeply evocative. But the work of one man—O. Winston Link, a New York City-based commercial photographer—covering one railroad, the Norfolk & Western, stands out from the rest as a composite document of steam's dying days.

In what was truly a labor of love, Link made numerous trips to the railroad in the late 1950s, photographing the machines and, significantly, the people who worked on and around them. His project was unique, especially since most of the images were made at night,

AFTER ITS RETIREMENT FROM A CLINCHFIELD, CAROLINA & OHIO STEAM LOCOMOTIVE IN 1952, THIS BELL WAS ACQUIRED BY A RAILROAD ENTHUSIAST. OFTEN, RAILROADS PRESENTED BELLS TO CHURCHES AND SCHOOLS.

FACING PAGE (LEFT): PENNSYLVANIA RAILROAD'S IMMENSE LOCOMOTIVE MAINTENANCE FACILITIES AT ITS PITTSBURGH, PENNSYLVANIA, ROUNDHOUSE WERE TYPICAL OF STEAM TERMINALS.

THE ONCE-MIGHTY FELL QUICKLY WHEN RAILROAD ACCOUNTANTS BEGAN TOTALING UP THE COSTS OF STEAM OPERATION AND MAINTENANCE VERSUS THOSE OF THE DIESEL. RETIRED PENNSYLVANIA RAILROAD STEAM IS SHOWN IN STORAGE AT THE COMPANY'S ENOLA, PENNSYLVANIA, YARDS IN THE 1950S.

allowing a degree of graphic control not possible in daylight. The pictures were created with a keen sense of composition and an inventiveness that bordered on the madcap, so elaborately constructed were such scenes as a Class A roaring past a drive-in movie theater. Complex syncronized flash set-ups were required in many cases, and the technical expertise was remarkable throughout. Hundreds of images—published in *Steam, Steel, and Stars* (1983) and *The Last Steam Railroad in America* (1995)—create a richly human portrait that has gained a wide and general audience.

Though the diminution and eventual demise of steam was the beginning of the depersonalization of railroading, the process didn't happen overnight. Centralized Traffic Control (CTC) dates back to 1927, when it was introduced on the New York Central, but the 1950s were still rich in train-order railroading, with "flimsies" (orders were generally written or typed on tissue) hooped up to engineers and conductors by agents and operators at thousands of depots and inter-

THE LAST OPERABLE "CHALLENGER," UNION PACIFIC 4-6-6-4 NO. 3985, CONTINUES TO DEMONSTRATE THE SUPERIOR QUALITIES OF "SUPER POWER" POSTWAR STEAM OF THE 1940S. KEPT FOR EXCURSION DUTIES, NO. 3985 HAS EASILY PULLED CONTEMPORARY HIGH-SPEED FREIGHTS.

FACING PAGE (RIGHT): TWO PASSENGER LOCOMOTIVES FORMERLY BELONGING TO THE SOUTHERN PACIFC WERE REUNITED AT CALIFORNIA STATE RAILROAD MUSEUM'S RAILFAIR 1991. AT THE END OF THE CELEBRATION, BOTH ENGINES JOINED COUPLERS FOR AN EXCURSION FROM SACRAMENTO TO OAKLAND. SEEN ROMPING OVER SP'S YOLO CAUSEWAY TRESTLE NEAR DAVIS, NO. 2472 LEADS NO. 4449 WEST IN A SCENE RIGHT OUT OF THE 1940S.

IMMEDIATELY FOLLOWING THE END OF WORLD WAR II, SOUTHERN PACIFIC, LIKE MANY OTHER RAILROADS, BEGAN STORING HUNDREDS OF STEAM LOCOMOTIVES AS DIESELS BEGAN TO REPLACE THEM. SOON, ALL THESE LOCOMOTIVES WOULD BE TOWED TO SCRAPPERS.

locking towers across the country. Though radio was coming in, replacing lantern signals as the preferred communication mode between train and engine crews, it would be years before operating authority could be transmitted over the air. Meanwhile, there were railroaders spread all along the line—and riding the cabooses that trailed every train.

Postwar America through the decade of the 1950s still had the appearance of a railroad country. In 1944, Class 1 railroad mileage totaled 215,493; by 1960 it had actually increased slightly, to 217,552. Over those rails during the decade and a half after the war, a heady mixture of steam and diesels had powered an impressive array of lightweight and heavyweight passenger trains—illustrious all-Pullman flyers, humble locals, and everything in between—and freight trains that ranged from hot "redball" merchandisers to coal drags, as well as "way freights," serving industries both large and small.

The 40-foot box car was still the emblematic and most common freight car. Stock still moved to slaughterhouse by rail. Many refrigerator cars were still ice-cooled, with huge blocks being wrestled from icing platforms through roof hatches of refrigerator cars. "Loose-car railroading" remained the order of the day, and the unique ability of a train to be combined and recombined at classification yards was held as a primary virtue. If you ordered merchandise, it was still likely to reach you courtesy of the Railway Express

WELL INTO THE MODERN ERA, PASSENGER CARS FROM THE CLASSIC AGE OF RAILROADING SURVIVED IN WORK-TRAIN SERVICE. THIS IS THE DINING ROOM OF THE C&O X-66, A KITCHEN-DINER-BATH CAR USED BY A WORK GANG AS THEIR "HOME AWAY FROM HOME."

THIS INGENIOUS DEVICE IS A "TRAIN ORDER HOOP." ORDERS OR MESSAGES FOR THE CREW OF A PASSING TRAIN WOULD BE TIED TO A LOOP OF STRING CLIPPED INTO THE CROOK OF THE HOOP. ONE OF THE CREW WOULD THEN REACH DOWN TO THE HOOP (HELD BY A BRACKET OR ANOTHER RAILROADER) AND "SNAG" THE STRING WITH AN OUTSTRETCHED ARM.

Agency, whose green baggage carts stood on the platforms of thousands of depots from coast to coast. So-called L.C.L. shipments ("less than carload lot") shipments were a routine and welcome aspect of the rail freight business.

The *Official Guide of the Railways* was still a rewardingly hefty tome, rich in routes and trains. The modern merger movement lay ahead, so most of the railroad names therein had been familiar ones for generations. Other than the colorful addition of diesels and streamliners, it might seem that little had changed, but forces were already in motion that would soon have serious implications for railroading.

In May of 1949, an ominous milestone was passed. For the first time, airline passenger-miles exceeded those of the Pullman Company.

THE SHIPPING OF FRESH-PICKED PRODUCE AND OTHER PERISHABLE FOODS ACROSS THE NATION WAS WHOLLY DEPENDENT ON THE MANUAL ICING OF REFRIGERATOR CARS, OR "REEFERS," UNTIL THE LATE 1960S WHEN MECHANICAL COOLING UNITS WERE ADDED TO INSULATED BOXCARS.

Steaming to the Scrap Heap

No sight was more melancholy than the long lines of out-of-service steam that piled up in railroad yards across North America through the 1950s.

In the steam-to-diesel transition, locomotives "stored serviceable" did sometimes come briefly to life to meet some seasonal upswing in traffic. These reprieves were brief, however, and eventually the steam locomotives all ended up in the same place—the "elephants' graveyard," where these hulking, once-powerful creatures lay lifeless.

The scrapper's torch completed the final chapter for virtually all of the nearly 40,000 engines under steam at the end of World War II. There were, however, a few survivors. Many railroads gave locomotives to on-line communities to be "stuffed and

THE RAILROADS USED PROCEEDS FROM SCRAPPED STEAM TO PAY FOR THEIR NEW INTERNAL COMBUSTION POWER. EVEN AT A RATE OF LESS THAN A QUARTER OF A DOLLAR PER POUND, SCRAP STEEL FROM RETIRED STEAM MADE ECONOMIC SENSE.

mounted" for display in parks, or by railroad stations. Regrettably, 40 years of exposure to the elements has made many of these exhibits good for little today but belated scrapping, though a few locomotives have emerged from display to be triumphantly restored for excursion service.

Some railroads simply sent trains to scrap, saving next to nothing. New York Central is a classic example. Nary a Hudson nor a Niagara survived.

Competitor Pennsy, on the other hand, set aside examples of most major classes of steam. After languishing in Northumberland, Pennsylvania, for many years, they eventually became the core of the Railroad Museum of Pennsylvania's fine collection at Strasburg.

In the 1950s, President Eisenhower signed into law the act creating the Interstate Highway System. America was unmistakably in love with its automobiles, and the federal government decided to make a monumental investment in the roads they would require to dominate the country's surface transportation system.

On March 29, 1957, the New York, Ontario & Western was abandoned. Though this charismatic road has become better loved in death than it ever was in life, the loss of a Class 1 carrier undoubtedly was shocking—a further loss for an industry destined to become increasingly aware of its mortality.

On March 27, 1960, regularly scheduled passenger steam service in the United States came to an end (except for special excursions like Rio Grande's *Silverton* Train) when Grand Trunk Western pulled its Northerns out of Detroit-Durand local service. Two days later the Canadian Pacific mixed train between Megantic, Quebec, and Brownville Junction, Maine, was dieselized, making moot the question of whether a mixed train was a passenger train.

On May 6, 1960, the Norfolk & Western dieselized, and the twilight of steam faded into night.

In the final years of steam, railroads all across the land became instant photo subjects for rail aficionados. Dieselization was well underway everywhere when this Pennsylvania K-4s 4-6-2 was called upon to pull a farewell excursion.

Chapter 7

AN INDUSTRY ON THE ROPES

By the time the 1970s ended, the glory days of railroading were over. Emblematic of the period was the case of Pennsylvania Railroad, which in 1968 merged with arch-competitor New York Central. The result, Penn Central, went bankrupt in 1970, becoming the centerpiece of government-sponsored Conrail in 1976—which itself struggled for years before finally landing on its feet.

*A*s the 1960s dawned, steam's departure had left a vast void in the railroad landscape. Gone were the mournful whistles in the night, the hiss of steam and clamor of exhaust, the rich smells of hot grease and coal smoke. Lacking such sensory delights, the diesel seemed pale in comparison. Steam locomotives had been manifestly alive. They also had been endlessly various, precisely the characteristic that gave the readily standardized diesel its superior competitive edge.

The demise of steam surely contributed to railroading's slow, inexorable slide out of the public eye. In the decade's early years, on the other hand, the fleet of colorful streamliners introduced in the immediate postwar era remained largely intact, speeding across the country behind sleek diesels— Electro-Motive's E-units, Alco's PAs, plus the occasional Baldwin or Fairbanks-Morse unit. The feature trains still ran: the *Chiefs*, *Rockets*, *Daylights*, *Zephyrs*, and *Limiteds* (named *Broadway*, *Twentieth Century*, *Panama*, *Merchants*, and *North Coast*), as well as the ever-popular *Empire Builder*, *Silver Meteor*, and *City of Los Angeles*.

Still, a huge change occurred in the way the nation traveled. What had been a railroad country was now an automobile country. Between 1945 and 1964, non-commuter rail passenger travel declined an incredible 84 percent, as just about every American

THE CHICAGO, ROCK ISLAND & PACIFIC WAS ABOUT TO DROWN IN A SEA OF RED INK WHEN THIS PHOTO WAS TAKEN AT THE ROCK'S DES MOINES, IOWA, DEPOT. MULTIPLE BANKRUPTCIES AND SEEMINGLY ETERNAL MISMANAGEMENT LEFT IT WITHOUT A CHANCE TO SURVIVE BEYOND THE 1970S.

DEEP IN THE HEART OF FORMER NEW YORK, NEW HAVEN & HARTFORD TERRITORY, ANTIQUATED SUBURBAN PASSENGER SHELTERS LINE THE ELECTRIFIED AMTRAK RIGHT-OF-WAY AT BRIDGEPORT, CONNECTICUT.

By absorbing the large Rail Diesel Car (RDC) fleets of the New York Central and New Haven railroads, Penn Central managed to provide marginal passenger services until the arrival of Amtrak. One such run along old New Haven trackage in Connecticut was covered by this ex-NYC "Beeliner" RDC.

who could afford it climbed into his or her own automobile, relishing the independence. What changed was not just the way Americans traveled, but also the way they worked, shopped, and played.

Before World War II, the country's growing urban population was starting to expand into the suburbs, but these by and large were "railroad suburbs" or "streetcar suburbs," dependent on these transportation modes and essentially pedestrian. The Levittowns and all their postwar kin, on the other hand, were clearly *automobile* suburbs: scattered, sprawling, without definable downtowns, and not negotiable on foot. Not far behind came the supermarket, shopping center, drive-in this-and-that, and the proliferation of motels. Rail-focused downtowns withered, and with them the hotels and Main Streets that had been their anchors.

As a result, businesses that once needed railway access now gravitated toward highways—particularly the interstates, into which the federal government poured billions of dollars, while simultaneously squeezing taxes from the railroads on rights-of-way and other company assets, including increasingly unused depots.

Branch-line passenger services were the first to go, then secondary services on the main lines. Finally, as the 1960s wore on, the flagships began to fall. One early and dramatic casualty came in May of 1961, with the discontinuation of the Milwaukee Road's Chicago-Seattle/Tacoma *Olympian Hiawatha*. This was a splendid train, with a full-length dome car, diner, sleepers, and distinctive "Skytop" observation car. Its route was exceptionally scenic, but the ridership just wasn't there.

Other trains followed—many others. The roll call went on and on, as railroads presented their cases for discontinuance to the Inter-

THE ERA IN REVIEW

1960:
The Erie Railroad merges with competitor Delaware, Lackawanna & Western to form the Erie Lackawanna Railroad.

1963:
After a U.S. ship is attacked, Congress endorses the Tonkin Gulf Resolution, authorizing U.S. involvement in the Vietnam War.

New England's troubled Rutland Railroad is abandoned. Sections of the line soon reopen as the Vermont Central Railroad and the Green Mountain Railroad.

1965:
New York City's Pennsylvania Station is razed in December, sparking a landmarks preservation movement that continues to this day.

1968:
Pennsylvania Railroad and New York Central merge to form Penn Central.

1969:
The Pullman Company's staffing of sleeping cars ends as of January 1.

1970:
In this frenzied time of mergers, Chicago, Burlington & Quincy; Great

state Commerce Commission (then the arbiter of transportation issues) and in most cases got the nod: *State of Maine, Ambassador, Pacemaker, Commodore Vanderbilt, Wolverine, Ohio State Limited, Knickerbocker, Maple Leaf, Phoebe Snow, Pocono Express, Owl, Blue Bird, Penn Texas, Golden Triangle, Pittsburgher, General, Admiral, Columbian, Erie Limited, Lake Cities, Thoroughbred, Powhatan Arrow, Cavalier, Sportsman, Southerner, Peach Queen, Pelican, Ponce de Leon, Humming Bird, Dixie Flyer, Havana Special, Green Diamond, Meteor, Sunnyland, Texas Special, Shreveporter, Southern Belle, Colorado Eagle, Royal Gorge, Prospector, Pioneer Limited, Copper Country Limited, Golden State, Shasta Daylight, Lark, Rocky Mountain Rocket, Corn Belt Rocket, Sam Houston Zephyr, Black Hawk, Ak-Sar-Ben Zephyr, Laker,* and *Winnipeger.*

The names represent only a part of the landslide of "train-offs" that the I.C.C. approved in the course of the decade. A number of Class 1

THE LAST OF THE ZEPHYR TRAINS, THE SALT LAKE CITY-BOUND RIO GRANDE ZEPHYR, PAUSES AT GRAND JUNCTION, COLORADO.

THE ERA IN REVIEW

Northern; Northern Pacific; and Spokane, Portland & Seattle combine, forming Burlington Northern.

The Interstate Commerce Commission reluctantly allows the demise of the legendary California Zephyr.

1971:
Amtrak takes over most passenger-train operations in the United States.

Auto-Train begins service in December, carrying automobiles and their occupants between Lorton, Virginia, and Sanford, Florida.

1973:
A fleet of French-built Turboliners are delivered to the United States, marking fledgling Amtrak's first new equipment acquisition.

1976:
Conrail begins operation as a result of the consolidation of Penn Central; Erie-Lackawanna; Reading; Lehigh Valley; Jersey Central; Lehigh & Hudson River; and Pennsylvania-Reading Seashore lines on April 1.

1979:
The first double-deck Superliner cars enter service for Amtrak.

railroads had previously gone freight-only, and more joined the list in this period, including the Lehigh Valley, Katy, Monon, Kansas City Southern, and Frisco lines. Some of the very greatest train names were erased from the *Official Guide*, including, unthinkably, the *Twentieth Century Limited*, New York Central's famous New York-Chicago flyer. On December 3, 1967, it lost its name, and, with it, its cachet, along with its beautiful deep-windowed observation cars (though downgraded overnight service remained on roughly the same schedule over the route).

By 1966, less than 2 percent of all intercity passengers were traveling by rail. Worse still, passenger trains faced critical problems in addition to this defection of patrons to auto travel. For one thing, railroads were hopelessly out of date in dealing with those patrons who did remain. They failed to enlist travel agents as valuable allies, and they even refused to accept the major credit cards.

Prevailing railroad work rules reflected century-old conditions and equipment, meaning that crew costs were astronomical. Even the newest equipment was a decade or two old, and more often than not, maintenance had been deferred as economics soured.

Meanwhile, the Post Office was systematically stripping passenger trains of the mail cars (RPOs) that had provided substantial (and increasingly critical) revenues since passenger trains

LESS THAN 50 YEARS AFTER ITS GRAND OPENING, THE PENNSYLVANIA STATION IN NEW YORK CITY WAS DEMOLISHED FOR THE CONSTRUCTION OF TWIN OFFICE TOWERS AND A NEW MADISON SQUARE GARDEN ARENA. THE TERMINAL'S DESTRUCTION SPARKED THE NATIONAL LANDMARK HISTORIC PRESERVATION MOVEMENT.

NEW YORK CENTRAL'S POSH TWENTIETH CENTURY LIMITED SAILED FROM GRAND CENTRAL TERMINAL IN MANHATTAN FOR THE LAST TIME ON DECEMBER 30, 1967. WHEN THE RED CARPET WAS ROLLED UP FROM THE BOARDING PLATFORM, A GRAND CHAPTER IN TRANSPORTATION HISTORY HAD ENDED.

By the close of 1960, mainline steam had vanished from North American rails and was running on borrowed time on a handful of shortlines: the Buffalo Creek & Gauley, the Mississippian, the East Tennessee & Western North Carolina, and others. But while working steam was chugging its final miles in common-carrier service, another phenomenon—recreational steam—was gathering momentum.

A number of railroads—Santa Fe, Burlington, Missabe Road, and Norfolk & Western, among them—ran steam excursions at the same time they were dropping the fires on regular-service steam. Reading's "Iron Horse Rambles" with various T1-class 4-8-4s crisscrossed anthracite country for five years beginning in 1959. In 1960, Union Pacific fired up Northern No. 844 for excursionists; the loco-

ATTRACTING THOUSANDS OF RIDERS YEAR AFTER YEAR IN THE EARLY 1960S, THE LAST READING COMPANY T-1 4-8-4S BECAME THE STARS OF THE STEAM EXCURSIONS THAT CAME TO BE KNOWN AS THE "IRON HORSE RAMBLES."

motive, subsequently joined by 4-6-6-4 "Challenger" No. 3985, is still going strong today. In 1967, Southern kicked off its famous, long-running, and now lamented steam excursion program with a privately owned 2-8-2.

Steam-powered tourist railroads, a concept that goes way back to 1947, when the Edaville Railroad opened in Massachusetts, also started popping up in greater profusion, often using locomotives made available by recent shortline dieselizations. Among the most notable was the East Broad Top's start-up in 1960. After this Pennsylvania coal-hauler had shut down in 1956, it was purchased for salvage. Virtually nothing was scrapped, however, and four years later its owner was persuaded to reopen the line for excursionists.

were in their infancy. At the same time, country depots were being boarded up. In 1965, New York City's Pennsylvania Station was demolished—an act of corporate vandalism that awoke the citizenry to the potential loss of our best buildings and sparked a landmarks preservation movement.

No doubt the most noted, rancorous, and painful of all passenger train-off decisions involved the illustrious *California Zephyr*, the San Francisco-Chicago service shared by Western Pacific, Rio Grande, and Burlington. By the time the Interstate Commerce Commission had reluctantly allowed this marvelous train to die, public opinion was thoroughly stirred up, and editorial writers

throughout the land called to task not only the railroads, but also the federal government, for lack of a balanced and coherent transportation policy that could save long-distance trains.

In June of 1969, Colorado Senator Gordon Allot spearheaded passage of a resolution calling for a federal study aimed at saving the passenger train. This led in time to the creation of Railpax, which would be called Amtrak by the time this quasi-governmental corporation took over virtually all of the nation's long-distance passenger trains on May 1, 1971.

Though the 1960s were preeminently the decade in which the privately operated passenger train languished and then died, other significant

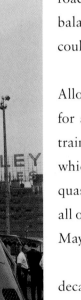

DURING THE 1960S, NEW YORK CENTRAL INSTALLED A SET OF JET ENGINES ON ONE OF ITS BUDD RDC CARS. ON A TEST RUN IN RURAL OHIO AND INDIANA, M-497 NOISILY SET A NEW U.S. RAILROAD SPEED RECORD OF 183.85 MPH. PRESIDENT ALFRED E. PERLMAN WAVES TO THE PHOTOGRAPHER PRIOR TO THE DEMONSTRATION TRIP.

ON THE FORMER ERIE RAILROAD MAINLINE BETWEEN BUFFALO AND CHICAGO, ERIE-LACKAWANNA DIESELS ROLL BOXCAR FREIGHT THROUGH KENT, OHIO. WITHIN A DECADE, OHIO'S INDUSTRIAL ECONOMY WILL BE TRANSFORMED, THE E-L WILL DISAPPEAR INTO CONRAIL, AND THE TRADITIONAL BOXCAR WILL GIVE WAY TO INTERMODAL CONTAINERS.

forces were at work, changing forever the face of railroading. For one thing, 1960 kicked off the modern merger movement, with competitors Erie Railroad and Delaware, Lackawanna & Western banding together in October to form Erie Lackawanna. For students of the railroad scene, this amalgamation wasn't that great a shock. Both names survived essentially intact, as DL&W was commonly called "the Lackawanna." Lackawanna's lovely passenger-train paint scheme of maroon, yellow, and gray would adorn all locomotives, but the EL circle-in-a-diamond logo descended directly from the Erie herald.

The next major merger was quite different. In October of 1964, when the Wabash, Nickel Plate Road, and Pittsburgh & West Virginia were merged into the Norfolk & Western, their names, colors, and logos vanished down the corridors of time—as the Virginian's had earlier, after its acquisition by the N&W in 1959.

SIGNIFICANT CULTURAL CHANGES BROUGHT BY RAILROAD MERGERS BEGINNING IN THE LATE 1960S INCLUDED THE LOSS OF HUGE NUMBERS OF DECORATIVE RAILROAD SEALS AND LOGOS. THE NORTHERN PACIFIC RAILWAY'S "MONAD" BORROWED THE YIN AND YANG, ANCIENT CHINESE SYMBOLS, TO PROMOTE ITS RAILS TO THE PACIFIC NORTHWEST AS THE GATEWAY TO ASIA.

In 1967, a combination of Seaboard Air Line and Atlantic Coast Line produced Seaboard Coast Line. Then came the merger that characterized the decade—the disasterous coupling on February 1, 1968, of the Pennsylvania Railroad and New York Central into Penn Central, with the decrepit New York, New Haven & Hartford thrown in later (against the wishes of the principal partners). The newly formed railroad's locomotive color scheme was basic black with no adornments. This proved all too appropriate. The new logo, an intertwined "PC," was sometimes called the "mating worms."

More mergers were soon to come, most notably the creation in 1970 of mammoth Burlington Northern from the Chicago, Burlington & Quincy, Great Northern, Northern Pacific, and Spokane, Portland & Seattle.

EVEN AS THE ONCE MIGHTY PENNSYLVANIA RAILROAD SUCCUMBED TO MERGER AND, FINALLY, BANKRUPTCY, ITS CLASSIC GG-1 ELECTRIC LOCOMOTIVES SOLDIERED ON. HERE, NO. 4924—A "WAR BABY" FROM 1942—LEADS A PENN CENTRAL PASSENGER TRAIN ON THE NORTHEAST CORRIDOR IN THE EARLY 1970S.

Santa Fe's Super C

In January of 1968, the Atchison, Topeka & Santa Fe caught the attention of the trade press (and shippers) with the inauguration of the *Super C*—a 40-hour piggyback and container train on the 2,200-mile route between Chicago and Los Angeles. This six-days-a-week service was as fast as the *Super Chief*—hence the name; average speed was more than 55 miles an hour, topping out at 79.

Trains were light. No more than about 20 cars were projected, though in reality they would often run with as few as two or three. As originally conceived, the trains were a straight shot— no classification, no pick-up or drop-off. There were, however, 17 crew changes en route, an indication of the antediluvian nature of the work rules at that time.

MINUTES BEFORE STARTING ITS FIRST RECORD-BREAKING 39-HOUR DASH TO LOS ANGELES FROM CHICAGO, THE ATCHISON, TOPEKA & SANTA FE'S INTERMODAL SUPER-C FREIGHT WAITS WHILE THE LAST COMPANY EXECUTIVES BOARD BUSINESS CARS BEHIND THE ENGINE FOR THE RIDE OF THEIR LIVES.

Naturally, the *Super C* was a premium-price service, costing about double the usual COFC/TOFC rates, in fact. Because of the high cost, the train had some difficulty attracting a steady clientele. The operation's purity was further compromised by the addition of a Kansas City pick-up, as well as combinations with trains west of Barstow, California.

At the same time, Northern Pacific was fielding a similar service on the 1,875-mile Seattle-Minneapolis *Tokyo Express*, which averaged 51 miles per hour and was thus faster than the *North Coast Limited*, NP's premier passenger train. Neither this train nor the *Super C* would linger for long, but they proved how quickly intermodal freight could move by rail.

In the 1970s, the process of merging would only accelerate. Illinois Central and Gulf, Mobile & Ohio merged to form Illinois Central Gulf, while the Chessie System was created from the Baltimore & Ohio, Chesapeake & Ohio, and Western Maryland lines. In a merger of mergers, Seaboard Coast Line joined with Louisville & Nashville (which earlier had acquired the Monon) and the Clinchfield Railroad to create Family Lines. In 1980, Chessie and Family Lines would come together to form CSX—in effect, a merger of merged mergers.

The greatest combination of the era wasn't the result of a merger, strictly speaking, but of a government bailout. By the mid-1970s, railroading in the Northeast was in complete disarray. Not only was Penn Central in bankruptcy, but so were Erie Lackawanna, Lehigh & Hudson River, and the "anthracite roads" that had once thrived in eastern Pennsylvania's hard-coal country: Lehigh Valley, Reading, and Jersey

AS A COMBINATION OF THE ILLINOIS CENTRAL AND THE GULF, MOBILE & OHIO, THE ILLINOIS CENTRAL GULF KNIT TOGETHER A 2,687-MILE MAINLINE SERVING ITS NAMESAKE REGION. AS A SUBSIDIARY OF ILLINOIS CENTRAL INDUSTRIES, THE ICG LATER WAS ALLOWED TO OPERATE INDEPENDENTLY, AGAIN AS THE ILLINOIS CENTRAL RAILROAD.

THE FORMER CHICAGO, BURLINGTON & QUINCY TRACKS RUNNING WESTERLY THROUGH ILLINOIS, IOWA, AND NEBRASKA HAVE GIVEN SUCCESSOR BURLINGTON NORTHERN A SPEEDWAY TO WESTERN MARKETS. HERE A TRAINLOAD OF NEW AUTOMOBILES RACES INTO THE SETTING SUN BEHIND EMD AND LEASED LMX/GE DIESELS.

FACING PAGE (LEFT): THE FICTIONAL KITTEN DUBBED "CHESSIE," FIRST PROMULGATED BY THE CHESAPEAKE & OHIO IN THE 1940S AS A SYMBOL FOR ITS SMOOTH PASSENGER SERVICES ("YOU CAN SLEEP LIKE A KITTEN"), WAS THE BASIS FOR THE MERGED CHESSIE SYSTEM MONOGRAM CARRIED ON LOCOMOTIVES AND ROLLING STOCK.

Central. On April Fool's Day in 1976, these railroads (plus a subsidiary, Pennsylvania-Reading Seashore Lines) were consolidated to form Conrail.

So the operative word in stories of 1960s and '70s railroading is "ended." Passenger trains were discontinued in swelling numbers, and the very concept of passenger transportation by private railroads eventually became obsolete. Great railroad names vanished by the score.

The abandonment of unprofitable branch lines likewise gathered force. What began as a leak in the 1960s would slowly turn into a torrent. Between 1960 and 1980, approximately one fourth of the nation's route miles were abandoned, as branches were pruned and mergers resulted in redundant trackage.

The last Railway Post Office (RPO) car operated on June 30, 1977, between New York City and Washington, D.C. The last non-urban, heavy-duty, mainline, electrified rail service had ended in 1974, when

CREATED TO RESCUE THE REMNANTS OF THE FAILED PENN CENTRAL MERGER, THE CONSOLIDATED RAIL CORPORATION SPENT MILLIONS OF DOLLARS IN GOVERNMENT SUBSIDIES BEFORE DEREGULATION FREED IT FROM ARCHAIC LEGAL AND LABOR RESTRICTIONS. AFTER BEING FULLY PRIVATIZED, CONRAIL BECAME ONE OF THE MOST DYNAMIC RAILROADS IN THE LAND.

ONCE CONRAIL TRIMMED AWAY ITS REDUNDANT TRACKAGE, IT SET ABOUT BECOMING A STEADY AND VERSATILE CARRIER OF CONTAINERIZED FREIGHT BETWEEN NEW YORK, PHILADELPHIA, BOSTON, AND POINTS WEST. HERE, CONRAIL'S TRAIN TV-301 SCURRIES ACROSS MOODNA VIADUCT AT SALISBURY MILLS, NEW YORK.

the Milwaukee Road de-energized its track across Montana and Idaho.

There were, of course, some new beginnings, and Amtrak was perhaps the most notable—a fragile phoenix of intercity rail service rising from the ashes of the languishing streamliners of the private railroads. Amtrak began operation on May 1, 1971, as a quasi-public corporation that had its genesis in the battles over the *California Zephyr*, as well as other discontinuances and downgradings. If a single individual can be called the father of Amtrak, it's probably Anthony Haswell, who in 1968 founded the National Association of Railroad Passengers (NARP), a lobbying and advocacy group that remains a critical force in rail preservation today.

With Haswell agitating, the press providing coverage, and the government getting into the picture following the 1969 resolution led by Colorado's Senator Allot, things began to move. The Federal Railroad Administration (FRA) appointed a task force, while the Department of Transportation (DOT), previously opposed to passenger trains, but apparently in a more positive mood under new head John Volpe, on January 18, 1970, released a preliminary plan for what would eventually become Amtrak.

On May 1, exactly one year before final implementation, the Rail Passenger Service Act of 1970 was introduced, providing for the formation of the National Railroad Passenger Corporation—or Railpax. A reluctant President Nixon signed the bill into law on October 30.

All railroads then operating long-distance passenger trains (as opposed to commuter services) were eligible to join Amtrak. The cost of admission: roughly half of 1970 losses on passenger service, payable in equipment, cash, or services. The benefits offered in return were enormous, as participating railroads would be free of all future pas-

AMTRAK'S ADOPTION OF BUDD-BUILT AMFLEET COACHES IN THE 1970S ENABLED THE NATIONAL SYSTEM TO ACHIEVE GREATER SAVINGS AND ON-TIME RELIABILITY. PASSENGERS ABOARD TRAIN NO. 475 ENJOYED THE SHOW OF AUTUMNAL COLORS FROM THEIR AMFLEET COACH SEATS NEAR WEST WARREN, MASSACHUSSETTS.

The Death of the California Zephyr

The CZ's death was slow, painful, and public. Western Pacific, the weakest of its three operators, was the first to go to the I.C.C. to ask out—in September of 1966. The Commission was on the horns of a dilemma, since the line was clearly demonstrating significant losses, yet the train was running full in summer, with a year-round load factor of 78 percent.

Furthermore, a survey showed a 95 percent approval rating by passengers. Although Rio Grande claimed losses, it still stood firm with pro-passenger Burlington in supporting the train. The I.C.C. deliberated for five months, then ordered Western Pacific to run the train for another year.

WP was back, hat in hand, as that term expired, only to be rebuffed again by the I.C.C., which felt that the railroad was only half-heartedly trying to improve the train's faltering balance sheet.

Then, in May of 1969, the Rio Grande asked to discontinue its portion of the run, citing annual losses of almost $2 million. By now, passengers were finally beginning to desert the CZ, disillusioned by poor timekeeping, deteriorating equipment, and years of discontinuation notices. The end came in February of 1970, when the I.C.C. ruled that the WP could end its segment, with Rio Grande dropping back to tri-weekly runs, connecting at Salt Lake City with Southern Pacific service to San Francisco.

The *California Zephyr* made its last run just over a month later.

AMTRAK'S SUPERLINER CALIFORNIA ZEPHYR ROLLS HIGH ABOVE CRYSTAL LAKE, CALIFORNIA, ON ITS WESTBOUND TRIP OVER A PORTION OF THE FIRST TRANSCONTINENTAL RAILROAD. ON THE REAR IS A FORMER SANTA FE "EL CAPITAN" COACH, THE TYPE OF CAR THAT INSPIRED AMTRAK TO CREATE THE SUPERLINER FLEET.

senger-related losses. Virtually all carriers rushed to join, though a few declined. Rock Island, already financially perilous and less than a decade away from total abandonment, simply couldn't afford the fee, and thus stayed with its surviving pair of short-haul *Rockets*.

Under the leadership of Graham Claytor (who later served as Amtrak's president during one of the corporation's healthiest eras), Southern Railway opted to run its New York-New Orleans *Southern Crescent*, plus a few lesser trains, on its own. The Rio Grande, not wanting to give Amtrak free rein on its highly scenic, single-track line through the Colorado Rockies, confused Amtrak's Chicago-to-San Francisco plans by staying out and running its own Denver-to-Salt Lake City *Rio Grande Zephyr*, using what used to be *California Zephyr* equipment.

At first, those passenger trains that survived—and about 60 percent did not—ran pretty much as before, but with Amtrak footing the bills. By fall, however, Amtrak had determined to purchase 1,200 of the best available cars from nine of the 20 joining railroads. In time, it would become the direct employer of all of its crews—not just on-board service personnel, but engineers and conductors, too. In 1976, on the occasion of Conrail's formation, Amtrak

PASSENGERS ENTERING THE DINING CAR ON BOARD DENVER & RIO GRANDE WESTERN'S RIO GRANDE ZEPHYR WERE GREETED BY THE COMPANY'S LOGO. WITHIN THE SEAL, "THRU THE ROCKIES" WAS A SUBTLE REMINDER THAT D&RGW'S COMPETITORS (UNION PACIFIC AND AMTRAK) TOOK A LESSER ROUTE ACROSS GRASSY WYOMING PRAIRIES.

IN LATER YEARS, ONE OF THE BEST-KNOWN PASSENGER TRAINS IN NORTH AMERICA WAS THE CALIFORNIA ZEPHYR AND, SHOWN HERE, ITS TRUNCATED SUCCESSOR ON THE DENVER & RIO GRANDE WESTERN, THE RIO GRANDE ZEPHYR.

took over ownership of the Northeast Corridor—Boston to Washington, plus the spur from Philadelphia to Harrisburg—but otherwise continued to be a tenant on the tracks of the freight railroads.

Amtrak's first locomotives and cars were all veterans purchased from participating railroads, but within a few years the corporation went shopping for new equipment. These early acquisitions—diesel locomotives, electric locomotives, coaches, and integrated trainsets—all proved unsuccessful.

This shouldn't have been surprising, since the technology of passenger railroading in the United States had been stagnant for 30 years. The new cars and locomotives appearing in profusion immediately after the war were modestly upgraded versions of prewar designs. Per-

THE VISTA-DOME RIO GRANDE ZEPHYR SCURRIES ACROSS A PARK AT FRASER, COLORADO, BENEATH THE MAJESTIC ROCKY MOUNTAINS. FROM FRONT TO BACK, THIS CLASSIC STREAMLINED AMERICAN PASSENGER TRAIN WAS THE LAST TRUE ZEPHYR.

haps the one significant exception was the self-powered high-speed Metroliner, which the Penn Central introduced on its New York-Washington speedway in 1969. These tubular cars, built by the Budd Company, were airplane-like, with unnecessarily cramped interiors and what probably are the smallest windows ever built into a modern passenger car anywhere in the world. (Trackside rock-throwers along this largely urban route were a factor in that design decision.)

Unfortunately, when Amtrak needed some new coaches for short-haul service, the only option not involving unacceptable delays and costs for design and retooling were "Metroshells"—Metroliners without their traction motors. Dubbed the "Amfleet," these cars, 492 in number, have been the staple of Amtrak daytime services since the first one was delivered in 1975.

Off-the-shelf passenger locomotives were no more available than coaches, so Amtrak bought diesels (SDP40Fs from EMD) and electrics (E60s from GE) that were only slightly modified freight-haulers. Both of these designs incorporated six-wheel trucks, and both proved derailment-prone at high speeds, severely limiting their utility. Amtrak did better with its next major motive-power selections, opting for four-wheel-truck locomotives. EMD began delivering a fleet of F40PHs in 1976, and the diesels be-

THE RIO GRANDE ZEPHYR'S F9A-UNIT NO. 5771 BECAME A CHERISHED FACE BETWEEN SALT LAKE CITY AND DENVER, ATTRACTING PHOTOGRAPHERS IN ITS WAKE MUCH AS THE LAST MAINLINE STEAM HAD DONE 30 YEARS BEFORE.

GENERAL ELECTRIC VAUNTED ITS E-60CP ELECTRIC PASSENGER LOCOMOTIVES AS A REPLACEMENT FOR THE GG1 LOCOMOTIVES AMTRAK USED ON ITS ELECTRIFIED NORTHEAST CORRIDOR, BUT THE E-60 DEMONSTRATED A TENDENCY TO DERAIL AT SPEEDS ABOVE 95 MPH AND HAD TO BE REPLACED.

The New York-Montreal Adirondack

As Amtrak went about saving the American passenger train in the 1970s, the corporation instituted significant changes. One that was distinctly two-edged, however, was the standardization of richly varied ancestors into look-alike trains.

One colorful exception was the *Adirondack*, a day train between New York and Montreal that was funded in part by the State of New York under a provision of the Amtrak Act that allowed states to mandate service by funding a percentage of the cost—two-thirds originally, later one-half.

The Delaware & Hudson was a willing operator of this train between Albany and Montreal—a wonderfully scenic ride, much of it along the shore of Lake Champlain—but on its terms, which were that the equipment used would be its own, refurbished at state

DELAWARE & HUDSON OPERATED THE ADIRONDACKS FOR THE STATES OF VERMONT AND NEW YORK, POWERING THEM WITH PAIRED ALCO PAS. THE LAST OF THESE STREAMLINED DIESELS IN NORTH AMERICA, THEIR HANDSOME COLORS ECHOED THE SANTA FE "WARBONNET" LIVERY.

expense and painted in a fetching blue, yellow, and gray. The locomotives would be four distinctive Alco PAs, handsome locomotives that D&H had purchased from Santa Fe in 1967 for service on the *Laurentian* and *Montreal Limited*.

Because D&H under Carl B. Sterzing, its feisty young president, wanted its identity front and center, Sterzing and Amtrak struck sparks virtually from the time of the train's inauguration on August 5, 1974.

After the leased CP domes were returned, Amtrak provided dome coaches in their stead, which D&H painted in its own colors, outraging Amtrak officials. Amtrak's blue and red promptly returned, and the passenger corporation played its trump card in this identity battle in 1977 by bumping the D&H equipment entirely with Turboliner trainsets.

came the backbone of the Amtrak fleet nationwide for the next two decades. The following year, the corporation ordered the first of what would be a substantial fleet of AEM7s, diminutive but powerful electrics of Swedish design built by EMD and the Budd Company. (Earlier, Amtrak had turned to Europe for inspiration when it purchased six Turboliner trainsets from France, then had an additional seven similar sets built domestically by Rohr.)

Amtrak's improving success with equipment purchases extended to cars as well. In 1975, the corporation ordered from Pullman-Standard the first of what would be an extensive fleet of double-deck "Superliners," inspired by bilevel cars that Santa Fe had operated on its *El Capitan*, a luxury coach train. By late 1979, when the Superliners began entering service on the long-haul Western trains for which they were intended, they were two years off schedule. Before long, however, they were running throughout the West and proving popular with passengers.

The Superliners would, in fact, significantly fuel the Amtrak resurgence that began in the late 1970s and gained real momentum through the 1980s. In the '60s and even earlier, the nation's Western trains—the *California Zephyr*, the Union Pacific's fleet of "City" trains (the *City of Los Angeles*, *City of Portland*, and so on), the Santa Fe's *Chiefs*, and others—were deservedly considered superior to their eastern counterparts. The advent of the Superliners only heighted the disparity.

AMTRAK CREWS SERVICE A FLEET OF BI-LEVEL SUPERLINERS IN CHICAGO. IN THIS REDESIGNED YARD, CARS ARE INSPECTED, CLEANED, AND RESTOCKED BEFORE BEING SWITCHED INTO TRAINS HEADED WEST AND SOUTHEAST FROM UNION STATION.

ALTHOUGH UNABLE TO MEET THE TIGHTLY DEFINED STANDARDS ONCE PROVIDED BY SANTA FE RAILWAY, AMTRAK SUPERLINER SOUTHWEST CHIEFS CONTINUE TO PROVIDE QUALITY SERVICE ALONG THE LEGENDARY SANTA FE TRAIL FROM CHICAGO TO LOS ANGELES. HERE, NO. 3 MAKES A QUICK LATE-NIGHT STATION STOP AT FLAGSTAFF, ARIZONA.

Clearances prohibited the operation of these bilevels in the East, where long-distance service was handled by the veteran sleepers, diners, and lounges inherited from the private railroads in 1971. Beginning in 1977, many of these old cars were upgraded and converted to "head-end power" (in which electricity generated by the locomotive replaces steam and axle-generators as the source of power for heating, air conditioning, and lighting). These reconditioned cars, dubbed the "Heritage Fleet," were actually quite attractive, but they were old.

With this new and refurbished equipment, its own railroad between Boston and Washington, and crews under its direct control, Amtrak grew through the 1970s into a creditable entity. It remained a political football, as it has ever since, but the corporation's staying

AMTRAK'S WESTBOUND CALIFORNIA ZEPHYR CROSSES THE SUISUN MARSHES AT BAHIA ON THE LAST LAP TOWARD ITS SAN FRANCISCO BAY TERMINAL CITIES OF EMERYVILLE AND OAKLAND.

The GG1: A Mighty Locomotive

The United States never embraced railroad electrification in a big way. Distances were generally too great and traffic densities too low for electrification's expensive infrastructure to make sense. The Pennsylvania Railroad's multitrack main line between New York and Washington was a dramatic exception.

By 1934, Pennsy had developed the locomotive that would become the operation's mainstay for almost half a century—the mighty GG1. The prototype, No. 4800, was cloaked in a somewhat ungainly, riveted shell. Fledgling industrial designer Raymond Loewy was given the important assignment of turning this proverbial ugly duckling into a swan.

The result was a shiny dark green carbody tricked out with five elegant gold pinstripes that plunged to vanishing points on the locomotive's shapely nose. Small red keystones provided dis-

PENNSYLVANIA RAILROAD'S NO. 4935 BASKS IN THE GLOW OF ADMIRERS AT HARRISBURG, PENNSYLVANIA.

creet splashes of color. One hundred and thirty-nine GG1s were built.

By the 1970s the GG1s were aging; though still able to outhaul anything in sight, their days were numbered. To provide a fitting finale, a group called "Friends of the GG1" restored one of Amtrak's "Gs" to its original pinstripe scheme. On May 15, 1977, GG1 No. 4935 was rededicated at Washington Union Station and put back into service.

Four years later, the Jersey Central Railway Historical Society and NJ Transit restored GG1 No. 4877 to glorious Loewy pinstripes—but in this case in Tuscan red (worn by a handful of Gs in the fifties). Like No. 4935, 4877 entered regular service and was on hand for the bittersweet ceremony on October 29, 1983, when the last active GG1 was retired from service on Transit's North Jersey Coast Line.

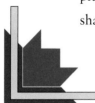

power has surprised many critics who suspected that its creation might have been intended as nothing more than prolonged euthanasia for the passenger train.

Whatever else it may or may not have been, Amtrak was unarguably monolithic. Though the corporation chose to preserve many of the great train names from the past, it cloaked all its equipment in "platinum mist" (or, alternatively, natural stainless steel) adorned with red and blue. Gone were the rainbow colors of the private railroads' trains, as well as their individualized services. Standardization—of menus, accommodations, and services—was the hallmark.

The rash of mergers had a similar effect on the face of railroading in general, and the demise of the weaker diesel builders led to greater standardization in motive-power as well. Fairbanks-Morse ended production in 1963. Alco threw in the towel in 1969. Baldwin-

FACING PAGE (RIGHT): JUST OVER THE NEVADA-CALIFORNIA BORDER, THIS TRIO OF NEWLY BUILT GENERAL ELECTRIC AC-4400CWS LEADS A STRING OF COAL HOPPERS WESTWARD ALONG THE EASTERLY FLOWING TRUCKEE RIVER AT FLORISTON, CALIFORNIA.

THE RESURGENCE OF SHORTLINE RAILROADS HAS RESULTED IN NEW COLOR SCHEMES AND A DIVERSE GROUPING OF OLDER LOCOMOTIVES. CALIFORNIA NORTHERN AND PARENT ARIZONA & CALIFORNIA ADORN THEIR DIESELS WITH PALE TAN, GREEN, AND YELLOW-GOLD, AS WORN BY THIS FORMER DULUTH MISSABE & IRON RANGE SD-9 ROADSWITCHER.

Lima-Hamilton had built its last locomotive way back in 1956. That left General Electric and Electro-Motive Division, the latter still the dominant force in diesel-building.

The look and mix of units on the diesel-ready tracks changed radically between 1960 and 1980. Streamlined "cab-unit" diesels were everywhere, wearing the classy, multicolored schemes created in many cases by EMD stylists. "Hood units"—preeminently Alco's RS3s (RS for "road switcher") and EMD's GP7s and later, GP9s (GP for "general purpose")—were essentially the same under the skin as the cab units, but with better visibility and easier access to machinery.

The next evolutionary step was to "chop" the short hood for better forward visibility, an innovation of the early 1960s that would typify diesel aesthetics for the next two decades (until the boxy, blunt "safety cabs" of the 1980s). Streamlining and fancy paint schemes seemed superfluous in this hunkered-down era of railroading, charac-

THE SECOND GENERATION OF AMERICAN DIESEL LOCOMOTIVES WAS STYLIZED BY ELECTRO MOTIVE'S NEW F-SERIES WITH THE DELIVERY OF 40 F-45S TO THE SANTA FE BEGINNING IN 1968.

REBUILT FP-45S, CALLED SDFP-45S BY SANTA FE, ARE NOW APPROACHING THEIR 30TH BIRTHDAYS HAULING HIGH-SPEED FREIGHT TRAINS ACROSS THE SOUTHWESTERN LINES OF BNSF.

terized by boarded-up depots, abandoned branch lines, and weed-infested rights-of-way. First-generation diesels from all the builders joined steam trains in the scrap yards. Utilitarian "chop-nosed" units in a limited number of basic models from EMD and GE were the locomotives appropriate to this era of dramatically lessened expectations. For much of the industry, particularly in the East and Midwest, where the traffic base had eroded badly, survival was virtually all that could be hoped.

But even in these dark days, when the future looked bleak indeed, railroading had begun to reinvent itself. Diesel standardization, and perhaps the example of locomotive pooling that occured naturally in mergers, led to increased power run-throughs from one railroad to another—an efficient and time-saving practice. Intermodal traffic (trailers and containers on flatcars, otherwise known as TOFC and COFC)—became a significant growth sector, doubling between 1965 and 1980, with the greatest explosion still to come.

Railroads began to exploit other niches with "unit trains" of a single commodity, such as grain or coal. (In 1979, in a rare example of route expansion, Burlington Northern opened its new Powder River Line, tapping rich coalfields in Wyoming.) Centralized traffic control, an idea that was already many decades old, became the norm, along with welded rail.

Railroading is an old-line industry, capital-intensive and labor-intensive, with a thoroughly unionized workforce. Though every gain was won only after a fight, essential work-rules rationalization was begun. The process of eliminating firemen on locomotives, for instance, started as far back as 1964. Crew operating districts, based on divisions that often dated back to railroading's early days (and thus re-

Burlington Northern Railroad's haulage of low-sulphur, high-BTU steam coal from Wyoming has created a virtual conveyor belt of coal trains that fan out across Colorado to the Midwest and South.

IN SOUTHERN COLORADO, THE BURLINGTON NORTHERN SANTA FE'S TRAINS OPERATE OVER THE SO-CALLED "JOINT LINE" FROM DENVER TO PUEBLO. THE TRACKS, ENGINEERED IN THE 1880S AS A NARROW-GAUGE LINE HEADED FOR MEXICO, WERE STANDARD-GAUGED AFTER THE TURN OF THE CENTURY.

THE POWDER RIVER SUBDIVISION OF THE BURLINGTON NORTHERN WAS NEWLY CONSTRUCTED TO SERVE THE MINES OF THE SAME NAME. MULTIPLE TRACKS, PLUS THE MOST MODERN SIGNALING, LOCOMOTIVES, AND ROLLING STOCK, HAVE TURNED BN INTO A SUPER RAILROAD.

VIA Rail: Canada's Answer to Amtrak

The Canadian railroad scene has differed radically from that of the United States in that it has been dominated by two giant, transcontinental carriers: Canadian Pacific, a private road, and Canadian National, a ward of the government. But despite a gallant, creative effort by CN in the '60s to reinvigorate passenger service with refurbished equipment, aggressive marketing, and flexible pricing, Canadian passenger trains eventually came to be beset with problems much akin to the woes faced by their U.S. counterparts.

In the mid-1970s, the Canadian government chose a solution that mirrored Amtrak, and VIA Rail Canada evolved. First, CN's services came under the VIA banner. Then, with the change from Daylight Saving Time to Standard Time in the fall of 1976, a joint VIA timetable included both CN and CP trains. Finally, in September of 1978, Canadian Pacific's passenger trains came directly under VIA's auspices.

VIA's creation from two railroads' passenger trains was enormously simpler than Amtrak's amalgamation of 20 different companies' services. For years, not much changed in operational patterns.

Canada's greatest train, CP's stainless-steel *Canadian* (Budd-built in 1954), continued to ply its outrageously scenic route between Montreal/Toronto and Vancouver—basically with its original equipment, including a pair of domes, though former Canadian National "Daynighter" coaches (with wide spacing and leg rests, for overnight travel) were added. Their smooth, Cor-Ten steel sides, painted VIA blue with yellow stripes, clashed with the fluted cars of Budd's *Canadian*.

Though in later years VIA would fall on hard political times and suffer massive train-offs in the process, passenger railroading north of the border was (and, selectively, remains) a fine experience in the VIA era.

sulted in operating crews receiving a day's pay for a few hour's work) in some cases were revised.

In the final months of 1980, several important events occurred. In December, The Pullman Company was dissolved as a legal entity (though it had ended its staffing of sleeping and parlor cars 11 years earlier), and Northwestern Steel & Wire in Sterling, Illinois, dropped the fires on its refugee fleet of steam locomotives—engines that this huge scrapyard had chosen to operate, squeezing out a last few useful miles before melting them down for razor blades. This was the last daily, non-tourist steam operation in the United States.

Less than two months earlier, on October 14, President Jimmy Carter had signed into law the Staggers Rail Act, partially deregulating the railroads. This event was significant. It was the go-ahead for the railroad industry, however dramatically redefined and slimmed down, to "highball it" once again.

SOUTHERN PACIFIC AC-POWERED DIESELS ROLL HIGH-BTU, LOW-SULPHUR STEAM COAL TO HUNGRY POWER PLANTS. SOUTHERN PACIFIC HAS BLENDED ITS USUAL GRAY AND SCARLET COLORS WITH A VARIATION OF RIO GRANDE'S SPEED LETTERING FOR A PROGRESSIVE NEW LOOK.

Chapter 8

INTO THE NEW CENTURY

*Thanks to deregulation, gains in productivity, and the
use of cutting-edge technology, the nation's railroads are
moving more goods than ever before. As the number of
railroads has dwindled because of mergers, the industry
has become more profitable, even while slashing rates
and employing fewer workers. With more mergers and
technological breakthroughs on the horizon, railroads
seem poised to become the nation's arteries of commerce.*

Turning points in history are often hidden and difficult to distinguish, but this was not the case in the rebirth of the American railroad industry. It happened on October 14, 1980. That's the day that President Jimmy Carter signed the Staggers Rail Act into law.

The legislation gave the railroads a freedom they'd not had in 75 years—that is, the right to adjust their prices in response to market conditions. The transformation literally took an act of Congress, but it would spawn thousands of mini-revolutions within the industry, creating an era of the railroad reborn.

After years of strangling the industry with regulation, Congress took the action partly because deregulation was popular, but also because Conrail had by this time already gone through approximately $3 billion in federal assistance, with no end in sight. Giving Conrail—and the rest of the nation's railroads—the freedom to run their businesses

ONE OF THE LEGACIES OF THE FORMER PENNSYLVANIA RAILROAD IS THE ALTOONA SHOPS, A SPRAWLING LOCOMOTIVE REPAIR FACILITY NOW A PART OF CONRAIL. PRECISION WORK DONE WITH PRIDE HAS LONG BEEN ASSOCIATED WITH ALTOONA, AS DEMONSTRATED BY MACHINIST KERMIT ALWIRE, GAUGING THE TRUENESS OF A REMANUFACTURED DIESEL CRANKSHAFT.

THE DISASTROUS MERGER THAT CREATED PENN CENTRAL LEFT ITS OFFSPRING, CONRAIL, WITH REDUNDANT TRACKAGE AND A BURDEN OF DEBT. FOLLOWING FEDERAL DEREGULATION, CONRAIL BEGAN TO ECONOMIZE, GRADUALLY BECOMING EFFICIENT AND PROFITABLE.

without cumbersome government agencies second-guessing them breathed new life into America's iron horse.

The Interstate Commerce Commission was given limited authority to hear complaints from shippers about railroad rates, while overseeing abandonments and mergers. The Federal Railway Administration, meanwhile, took on the job of policing railroad safety.

L. Stanley Crane, Conrail's CEO, later recalled the era. "We lived out 100 years of railroad history—moving from the restrictive regulation and capital-starvation of the past into the market-driven, innovative, and successful company of today and tomorrow," he said.

Few could have foreseen the thousands of changes that would take place as railroads exercised their freedom to operate as a free-market business instead of a regulated utility. The change that began with the Staggers Act came full circle in 1987, when a profitable Conrail became a publicly traded company on the New York Stock Exchange. Starting at $28 a share, the stock rose to more than $84 within a few years.

Conrail's experience was similar to that of many railroads in the 1990s. The road focused more on customer expectations. It trimmed expenses and abandoned or sold off unprofitable lines. The focus on reliability even led the company to paint its buzz phrase—"Conrail Quality"—in huge letters on all of its locomotives.

The railroads of the 1990s look almost nothing like they did a few years ago, and changes anticipated over the next 15 years will probably make for even more dramatic contrasts.

WHEN BUSINESS ON SOUTHERN PACIFIC'S OVERLAND ROUTE FELL IN THE 1970S, MILES OF DOUBLE TRACK WERE REDUCED TO A SINGLE LANE. THE TRACK WAS REUSED IN TEXAS, WHERE DOUBLE-TRACKING BECAME A NECESSITY.

Railroads of the modern era jumped at the chance to become bigger and more efficient. For years, the largest of the railroads were referred to as the Super Seven. Today, that number has been whittled down even further. The stage is set for a day in the near future when there will be two major rail systems in the West; three in the East; a few regional railroads running secondary rail lines unwanted by their larger cousins; and hundreds of shortlines taking over smaller branch lines.

Through a series of mergers, several super-railroads have been created. These giant railroads take several forms. Some are the creation of a marriage of equals—such as Chessie System and Family Lines, or Norfolk & Western and Southern, or the combination of Burlington Northern and Santa Fe in the mid-1990s.

The Burlington Northern-Santa Fe merger created the nation's largest railroad, with almost 30,000 miles of track. Even before the

THE ERA IN REVIEW

1980:
The Staggers Rail Act becomes law on October 14, beginning deregulation and giving railroads the right to set rates.

Chessie System and Seaboard Coast Line Industries merge to form CSX.

Burlington Northern acquires Frisco, connecting Pensacola, Florida, and Seattle, Washington.

1981:
Union Pacific merges with Missouri Pacific and Western Pacific, tapping new markets in Texas, Louisiana, and the San Francisco Bay area.

1982:
Southern and Norfolk & Western merge to create Norfolk Southern. The innovative NS establishes itself as a major coal hauler and freight line.

1985:
The Soo Line purchases the remnants of the once mighty Milwaukee Road.

1986:
Norfolk Southern begins regular operation of its RoadRailer units— versatile containers that can ride the rails or the highways.

CHESSIE SYSTEM WAS CREATED BY THE MERGING OF THE *CHESAPEAKE & OHIO*, *BALTIMORE & OHIO*, AND *WESTERN MARYLAND* LINES IN THE 1970s. MERGED AGAIN IN 1980 WITH *FAMILY LINES*, *CHESSIE* HAS BECOME *CSX CORPORATION*, A PROFITABLE FREIGHT CARRIER THAT COMPETES HEAD-TO-HEAD WITH MIGHTY NORFOLK SOUTHERN.

THE ERA IN REVIEW

1987:
Conrail goes public in the largest stock offering in U.S. history.

1988:
Rio Grande and Southern Pacific unite as Southern Pacific Lines.

The Missouri-Kansas-Texas line becomes part of Union Pacific.

1991:
Canadian Pacific buys Delaware & Hudson, increasing its presence in the northeastern United States.

1992:
Amtrak begins operating Virginia Railway Express commuter trains around Washington, D.C.

1994:
The first diesel locomotives powered by AC (alternating current) enter service on Burlington Northern.

1995:
Burlington and Santa Fe merge.

Union Pacific acquires Chicago & North Western, then announces plans to merge with Southern Pacific.

merger, Burlington was the nation's biggest coal hauler. Thanks to the demand for low-sulphur coal from Wyoming's Powder River Basin, BN hauls more coal for utilities than any other railroad in the nation. Santa Fe's specialty was the high-speed piggyback train, toting truck trailers and containers across the nation. From Chicago to Los Angeles, Santa Fe's silver and red "war bonnet" paint scheme led some of the country's fastest TOFC (Trailer On Flat Car) runs.

Taking a different approach, Union Pacific has grown by purchasing railroads. Over the last 15 years, the UP has acquired the Western Pacific, Missouri Pacific, Missouri-Kansas-Texas, and Chicago & North Western, Southern Pacific, and Denver & Rio Grande Western lines, creating a blanket across the West and the Midwest.

At the end of 1995, Union Pacific sought to bring Southern Pacific—itself a combination of the SP and Rio Grande—under its con-

SANTA FE'S MOST MEMORABLE ICONS OF THE DIESEL AGE ARE ITS "CHIEF" LOGO AND THE RED, SILVER, YELLOW, AND BLACK COLOR SCHEME OF ITS LOCOMOTIVES. THE LAST PRESERVED PAIR OF PASSENGER DIESELS BEARING THE RESTORED FLASHY FINISH NOW RESIDE AT SACRAMENTO'S CALIFORNIA STATE RAILROAD MUSEUM.

THANKS TO POWDER RIVER COAL, BURLINGTON NORTHERN WAS FACED WITH THE NEED TO CREATE A NEW BREED OF LIGHTWEIGHT ROLLING STOCK AND HIGH-HORSEPOWER DIESELS. ALUMINUM HOPPERS TO CARRY THE COAL AND MICROPROCESSOR-EQUIPPED, AC-POWERED LOCOMOTIVES TO PULL THEM WAS THE RESULT.

trol to counterbalance the BN-Santa Fe combination. That made the UP the nation's largest railroad with slightly more than 30,000 miles. The move came more than a decade after an early 1980s attempt to merge the Santa Fe and Southern Pacific. That deal went awry when the I.C.C. failed to give its approval.

Ironically, the dream of a true transcontinental railroad remains just that—a dream. In all of the mergers of recent years, none has dared unsettle the balance of trading partners on either side of the Mississippi River. That is likely to change some time in the twenty-first century. Industry experts point out that it is only a matter of time before mergers between the remaining East Coast and West Coast railroads take place. The U.S. railroad map may eventually show three, or perhaps two, major rail systems crisscrossing the mighty Mississippi.

The super-railroads of today are a reflection of other U.S. mergers and mega-companies of the modern era. As railroad companies merge, they are able to concentrate more authority in fewer managers, dictating orders across a wider area.

As is often the case, unproductive parallel rail lines and antiquated equipment typically become surplus after a merger. In the case of many mergers, these surplus lines quickly become fodder for re-

THE WESTERN PACIFIC, AMERICA'S LAST TRANSCONTINENTAL LINE, FOUGHT INSOLVENCY AND ITS RIVAL, SOUTHERN PACIFIC, UNTIL IT COULD NO LONGER MAINTAIN INDEPENDENCE. ABSORBED BY THE UNION PACIFIC IN 1981, THE FORMER WP HAS BEEN REBUILT INTO A BUSY MAJOR LINK IN UP'S CALIFORNIA CONNECTION.

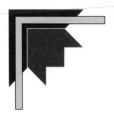

A Shortline Resurgence

Even as super-railroads began to dominate the industry and become even larger in the 1990s, smaller railroads were beginning to proliferate.

From 484 shortlines in 1987 to 519 in 1994, America's shortline railroad industry was growing. By 1995, shortlines represented about 25 percent of the nation's rail system, according to the American Association of Railroads.

As trunk railroads became larger, they began to focus on heavily used corridors and quantity shippers of intermodal, containerized, and bulk freight moving *en masse*. On many occasions, they sold or leased secondary mainlines or branch lines

THIS TWILIGHT SCENE OF A CONTEMPORARY SOUTHERN PACIFIC FREIGHT LEAVING THE SAN FRANCISCO BAY AREA ELOQUENTLY SYMBOLIZES THE RAILROAD'S POSSIBLE MERGER INTO THE UNION PACIFIC.

to independent operators with lower overhead costs. The Santa Fe even sold the branch line to its namesake city in New Mexico.

Most shortlines were built on hustle. For example, the manager of one such rail line might have the office and telephone for his business in his house. When a shipper needs a freight car moved at 4 A.M., he can call and arrange a special move. No problem.

The mergers of the Burlington Northern and Santa Fe, as well as the proposed merger of Southern Pacific and Union Pacific, have presented new opportunities for shortlines. For now, at least, their future appears secure.

gional railroads, shortlines, and railroad museums. Regionals and shortlines often succeeded where the super-railroads failed, due to lower costs and less restrictive work rules.

Several of these lines have found a niche. Montana Rail Link, for example, began operating Burlington Northern's former Northern Pacific line, no longer needed because of plenty of capacity on the paralleling Great Northern line. Today, Montana Rail Link is a healthy company, with almost 1,000 miles of track and almost 100 diesel locomotives moving paper, forest products, grain, and other commodities. Other companies, such as RailTex, of San Antonio, Texas, operate several shortlines of less than 100 miles each from one central headquarters.

The efficiency of the super-railroad is a stunning example of American business at work. Railroad stocks have outperformed the overall U.S. stock market since 1991. At the same time, freight rates have fallen in inflation-adjusted dollars. The industry has begun to take back traffic it lost to trucks and barges in the years since World War II. Freight shipments reached record levels for seven years in a row through 1994. The railroads' share of intercity freight rose to 39.2 percent in 1994, up from 38.1 percent in 1993 and 37.5 percent in 1992.

Even before they adopted a new paint scheme on their locomotives, the Burlington Northern and Santa Fe went to work immediately after

TROPICANA BEGAN SENDING ITS FLORIDA CITRUS PRODUCTS TO MARKET IN SOLID TRAINS OF INSULATED CARS IN THE 1970S. SUCH DEDICATED SHIPPER RUNS WERE THE FORERUNNERS OF TODAY'S CONTAINER TRAINS.

CREWS OF TWO OR THREE AND A FLEET OF REBUILT LOCOMOTIVES, SUCH AS THESE FORMER CHICAGO & NORTHWESTERN EMD GP-15TS, KEEP CALIFORNIA NORTHERN RAILROAD, A NON-UNION RIVAL OF THE SOUTHERN PACIFIC, ON THE MOVE.

Preserving Railroading's Heritage

It has been left to an army of volunteers, numerous museums both great and small, and a few caring railroad companies to document and put aside for posterity at least a sliver of railroad history.

Volunteer railway historical societies, some of them numbering their members in the hundreds, sprouted to cover every major trunk line. Organizations with a broader mission, such as the Railway & Locomotive Historical Society and National Railway Historical Society, have seen their memberships increase as well.

FORMER SOUTHERN PACIFIC "DAYLIGHT" GS-4 No. 4449 REMAINS THE PRIZED AMBASSADOR OF THE CITY OF PORTLAND, OREGON, ITS OWNER.

Museums took root in depots across the country, as well as in former shop complexes, such as those in Scranton, Pennsylvania, Savannah, Georgia, and Spencer, North Carolina. Some museums were provided with handsome new buildings paid for with tax dollars. The California State Railroad Museum in Sacramento opened in 1981 with a collection spanning Golden State railroading from its earliest days in the 1860s to the modern era. Similarly, the Railroad Museum of Pennsylvania, in Strasburg, presents an impressive sampling of the Pennsylvania Railroad's roster—from the smallest steamer to the biggest diesel.

Some of the major railroads have run steam-powered excursions periodically. Southern Railway and its successor, Norfolk Southern, have operated a popular weekend excursion train. Likewise, the Union Pacific, always mindful of its place in the nation's history, has preserved two giant locomotives for display and occasional operation.

their merger in 1995 to streamline their operations and launch an intermodal train service between California and the Southeast. The new service bypassed the Burlington, whose lines were packed with coal trains bound from the Powder River Basin in Wyoming to utility plants in the South, in favor of the higher-speed Santa Fe lines across the West. The improvement sliced 24 hours from the scheduled run between San Bernardino, California, and Atlanta, Georgia.

On some railroads where the norm has been to reduce costs and eliminate rail lines, old shops, and unused equipment, a reverse trend has taken hold. Many rail lines have struggled to keep up with all of the traffic.

At Union Pacific, business was so good in 1995 that the company leased 75 diesel locomotives from Norfolk Southern. The three-track Union Pacific mainline across Nebraska, a venerable funnel of Amer-

AC-MOTORED GENERAL ELECTRIC AC44CWS, THE NEWEST POWER ON THE SOUTHERN PACIFIC, ROLL FREIGHT THROUGH THE TEHACHAPI MOUNTAINS OF CALIFORNIA.

PIONEERED TO MAXIMUM RELIABILITY, EMD SD-70MACS, USING AC MOTORS, MICROPROCESSORS, AND IMPROVED DIESEL PRIME MOVERS HAVE BROUGHT TO BURLINGTON NORTHERN MOTIVE POWER SUITABLE FOR THE DAWN OF THE NEW MILLENIA.

ican commerce connecting the West, Midwest, and East, is so packed that the line plans to add a fourth track. Likewise, Norfolk Southern plans to install a second track on much of its busily traveled route between Atlanta, Georgia, and Chattanooga, Tennessee.

Conrail, which had laid off employees for a number of years, hired 800 new workers in 1994. Southern Pacific, which had one of the oldest diesel locomotive fleets in the nation, spent more than $750 million on new power in the early 1990s, renewing almost half of its fleet.

Even General Motors, which quietly closed its LaGrange, Illinois, locomotive manufacturing shop in the late 1980s and considered selling its once-lucrative diesel business, took a second look. Although most diesels are still built at General Motors' Electro-Motive subsidiary in London, Ontario, production capacity was at such a high level in the 1990s that some engines had to be shipped unpainted for the railroads to finish in their own shops. Conrail even took diesel locomotive kits and finished them in the company's shops in Altoona, Pennsylvania, where steam locomotives were once constructed.

Earnings for the nation's railroads reached $3.3 billion in 1994. That's up from $2.5 billion the previous year. Railroad industry executives even credited deregulation with helping them become more safe. After the American Association of Railroads announced the safest year ever in 1994, association CEO Edwin Harper remarked that, since the enactment of

EVEN IN THE AGE OF MECHANIZED TRACK REPAIRS, STRONG-ARM LABOR IS STILL REQUIRED FOR SOME JOBS, SUCH AS THE ADJUSTMENT OF SWITCHPOINTS AND TIE RODS ON THESE TRACKS, IN THE PORTLAND, OREGON, YARDS OF THE UNION PACIFIC RAILROAD.

WHEN NATURE THROWS ITS WINTER WORST AT A RAILROAD LIKE SOUTHERN PACIFIC, THE COMPANY SENDS OUT ITS ARSENAL OF SNOW-FIGHTING EQUIPMENT—PLOWS, SPREADERS, FLANGERS, AND CREWS WHO KNOW HOW TO FACE THE HAZARDS CALMLY.

Requiem for the Caboose

One of railroading's most widely recognized symbols—the caboose—was lost during the 1980s. With new labor agreements reducing the number of crew members from as many as five to two or three, cabooses exited much in the same way steam locomotives had 30 years earlier. Henceforth, conductors would ride the diesel locomotive cab, which was becoming increasingly larger and more office-like.

Concerned about safety, railroads welcomed the end of the caboose. Crewmen in cabooses were often subjected to punishing jolts. One railroad, the Union Pacific, estimated that 90 percent of injuries among trainmen took place in cabooses.

Replacing the little red caboose—which by this time was also painted green, orange, gray,

ATCHISON, TOPEKA & SANTA FE RAILWAY CABOOSE NO. 999702.

blue, yellow, or a multitude of other colors—was FRED, short for Flashing Rear End Device, a 35-pound electronic beacon priced at around $4,000 that blinked a red warning signal and transmitted air-brake data to the front of the train. Compare that with an $80,000 price tag for a new caboose, which costs an additional 80 cents per mile to operate.

The majority of the nation's 11,000 cabooses went to the scrap heap. A few continued to operate on branches or shortlines where long back-up moves require a platform for the crew to ride.

At least 2,000 of them were sold to individuals or donated to museums, parks, and communities to be displayed along the tracks they once plied.

the Staggers Act and the resulting increase in railroad cash flow, "freight railroads have made capital expenditures in excess of $50 billion to improve track, signals, equipment, and information systems." Technological advancements, better freight car designs, and better operating practices all led to the improved safety record.

The railroad industry's robust health has come as a result of an improving U.S. economy, computerization of everything from dispatching to waybills, increased research and development, and breakthroughs in labor agreements.

Two of the most exciting technological developments have come with the introduction of double-stack containers and RoadRailers. Double-stacks rely on a flatcar with a sunken floor that allows two intermodal containers to rest one atop the other, doubling the capacity of a flatcar. Southern Pacific was the first major railroad to build these cars, in conjunction with ACF Industries.

Double-stack containers often arrive by ship, then continue their journey by train, with final delivery by truck. Double-stack trains have necessitated the rebuilding of many routes on the nation's mainline railroads to accommodate these ultra-high loads. The clearance of bridges and tunnels were raised in Pennsylvania in a multimillion-dollar

SUPER FLEET LOCOMOTIVES PAINTED IN THE CLASSIC WARBONNET LIVERY NOW RUSH DOUBLE-STACKED CONTAINERS, TRAILERS, AND COAL ACROSS SANTA FE LINES. THE BURLINGTON NORTHERN-SANTA FE MERGER HAS HAD LITTLE EFFECT; NEW LOCOMOTIVES STILL LEAVE THEIR BUILDERS IN WARBONNET PAINT, BUT WEARING BNSF LETTERING.

SOUTHERN PACIFIC HAS TREMENDOUS FAST-FREIGHT TRAFFIC ON ITS LINES ACROSS THE AMERICAN SOUTHWEST TO NEW ORLEANS, KANSAS CITY, AND CHICAGO GATEWAYS. HERE AT THE THROAT OF ITS WEST COLTON, CALIFORNIA, YARDS, SP DOUBLE-STACKS PASS EACH OTHER HEADED IN OPPOSITE DIRECTIONS.

project to get double-stack service to the port of Philadelphia. In Virginia, Norfolk Southern eliminated or renovated several tunnels on its hilly line into West Virginia to allow double-stacks to pass between Chicago and the port of Norfolk.

Double-stacks have won back much of the profitable perishable-goods business for the railroads. Replacing the traditional refrigerated boxcar is the 40-foot-long double-stack container, powered by a generator with an automatic backup in case the main generator fails. With double-stack trains running between Seattle and New York in only five days, everything from Alaskan king crab to photographic film can be shipped in temperature-controlled boxes.

NO MATTER THE SEASON, CONRAIL'S NEW YORK-TO-CHICAGO CORRIDOR VIA THE HUDSON RIVER VALLEY STAYS OPEN TO CARRY THE HOTTEST COMMODITIES FROM PORT-TO-PORT AND BEYOND. DOUBLE-STACKS ABOARD FREIGHT TV400-Y STREAM PAST THE ICE-ENCRUSTED HUDSON AT BEAR MOUNTAIN, NEW YORK.

In 1977, according to data from the Association of American Railroads, railroads carried only 0.2 percent of produce shipments. After deregulation, perishable traffic jumped to 15 percent. A container, which can make several trips in one month's time, easily outperforms refrigerated boxcars, which by comparison average only one trip a month.

On other railroads, particularly Norfolk Southern, RoadRailers are the current rage. Basically a truck trailer that can ride the rails or the highways, these lightweight, versatile containers operate in dedicated trains of 100 cars or more, moving everything from beer to cat litter. Detachable rail wheels make them easy to put on the tracks, while retractable wheels make them easy to put on the road. Both have meant big gains in productivity.

The railroads redesigned everything. They built new hopper cars to carry the nation's coal for electric power plants, switching to lighter

UNION PACIFIC'S APLA— THE DEDICATED AMERICAN PRESIDENT LINES CONTAINERS FOR LOS ANGELES—SNAKES ITS WAY ALONG THE DESERT GRADE NEAR FROST, CALIFORNIA.

CONRAIL TAKES FULL ADVANTAGE OF THE SMOOTH PROFILE GRANTED BY ITS FORMER NEW YORK CENTRAL "WATER LEVEL ROUTE" ALONG THE HUDSON RIVER.

THROBBING WITH ACTIVITY NIGHT AND DAY, RAILROAD YARDS ARE THE HEART AND SOUL OF RAILROADING. DIESELS GRUMBLE UP AND DOWN THE MANY TRACKS, PULLING A FEW CARS HERE, DROPPING SEVERAL OVER THERE, TO ASSEMBLE AND BREAK UP TRAINS AS THE FLOW OF BUSINESS REQUIRES.

and more durable aluminium designs, and they revamped the traditional wood-hauling car to make it easier to load and unload. They even replaced the wooden tie and spike with concrete ties and metal clamps.

Communications technology has also revolutionized some aspects of railroading. Throughout the industry's history, train crews have left their terminals with a manifest of pre-assigned duties, pick-ups, and set-offs. On the Union Pacific, the railroad started using a direct-link computer system between the crews and the marketing department. That means reporting immediately when cars are distributed or collected. It also means flexibility in sending service orders to a train on the road.

WITH THE AID OF ELECTRONICS, RAILROADS HAVE SUBSTANTIALLY CUT COSTS AND INCREASED PRODUCTIVITY WHILE STILL OPERATING SAFELY. RADIOS ASSIST SWITCHING CREWS IN RELAYING SIGNALS BACK AND FORTH, WHILE FRED—THE FLASHING REAR END DEVICE—MONITORS MAINLINE TRAIN OPERATIONS FROM THE REAR OF THE LAST CAR.

In Roanoke, Virginia, Norfolk Southern's giant freight yard resembles a big remote-controlled model railroad. Computers set the brakes on the cars being sorted in the railroad's hump yard. They also align the switches. Operators sitting in a strategically positioned tower even manipulate the pace of locomotives shoving cars through the yard.

New freight-car wheel designs have reduced the number of accidents resulting from wheel failure by 80 percent. By changing the shape of the wheel and subjecting the steel to heat treatment, professional engineers have literally reinvented the railroad wheel.

Advances in technology have had their price, however. Railroad employment has been particularly hard hit. Today's railroads haul more freight than they did at the beginning of the 1980s, but they do so with 40 percent fewer employees.

THE LEAST-CHANGED FUNDAMENTAL ASPECT OF RAILROADING FOR THE LAST 150 YEARS IS THE FLANGED WHEEL. TODAY'S STEEL WHEELS MOVE MILLIONS OF TONS OF FREIGHT AND PASSENGERS SMOOTHLY AND SAFELY.

The Age of Big Diesels

In a change symbolic of the entire railroad industry's metamorphosis, locomotives became more powerful and more dependable in the modern era.

In the mid-1990s, the nation's two largest locomotive builders began producing the first diesel locomotives with normal size but gargantuan strength. Both General Motors' Electro-Motive Division in LaGrange, Illinois, and General Electric in Erie, Pennsylvania, unveiled designs based on alternating current (AC) power.

Diesels have operated with direct current (DC) motors for some 70 years, but only recently has technology advanced far enough to make AC motors practical. The chief advantages of AC motors are fewer parts and less shop time, resulting in a more reliable locomotive.

A NEW GENERATION OF DIESELS IS REPLACING AGING UNITS LIKE THIS SP LOCOMOTIVE.

The two builders—along with newcomer Morrison Knudsen of Boise, Idaho—began offering locomotives with previously unheard of horsepower: 4,000, 5,000, and even 6,000 units. They were also loaded with luxuries such as self-steering wheel sets, self-diagnostic computers, and ultra-quiet cabs.

Officials at Burlington Northern, the first railroad to embrace the new technology, hailed the production of such super-engines as another step toward a fully scheduled railroad. The words were not just hype. On some of the railroad's most demanding runs, three of the new units replaced five of the old ones.

To put the revolution in perspective, BN Chairman Gerald Grinstein called it "the most dramatic step forward in locomotive technology since diesel replaced steam."

From 1979 through 1992, the output per hour in the railroad industry rose 8.1 percent, according to the Bureau of Labor Statistics. That made U.S. railroads the most productive in the world. Railroad productivity increased 157 percent from 1983 to 1992.

In addition, many sweeping labor agreements have changed the face of the industry. A 1982 agreement reduced the number of crew members on a freight train from four or five to two or three. Early 1980s agreements also spelled the end for the caboose—from then on, the conductor would ride in the locomotive with the rest of the crew.

After a strike in 1991, the Brotherhood of Locomotive Engineers won a wage hike that hasn't kept up with the rate of inflation. The union also gave up some health benefits and agreed to work more hours before getting overtime pay. As a result, an Amtrak passenger train that once required four crews to complete the trip from Washington, D.C., to Atlanta, Georgia, now operates with only two.

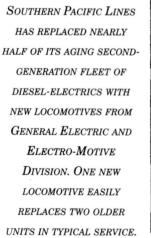

SOUTHERN PACIFIC LINES HAS REPLACED NEARLY HALF OF ITS AGING SECOND-GENERATION FLEET OF DIESEL-ELECTRICS WITH NEW LOCOMOTIVES FROM GENERAL ELECTRIC AND ELECTRO-MOTIVE DIVISION. ONE NEW LOCOMOTIVE EASILY REPLACES TWO OLDER UNITS IN TYPICAL SERVICE.

CHICAGO HAS LONG BEEN THE MOST DYNAMIC HUB OF THE NORTH AMERICAN RAILROAD BUSINESS. LIKE MANY OTHER AMTRAK TRAINS, THE TEXAS EAGLE CALLS THE WINDY CITY ITS HOME; HERE, PASSENGERS MAY DETRAIN FOR BUSINESS OR PLEASURE, OR BOARD ANOTHER TRAIN FOR DISTANT POINTS EAST AND WEST, NORTH AND SOUTH.

Such changes resulted in drastic reductions in employment at the nation's major railroads, whose work forces dipped from 475,000 at the dawn of the new era to some 191,000 at the end of 1993. The trend is expected to continue, as technology and computers make railroading safer and more efficient with fewer workers. Someday, through-trains may run by radio signal from remote-controlled dispatching centers, trimming the crew to a single person.

The railroad industry is taking a second look at virtually everything it does to squeeze more profit and efficiency from its operations. Freight cars once tracked by human clerks as trains entered yards now respond to radio signals that can beam their codes directly into a computer.

Amtrak, the nation's federally subsidized passenger railroad, has likewise begun moving toward a new era. With its budget tied directly to federal subsidies, however, it has weathered a difficult era in which money to buy new equipment has been tight.

The purchase of millions of dollars worth of new Super-liner passenger cars at the beginning of the 1990s and a newly de-signed car known as the Viewliner spelled the end for the stream-lined passenger-car fleet of the 1950s. The

CUSTOM-DESIGNED NEW LOCOMOTIVES FOR THE COMING DECADES HAVE BEGUN COMING ON-LINE IN THE FORM OF GENERAL ELECTRIC P-40BWHS. ONE SUCH 4,000-HORSEPOWER "GENESIS" UNIT ACCELERATES AMTRACK TRAIN NO. 3, THE SOUTHWEST CHIEF, THROUGH COAL CITY, ILLINOIS, EN ROUTE TO CALIFORNIA.

COMMUTERS IN BOSTON TAKE TO THE RAILS ABOARD MASSACHUSETTS BAY TRANSPORTATION AUTHORITY (MBTA) TRAINS. COACHES BUILT BY BOMBARDIER OF CANADA AND VERMONT PROVIDE ABOVE-AVERAGE LEVELS OF COMFORT.

Cutting-Edge Technology

*C*omputers have changed the way railroads conduct business. Today, companies can transmit orders and waybills from their own dispatching centers directly to trains nationwide.

Even the boxcar, the standard freight-carrying vehicle for more than 160 years, has gotten a nudge. Replacing it is the RoadRailer, a truck trailer with removable wheels that runs like a train when its on the tracks.

And even more dramatic changes may be on the way. One of the nation's major railroads, CSX, is developing a new concept called the "Iron Highway," which is a continuous ramp on which truck trailers can be loaded. It's a new twist to the well-established practice of hauling trucks on trains, and one that's supposed to make railroads more competitive in the short-haul market of a few hundred miles or less.

In Southern California, diesel locomotives are out at the Santa Fe and Union Pacific's giant terminals. The two roads are operating locomo-

tives powered by liquified natural gas to reduce emissions and meet clean-air standards.

Meanwhile, Amtrak recently unveiled its *American Flyer*, America's first high-speed (up to 150 mph) passenger trains, which will be in service between Washington, D.C., and Boston by the end of 1999. The company promises more high-speed "corridors" nationwide.

TAKING BACK AN IDEA FOOLISHLY REJECTED IN THE 1950S, NORFOLK SOUTHERN, CSX, UNION PACIFIC, CONRAIL, AND AMTRAK HAVE BEGUN TO OPERATE FLEETS OF DISTINCTIVE, LIGHTWEIGHT ROADRAILERS—HIGHWAY TRAILERS WITH RAILROAD WHEELS AND COUPLERS.

first of some 140 new Superliners resulted in entirely new versions of popular Amtrak trains such as the *Cardinal* and the *Capitol Limited*.

Steps to improve Amtrak service between Washington, D.C., and New York City have seen travel times trimmed, with steps being taken to increase speeds from the 120-miles-per-hour range into the 140s. Congress allocated millions of dollars to increase speeds through computer-aided dispatching, higher-speed track, and new electric locomotives.

Perhaps the most encouraging signs that Amtrak was ready to make a leap forward came in 1993. Amtrak tested the Swedish X2000, German ICE, and Spanish Talgo—all advanced trains. These new trains operate with special devices that allow them to travel at higher speeds on curves. Computer-controlled devices actually tilt the X2000 to give it the ability to flash through curves at speeds much higher than normal. Such trains are envisioned as the next step toward faster service between cities. In the extreme Northeast, they're seen as the key toward extending high-speed service from New York City into highly congested New England.

If successful, high-speed rail lines will spread from the Northeast into other sections

ONE OF AMTRAK'S NEW GENESIS HIGH-HORSEPOWER P-40BWHS LEADS THE LAKE SHORE LIMITED THROUGH COLD SPRING, NEW YORK.

Testing the Rails

Virtually every American industry has its own test laboratory. For the railroads, it's the Transportation Test Center in Pueblo, Colorado. Since 1982, the American Association of Railroads has used this remote, 52-square-mile area to put new concepts and railroad car designs through their paces.

Test machines "rock and roll" stationary freight cars, simulating vibration and speed to evaluate endurance. The center's obstacle course, consisting of 48 miles of test track, is where old and new locomotives and railcars, track components, and signal and safety devices are put through real-life testing.

For example, the center once put a locomotive pulling cars loaded with 125 tons of cargo each—an increase from the 100-ton limit—on a 2.8-mile loop of test track. The train circled continuously, completing a circuit every four minutes. The test was designed to see if the track would fall apart under the weight. It didn't,

proving that productivity could be increased by using fewer, but heavier, railroad cars.

The center also offers hands-on training for hazardous materials response teams. The course includes simulated derailments, crashes, and highway accidents.

It's a chance to test real operating practices before human lives and millions of dollars in equipment are at stake.

REMOTE-CONTROLLED SIGNAL SYSTEMS GOVERN THE BULK OF CLASS 1 RAILROAD MAINLINE OPERATIONS, YET THE NEED FOR HUMAN INTERACTION REMAINS, PARTICULARLY IN THE AREA OF TRAINING.

of the nation. Modern trains will glide along banked turns and fenced-off right-of-ways to move passengers from city to city in record time.

The University of Texas Center of Electromechanics, for example, has been awarded $2.9 million to develop an advanced passenger locomotive that can accelerate faster. If super-railroads, big technological changes, and sweeping labor reforms were unexpected at the beginning of the 1980s, the next few years could be even more surprising.

Just as the steel railroad car replaced the wooden one, and the diesel replaced the steam engine, it's reasonable to expect even more change from the major railroads in the years to come.

More and more powerful locomotives aided by computers that track everything from the adhesion of the wheels on the rail to the per-

THE SUPERLINER CALIFORNIA ZEPHYR CARRIES THE AMTRAK BANNER EASTWARD ON ITS JOURNEY FROM THE SAN FRANCISCO BAY AREA TO CHICAGO. CROSSING THE SACRAMENTO RIVER ON THE SUISUN BAY BRIDGE AT BENICIA, TRAIN NO. 6 HAS TWO EMD F-40PH UNITS LEADING THE WAY.

formance of the motors will be pulling trains in the near future. Dedicated trains in which each rail car is powered, thus providing for smooth starting, stopping, and operation, is one possibility.

Intermodal traffic, which has grown more than 60 percent in the last decade, is expected to jump another 60 percent in the next few years. Fast intermodal trains roll across the Colorado high plains on the Santa Fe line as Q-trains and on the nearby Union Pacific line as Z-trains or "Zippers."

Railroads will become better utilized thanks to satellite tracking and computerized signaling and safety devices. As the nation continues to wrestle with environmental problems, the railroads will continue to be an important resource, moving the same amount of freight with only a tenth of the pollution.

The first reviews on deregulation seem to be positive. A shippers group called CURE (Customers United for Rail Equity) sought to partially re-regulate the industry beginning in 1986, but made little progress. In vindication of the 1980 Staggers Act, the federal government in late 1995 dismantled the Interstate Commerce Commission. Debate focused on which remaining federal agencies would assume the I.C.C.'s duties to hear rate disputes and merger cases. The future of the railroad as a free-market industry looked secure.

Throughout their more than 170-year history, American railroads have reflected the development of this diverse and changing country.

A FLEET OF NEW EMD F-59PHI LOCOMOTIVES FOR AMTRAK CALIFORNIA HAS STARTED PULLING POPULAR INTERCITY TRAINS UP AND DOWN THE GOLDEN STATE.

ULTRASONICALLY INSPECTING EACH INCH OF EVERY RAIL, A SPERRY RAIL SERVICE CAR CREEPS STEADILY ALONG SEARCHING FOR HIDDEN FISSURES AND FLAWS IN THE TRACK UNDER ITS WHEELS. IF A FLAW IS DISCOVERED, THE OFFENDING SPOT IS PAINT-MARKED FOR QUICK REPAIR.

ANOTHER SHORTLINE SUCCESS IS THE NAPA VALLEY RAILROAD AND ITS WINE TRAIN. THE FORMER SOUTHERN PACIFIC BRANCH, DATING FROM 1866, OFFERS A DELUXE DINING EXPERIENCE ABOARD RESTORED PASSENGER CARS PULLED BY VINTAGE CANADIAN FPA DIESELS.

They grew up with the nation in the 1830s and spearheaded the drive West. They turned ever more complex and, by the turn of the century, became the province of wealthy speculators. They went to war twice in this century. And facing the new world after World War II, they struggled with old ways of doing things.

Today, they're obsessed with technology and productivity, as our society demands newer, faster, and better ways of doing things. In that sense, the railroad is a mirror of American culture. Never before has it been involved in so many new ways of doing what it does best—carrying freight and passengers. As many American industries are busy trying to "re-engineer" their companies, the railroads are well into almost one generation's worth of experimentation and change.

The UP-SP Merger

It is a dream nearly as old as the Transcontinental Railroad of 1869—a through-route connecting the Union Pacific and the Southern Pacific lines. It was a vision that almost came to be in 1909.

The announcement in 1995 that Union Pacific would buy Southern Pacific for $5.4 billion to create the largest railroad in North America was a fulfillment of sorts.

A SOUTHERN PACIFIC FREIGHT TRAIN CROSSES THE LUCIN CUTOFF ATOP GREAT SALT LAKE NEAR PROMONTORY POINT, UTAH.

After all, it was the UP and SP predecessor Central Pacific that joined the nation together with a ribbon of rails at Promontory Summit, Utah, in 1869. And it was the dream of one railroad builder, Edward H. Harriman, to combine the two lines just after the turn of the century. Harriman was a believer in super-railroads—giant systems that stretched from coast to coast, providing shippers with fast, efficient service.

Harriman, described by the New York Times as "the world's greatest railroad man" because of his incredible hold over several major railroads of the era, exercised control over the voting stock of both western giants briefly in 1909.

Alas, Harriman died before he could see the dream realized. The decades passed, and the UP and SP became fierce competitors. With the creation of the combined Burlington Northern-Santa Fe system in 1995, the next logical step was to combine always strong UP and financially weak SP for a balanced two-railroad West.

Harriman would have approved.

Need proof? Watch what happens south of Seattle late on a springtime afternoon. At a mainline crossing where both Union Pacific and Burlington Northern are within feet of each other, the gates flash and come down. The headlight of a southbound Burlington Northern train appears. Quickly, its two diesels and string of double-stack containers whizz by. The sound of the engines is a deep roar, like a baritone clearing his throat. The tracks sing as the cars pass beneath them. In the distance, a small beacon, the conductor of the twenty-first century, flashes red, sending out an electronic greeting.

Or watch on a sunny Sunday afternoon as a giant CSX coal train rolls through Marietta, Georgia, on its way from a Kentucky coal mine to a Florida power plant. Two AC-powered engines roll the 13,000-ton train south almost effortlessly. Gone forever are the laboring steamers, stopping regularly for water and coal.

Gone, too, are many of the doubts about railroading's future. The industry is headed full throttle toward the twenty-first century, and it's not looking back.

Some of the last great streamlined passenger equipment inherited by Amtrak from a variety of U.S. railroads rolled across the West in the late 1970s. Shown here is the winter-only Reno Fun Train, photographed high in California's Sierra Nevada.